Total
KEYBOARD

Library of Congress Cataloging-in-Publication Data
Available

10 9 8 7 6 5 4 3 2 1

This edition published in 2003 by
Sterling Publishing Co., Inc.
387 Park Avenue South,
New York, NY 10016

Copyright © Carlton Books Limited, 2000

Manufactured in Dubai
All rights reserved

ISBN 1 4027 0981 1

Production: Janette Davis/Marianna Wolf

Design: The Orgone Company

Photographs by Laura Wickenden

Total KEYBOARD

Terry Burrows

Sterling Publishing Co., Inc.
New York

CHAPTER 1
THE KEYBOARDS

INTRODUCING THE INSTRUMENTS

The term "keyboard" covers a wide range of fascinating musical instruments that can be heard gracing virtually every style of music, from the baroque harpsichord to modern-day digitally sampled dance music. The best-known and most popular keyboard instrument is the piano, and yet many are surprised to learn that given its high-profile position in the world of classical music, it was not until the early part of the 18th century that the instrument even came into being.

THE PIANO AND ITS ANCESTORS

The godfather of all keyboard instruments is the organ, the earliest known example of which was the hydraulis, invented around the 3rd century BC by Ctesibius of Alexandria. The instrument came about from an attempt to apply a mechanical wind supply to a large set of panpipes.

However, it was in Europe that the organ evolved, and where from the 8th century it exerted a strong influence over the early development of Western music. Strangely, though, it was not for another five hundred years that the "chromatic" keyboard—the familiar sequence of black-and-white notes that we still use today —was developed and applied to the organ.

During the early 16th century, other keyboard instruments began to appear, the most notable of which was the harpsichord. Each time a key on the harpsichord was pressed, a connected quill would pluck the string, creating the sound. For the next two hundred years, the harpsichord was one of the most important of European musical instruments.

The story of the piano began in 1709 in Florence, when the Italian harpsichord maker Bartolomeo Cristofori constructed what he called "Gravicembalo col piano e forte" (literally, "harpsichord with soft and loud"). Cristofori had replaced the plucking mechanism with a series of hammers, so that when the note was pressed, the hammer struck the string creating the note. One major difference, however, was in the dynamic control offered by the new instrument: unlike the harpsichord, the "pianoforte" (as it was abbreviated) allowed the player to vary the loudness of the sound depending on how hard the keyboard was pressed.

For many years after its development, the piano still continued to resemble the harpsichord.

The German-built Steinway grand, one of the best-known names in piano manufacture.

Whilst Cristofori received brief attention for his endeavors, interest soon waned. It was a further 20 years before the German Gottfried Silbermann learned of Cristofori's work and created his own model. By 1750, Silbermann's instrument had gained the approval of no less a figure than Johann Sebastian Bach.

The first great piano virtuoso was Carl Philip Emmanuel Bach, the second son of "JS." His book *Essay of the True Art of Keyboard Playing* was a significant and influential work. Although directed mainly at harpsichord players, Bach acknowledged the piano as an instrument of the future. By the time of his his death in 1788, the piano was widely viewed as the superior instrument: the harpsichord's time had passed.

At this time, grand pianos still bore a close resemblance to the harpsichord in size. However, some instrument makers had already begun experimenting with the shape. In 1760, an apprentice of Johann Silbermann by the name of Johannes Zumpe designed the "square" piano. Zumpe believed the instrument—then only affordable to the very wealthy—could catch on among the middle classes if suitably priced. His square piano was small, light and could be carried on the back of a single porter. The instrument was extremely popular until the end of the 19th century when the classic "upright" piano began to find its way into more and more ordinary homes.

Until well into the 20th century, the piano typically formed the centerpiece of communal family life in many homes throughout Europe and America. It wasn't until after the end of World War Two that other forms of home entertainment, such as radio, television and gramophone records, caused a decline in its popularity. Finally, when the rock and roll era arrived in the mid-1950s, the piano found it increasingly hard to compete with the glamor of the new electric guitar.

Nonetheless, the piano has remained a popular and well-loved instrument, somehow still finding a place for itself whatever new musical fashion comes along.

THE ELECTRONIC AGE

Although we may think of electronic instruments as a modern phenomenon, experimentation with the idea of harnessing electricity for musical uses has been going on for over 200 years. As long ago as 1762, the Bohemian Prokop Divis, invented what he called an "orchestrion" in an attempt to imitate the string and wind instruments of the orchestra.

It wasn't until Alexander Graham Bell's invention of the telephone in 1876 that a genuine breakthrough came. Bell showed that sound could be converted to electrical impulses and back again, creating a basic principle on which future electronic instruments would operate.

From that point onward, a wide variety of strange and exotic electronic instruments appeared, most of which caused a brief flurry of interest and then disappeared.

THE HAMMOND ORGAN

The first practical electronic keyboard to catch on was the Hammond organ, invented in the early 1930s by engineers Laurens Hammond and John Hanert. The principle on which the Hammond works is a series of notched metallic discs, known as tone wheels. By spinning in a magnetic field, the tone wheels create a voltage that produces a soundwave. Pressing a key on the organ can sound up to nine different soundwaves at different pitches; the volume of each soundwave is controlled by a drawbar on the organ's keyboard, thus creating the potential for brilliantly rich and varied tones.

The Hammond organ made its debut at New York's Radio City in April 1939. Although its intended use was as a domestic instrument that could sound like a church organ, by the 1950s it was more likely to be found outside the home, as jazz musicians such as Jimmy Smith took its potential in an altogether

Jimi Tenor represents yet another generation of young players who find a role for the Hammond in their music.

unexpected direction. Over the next two decades, the Hammond organ again found itself in unexpected territory at the heart of the sound of rock bands such as Deep Purple, Yes and Emerson Lake and Palmer.

Although the Hammond is the most famous electronic organ of them all, other notable models have existed. In the 1960s, for example, the budget Vox Continental and Farfisa organs were widely used, and still find favor among fans of the "cheesier" types of modern music.

Even though the popularity of electronic organs waned with the spread of synthesizers, there remains a steady demand for their characteristic sounds.

OTHER EARLY ELECTRONIC INSTRUMENTS

The most important useable early electronic instrument was the theremin, invented in 1920 by the Russian scientist Lev Theremin. His instrument appeared to be a large wooden box with two antennae sticking out. The sound was created by an oscillator tone, the volume and pitch of which were controlled by the proximity of the hand to the the antennae. Extraordinarily difficult to master, the theremin remains something of a cult instrument.

In a similar vein, in 1928, Frenchman Maurice Martenot produced an instrument known as the ondes martenot. Working on broadly the same principles as the theremin, the instrument was easier to play since pitching was controlled by passing the hand along a series of wires in front of a conventional keyboard.

The composer Varése worked with both instruments. For his composition *Ecuatorial* he intended to use two theremins. However, in performance he found them too difficult to control, and replaced them with a pair of ondes martenots. Both instruments are capable of great dynamic expression and almost vocal-like tones; both instruments were also popularly used on horror and science fiction soundtracks during the 1950s.

The most famous synthesizer of them all, the classic MiniMoog, was produced between 1971 and 1981.

THE BIRTH OF THE SYNTHESIZER

The theremin is widely viewed as the prototype for the modern synthesizer, but it was difficult to play, and failed to catch on in a big way. It was not until 1964 that electronic music took its next major step forward when Dr. Robert Moog presented his paper, *Voltage-Controlled Electronic Music Modules*, to the Audio Engineering Society of America. Although others were working on the same lines, it was Moog who is generally credited as having invented the "analog" synthesizer.

Moog's original models were broken down into their component parts of oscillators, filters, amplifiers and envelopes (*see page 138*). These elements were then patched together using cables to create a wide variety of different sounds. For this reason, the early synthesizers were complex beasts, featuring enormous banks of knobs and tangled patch leads. They could also cost as much as a small apartment to buy.

The Moog synthesizer first reached the public in a big way in 1968 when classical musician Walter Carlos recorded the hit album *Switched-On Bach* using only a synthesizer and a multitrack tape recorder. Although other manufacturers were making synthesizers by that time, the name Moog became synonymous with the instrument.

THE MINIMOOG

There were two main problems with the first generation of "synths": firstly, they were monophonic, meaning that only one note could be played at a time; secondly, the complex repatching required to create new sounds was impractical (or too difficult) for most live performers. Moog overcame the second of these limitations in 1971 with the creation of the most famous synth of them all, the MiniMoog. This revolutionary instrument condensed the different components into a single portable unit. Most important of all, though, was the fact that the patching had been simplified and automated in a way that would suit most users. It may not have had the same scope for altering sound as its big modular brother, but it was a much more playable and "musical" instrument.

The MiniMoog pretty well defined the sound and operation of synths for the next decade, selling over 13,000 units in its ten-year life span. When Japanese manufacturers such as Korg, Roland and Yamaha began to get in on the act, their models were invariably simplified versions of the MiniMoog. These companies also managed to make their products affordable to non-professional musicians, and as sales increased, gradually the Moog company lost its grip on the market.

SEQUENCING

A development that went hand in hand with the synthesizer was the automated sequencer. This was a way of programming notes to play and repeat automatically. The first sequencers were very simplistic, offering only eight-note cycles, but in 1977, Roland unleashed the MC-8 Microcomposer, which featured a 5,000-note memory and was designed to "trigger" sounds from synthesizers that were linked to the unit. These were the precursors to the modern-day MIDI recorders.

EVOLUTION OF THE SYNTHESIZER

By the mid-1970s, the synthesizer had already made its mark on the music world, with landmarks albums such as Tangerine Dream's *Phaedra*, Jean-Michel Jarre's *Oxygene* and David Bowie's *Low* not only selling in large quantities, but influencing a generation of young musicians. However, all of these synth-based works were only made possible by studio multitracking techniques. Since the instruments could only play one note at at time, chords had to be built up on tape one note at a time. The solution came in the form of the polyphonic synthesizer.

The first important polyphonic synth was the Sequential Circuits Prophet 5, which appeared at the end of 1977. This, as the name suggests, could play five notes simultaneously. The Prophet 5 was capable of producing a very rich and full sound. Such was its popularity that it could be heard on a sizeable proportion of hit pop singles into the early 1980s. The other significant polysynth of the period was the eight-voice Yamaha CS-80, a powerful keyboard which is now something of a collector's piece.

The Prophet 5 was revolutionary for another reason: its programmability. Until this time, if a player wanted to recall a specific sound, the only option was make a note of the positions of each of the controls, and reprogram them by hand. The Prophet 5 allowed the sounds to be stored digitally, meaning they could be recalled from a "preset" button. To give new players a start, the synths were sold with a number of sounds already loaded into the presets. An interesting by-product resulted from this, as service engineers who repaired and maintained Prophet 5s noted that in the vast majority of cases the factory presets had been unaltered. The implication here was that for all of the machine's sophistication, users were not spending their time coming up with radical new sounds, but simply flicking their way through the presets until they found a sound that they liked. This is perhaps one reason why so much of the music from that period has a homogeneous feel to it.

MIDI AND THE DIGITAL ERA

All of the synths mentioned so far worked along broadly the same principle—analog "subtractive" synthesis. In essence, this means that a sound starts off in a harmonically rich state and has filters applied to subtract unwanted harmonics, thereby creating a new sound. However, by the early 1980s, some of the Japanese manufacturers had begun to experiment with other ways of creating sound.

One breakthrough came in 1983 with the launch of the Yamaha DX7. Using a digital system of programming called "frequency modulation" (FM) synthesis, the DX7 was capable of producing extremely accurate likenesses of "real" instruments. Unlike its predecessors, it didn't feature banks of knobs and sliders, but numerous multi-function buttons.

Where the DX7 scored highly was in its preset program cartridges, each of which could produce 64 sounds. Like the Prophet 5 beforehand, the DX7's presets can be heard smothering numerous chart hits throughout the 1980s. Whilst digital FM synthesis was clearly capable of producing great sounds, it was far too complex and time-consuming for most ordinary users to comprehend. In spite of the fact the DX7 remains the biggest-selling synth ever, only a tiny proportion of its users bothered to progress beyond the preset buttons.

The Sequential Circuits company built the Prophet series, the first polyphonic programmable synthesizers.

However, the most significant development of the period was without question a communications protocol known as Musical Instrument Digital Interface (MIDI) (*see page 146*). This was a universal system that allowed synthesizers, sequencers and drum machines to communicate with one another. MIDI sequencers allowed keyboard performances to be captured and then altered afterwards. Much of the popular music from the mid-1980s onward relies on MIDI to some degree.

THE ANALOG TREND

By the end of the 1980s, digital synthesis was deemed to have killed off its analog counterpart. Yamaha's FM system was followed by other digital forms such as Roland's Linear Arithmetic (LA) programming, which combined digital sampling (*see below*) to create even greater realism.

However, there was also a growing view that digital sounds were overly harsh and clinical, and that they lacked the warmth of the old analog keyboards. Gradually, ancient pieces of technology like the MiniMoog became prized collector's items. This process was exacerbated by the birth and spread of Acid House music from the United States, the producers of which made extensive use of cheap "junked" technology. All of a sudden, old pieces of equipment that a few years earlier couldn't have been given away were changing hands at two or three times their original price. The continuing popularity of the various forms of dance music set the trend for most of the products that emerged throughout the decade that followed.

New technology continues to develop at an incredible pace, with the necessity for computer systems in recording and sound production becoming increasingly important. Hardware sequencers have largely been replaced by software-based MIDI recorders. Similarly, "soft synths" can create the most powerful sounds from within a basic home computer.

Running on an Apple Macintosh, the Vibra 9000 is one of the most powerful "soft synths" on the market.

DIGITAL SAMPLING

One of the most important technical developments of the past two decades was the birth of digital sampling. At its simplest, a keyboard that is equipped with sampling facilities can play back a digital recording of a real instrument. For example, if you feed in a recording of a violin playing the note C, it can be programmed to replay every time you press the note C on the keyboard.

Although sampling has dominated recorded pop music since its inception, its history can be traced back to the 1960s, and the British-built Mellotron keyboard. This worked in fundamentally the same way as a sampler except that each key of the instrument was linked to a cartridge holding a loop of magnetic tape that contained a recording of a real instrument playing the same note.

The first digital sampling system to come onto the commercial market was the Fairlight CMI system, developed in Australia in 1979. Although it was used extensively, at a cost of over $150,000 for a full system, only the wealthiest producers and musicians could afford it.

With the passing of time and rapid developments in technology, it was inevitable that the major Japanese synthesizer manufacturers would develop their own cheaper, user-friendly versions. Nowadays for little more than $500 it's quite possible to buy a sampling keyboard with extensive editing facilities and fifty times as much on-board memory as the Fairlight.

As well as providing a means for imitating real instruments, sampling evolved in a rather unexpected way, as dance music producers began to digitally record and play back snatches or loops of existing songs and build them into their own music. The most common use for this approach is in programming drum loops—particularly attractive for project or home studio users who lack the facilities or skills to record a real drummer. One particular snatch—the James Brown track "Funky Drummer"—has been overused in this way to the point of cliché, with Clyde Stubblefield's famous drum fill featuring on numerous dance and rap hits over the past fifteen years.

THE MUSIC AND THE MUSICIANS

From its creation less than 300 years ago, to the birth of recent electronic relatives, the piano was arguably the most important instrument in Western music. During the 18th and 19th centuries, its polyphonic capabilities and impressive dynamic range attracted the most sophisticated composers and musicians of the day. At the start of the following century, the piano again found itself at the centre of popular musical forms such as jazz and blues. During the rock era, the keyboard's position was somewhat usurped by the electric guitar, but fought back with the birth of synthesizer and other electronic relatives. However, the development of MIDI technology all but created the electronic dance boom of the past decade, placing the keyboard player once again at the very heart of music.

THE EARLY WORKS

One family name overshadows the early development of the piano, and compositions written for the instrument. At the start of the 18th century, Johann Sebastian Bach was known as an organist and composer of great standing. His initial encounter with the Silbermann piano in 1736 had not been a happy one—Bach was openly critical of the keyboard action and tone of the instrument—although by 1750 he was more impressed. Mostly remembered for his religious works, the 48 preludes and fugues of Bach's *The Well-Tempered Clavier* are still immensely popular among modern pianists.

Two other important keyboard composers of the same period were Georg Frederic Handel and Domenico Scarlatti. Like Bach, although they never composed specifically for the piano, which was still in its early crude stages of development, their works were widely adopted as a part of the standard piano repertoire.

It was in the hands of two of J. S. Bach's sons that the piano truly flourished. Christian Philipp Emanuel Bach was the second son of Johann Sebastian. A position as a musician and composer at the court of King Frederick the Great of Prussia made C. P. E. Bach an influential figure of his time. Not only was he the first significantly great pianist, he also wrote a seminal tutor—*Essay on the True Art of Keyboard Playing*. Above all though, it was his work as a composer that gave the piano a broader respectable repertoire during the transitory period that separates the Baroque and Classical eras.

Although it was in Germany that the piano had almost entirely evolved as a musical instrument, it was in London that the instrument and its music first became fashionable. It was there in 1768 that the piano received its first noteworthy public debut. Once again, it was at the hands of a Bach—this time Johann Christian Bach, the youngest son of J. S. Bach.

Following the death of his father, J. C. Bach had been brought up and taught by his elder brother before moving to

Italy where he became a composer of operas. In 1762, Bach took a position in London and became closely involved with the British royal family. Such were his connections with the establishment that he became known as "The English Bach". It was during this time that he became especially well-known as for his keyboard exploits.

Although Bach composed little for the piano, the sonatas *Opus 5* and *Opus 17* were acknowledged as an important influence on Wolfgang Amadeus Mozart, a young prodigy who from the age of seven travelled widely around Europe astonishing audiences with his genius at the harpsichord. By

One of the most important figures in the history of the piano, Franz Liszt astonished the music world when he retired from public performance at the age of 35.

Artur Rubenstein, widely thought to have been the 20th century's greatest interpreter of Chopin.

his late teens, Mozart had transferred his affections to the piano.

It was during the 19th century that piano matured, driven by some of the greatest composers ever to have lived. Having produced some of the best-known symphonic works, Ludwig van Beethoven also composed 32 sonatas for the piano, the most popular of which is *Op. 27, No. 2*—the so-called "Moonlight Sonata." Other important composers of music for the piano from the same period include Franz Schubert, Felix Mendelssohn, Frédéric Chopin and Robert Schumann.

The same period also saw the emergence of the greatest composer-virtuoso of them all, Franz Liszt. An incredibly prolific composer, by the time of his death in 1886 Liszt had written over 1,300 works, most of which were for the piano. Liszt is also arguably the greatest keyboard technician to have lived. With a passion for the piano that bordered on the obsessive, he was known to have practiced for up to fourteen hours a day. As a performer, Liszt could also have been described the pop star of his day, often inducing near-hysteria in women in his audiences. It was Liszt more than anyone else that provided the template for the modern-day concert pianist.

The 20th century saw a gradual subversion of the traditional approaches to harmony used in the Baroque and Classical eras. Composers such as Arnold Schoenberg championed a process of composition that abandoned the use of a tonal reference point. Although influential among other composers, mainstream audiences continue to be unimpressed—one reason why the most popular modern-day concerts are still more likely to comprise music written during the previous century.

The most highly rated performers of the past century were more often interpreters rather than outstanding composers in their own right. These include such illustrious names as Artur Rubenstein, Miecyzslaw Horszowski, Artur Schnabel, Glenn Gould, Sviatoslav Richter, Andras Schiff, Daniel Barenbohm and the great Ignace Paderewski.

BLUES AND JAZZ

Blues music evolved in the 19th century with the slave laborers who worked the cotton fields of the Deep South. Originally a vocal music, blues first developed through the "work songs" heard on the plantations. Gradually, this highly expressive form began to cross-fertilize with other cultural traditions brought in by migrants from Europe, such as hymns and the music of marching bands. From then on, the blues evolved in different directions, going on to influence pretty well every new musical form that appeared in to 20th century, from jazz and country to rock and roll.

Ragtime was the first piano-based music to be in any way influenced by the blues tradition. The most famous exponent of this form was the classically trained Scott Joplin, whose *Maple Leaf Rag*, published in 1899, made him a wealthy man, and is still widely performed today.

Jelly Roll Morton, the self-styled "Originator of Jazz, Stomps and Blues," was one of the first great stars of the piano in the United States. Although his story is peppered with wild and implausible exaggerations (he once claimed to have invented jazz in 1902—not bad for a twelve-year-old!) he was undoubtedly a ground-breaking musician. One of his early solo pieces, a rag called "Froggie Moore," was recorded in 1923 by King Oliver's band: featuring a young cornet player named Louis Armstrong, this is one of the cornerstones of jazz history.

By 1910 ragtime had evolved into what became known as "stride" piano and was a speciality of a number of Harlem-based musicians, whose leading member was James P. Johnson. One

One of the most important musicians of the 20th century, Art Tatum's technical wizardry took jazz piano in a new and exciting direction.

of his pupils was a young man named Thomas "Fats" Waller. By the late 1920s. Waller's name had become synonymous with the stride style. A gifted pianist and songwriter, Waller's popularity as a hammy, all-round entertainer overshadowed his true talent.

Two highly significant jazz pianists first came to public notice in the 1930s. Earl Hines was the first player to transcend the ragtime form, creating an identifiable style of jazz piano. Many of his finest recordings were made with Louis Armstrong—the most important musician in jazz history.

The same period also saw the emergence of jazz's greatest keyboard virtuoso. Almost blind from birth, Art Tatum started out as a stride player in the style of Fats Waller. His gifts were remarkable: not only did he have perfect pitch, but from only a single listen he could evidently play back any tune he heard in any key. However, the most awesome aspect of his playing was a technique that placed him in the same league as the likes of Liszt in the classical world. A typical Tatum solo saw the most basic of melodies embellished with fearsome complexity. He was a great influence on the bebop generation that followed, and not only to pianists.

Thelonius Monk, one of the founding fathers of bebop.

In 1953—three years before his death—Tatum embarked on a major series of recordings which resulted in the 13-album set, *The Tatum Solo Masterpieces*. This contains some of the finest examples of unaccompanied piano ever captured on vinyl.

The bebop movement of the 1940s saw jazz take a complex turn that required a different way of thinking and considerable dexterity to perform. The most important pianist to emerge from this scene—indeed, he was one of its founding fathers—was Thelonius Monk. Although his first recordings were in the early 1940s, his style of music was so advanced that it was well over a decade later that he was "discovered" by jazz critics. Monk was by no means a great technician—his playing was not always even that accurate—however his ability to improvise on a theme had a major impact on those who heard him.

The end of the 1950s was a transitional period for jazz. Although players such as Dave "Take Five" Brubeck achieved mainstream popularity, jazz began to lose its widespread appeal to young audiences, many of whom were turning towards other forms of popular music.

The decade that followed saw jazz further marginalized by the "free" style of playing. This lead some jazz musicians to seek other musical avenues. The most notable advance came in 1969 when "cool" jazz pioneer Miles Davis formed an all-electric band, which combined elements of free playing with others that were closer in spirit to James Brown-style funk. The album

The versatile Herbie Hancock is equally at home in the worlds of jazz, classical, funk or pop.

Bitch's Brew was a milestone that kicked off the whole jazz fusion movement that dominated the first half of the 1970s. Fusion peaked in 1973 when pianist Herbie Hancock recorded the synthesizer-heavy *Headhunters* album. This multi-million seller all but created the jazz-funk genre that followed. Other notable electronic jazz pioneers included the band Weather Report, lead by Joe Zawinul and Wayne Shorter, both former employees of Miles Davis.

LANDMARK JAZZ KEYBOARD ALBUMS

The term "jazz" encompasses many different styles of music. This list contains albums recorded by some of the most important keyboard players in jazz history.

- Geri Allen—*Etudes*
- Albert Ammons—*Boogie Woogie Stomp*
- Art Ensemble of Chicago (Muhal Richard Abrams)—*Fanfare For the Warriors*
- Eubie Blake—*Blues and Ragtime 1917-1926*
- Dollar Brand—*African Space Program*
- Dave Brubeck Quartet—*Time Out*
- John Coltrane (McCoy Tyner)—*The John Coltrane Quartet*
- John Coltrane (McCoy Tyner)—*A Love Supreme*
- Chick Corea—*Akoustik Band*
- Miles Davis (Bill Evans)—*A Kind of Blue*
- Miles Davis (Joe Zawinul)—*Bitch's Brew*
- Errol Gardner—*Concert By The Sea*
- Herbie Hancock—*Maiden Voyage*
- Herbie Hancock—*Head Hunters*
- Fletcher Henderson—*First Impressions*
- Earl Hines and his Orchestra—*Swinging in Chicago*

- Keith Jarrett—*Sun Bear Concerts*
- Keith Jarrett—*Shades*
- James P. Johnson—*Snowy Morning Blues*
- Scott Joplin—*1916*
- Thelonius Monk—*Brilliant Corners*
- Thelonius Monk—*Complete Blue Note Recordings*
- Jelly Roll Morton—*Complete Victor Recordings*
- Oscar Peterson—*Exclusively For My Friends*
- Bud Powell—*The Complete Blue Note Recordings*
- Horace Silver and the Jazz Messengers—*Horace Silver and the Jazz Messengers*
- Jimmy Smith—*The Sermon!*
- Sun Ra—*Atlantis*
- Art Tatum—*The Complete Pablo Solo Masterpieces*
- The Cecil Taylor Quartet—*Looking Ahead*
- Keith Tippett—*Mujician*
- Stan Tracey—*Under Milk Wood*
- McCoy Tyner—*The Real McCoy*
- Fats Waller—*Fractious Fingering*
- Weather Report (Joe Zawinul)—*I Sing the Body Electric*
- Weather Report (Joe Zawinul)—*Heavy Weather*

From Düsseldorf in Germany, Kraftwerk were a seminal influence on the development of electronic music.

KEYBOARDS IN POP AND ROCK

Although the piano undoubtedly played its part in the rock and roll sound that emerged from the United States during the 1950s, the birth of Leo Fender's solid-body electric guitar at the start of the decade heralded a new era in popular music. For the foreseeable future, the piano was widely viewed as a rather frumpy, unsexy instrument when compared to the freedom of the electric guitar. Furthermore, pianos were now becoming difficult to use in the context of the increasingly loud volumes of the rock era.

During the 1960s, the only realistic counterparts to the electric guitar were organs or electric pianos. The Hammond organ was by now a well-established instrument in its own right, and although it found some favor among some of the "progressive" bands, it didn't really create a very rocky sound.

Probably the best known keyboard band from this period was The Doors, whose use of the Vox Continental organ was at the very heart of their sound. In fact, keyboard player Ray Manzarek gave an accidentally prophetic glimpse of how keyboards might be used in the future. Since The Doors had

no bass guitarist, when the band performed live, Manzarek filled the role by playing the bass notes of an electric piano with this left hand.

THE EARLY DAYS OF THE SYNTHESIZER

Although the first synthesizers were available by 1965, they made little headway in the music world, initially being viewed as something of a novelty. Surprisingly, perhaps, the synthesizer made its first big impression in the classical world when Walter Carlos produced the multitrack epic *Switched-on Bach*.

Seemingly lost to the modern history books, among the first contemporary musicians to make extensive use of the synthesizer were the American duo Beaver and Krause. A veteran of electronic film scores, Paul Beaver was a master of the Moog modular synthesizer. Together he and Bernie Krause pioneered electronic "audio-expressionism" through albums such as 1969's *In a Wild Sanctuary*.

From the early 1970s, rock and pop bands began experimenting with the possibilities of new electronic sounds. Roxy Music's eponymously named 1972 album is one of the finest examples from this period, making extensive use of the

British VCS III synthesizer, played by Brian Eno. In fact, the original demos for the album show that—presumably in the interests of commerce—the band's electronic excesses were somewhat played down for the final recording.

Eno left Roxy Music soon afterwards to pursue a somewhat eccentric musical career. Setting up his own Obscure record label, he championed new approaches to music, introducing new composers, such as Michael Nyman and Gavin Bryars. His own contribution to the label was the album *Discreet Music*. Two sides of gently shifting tones, it was the first example of "ambient" music. Although his own music doesn't sell in massive quantities, he remains a major influence in electronic music.

SEVENTIES SUCCESSES

The synthesizer was unsurprisingly a big favorite with the flashy progressive groups of the mid-1970s. Rick Wakeman's fingers danced freely over the keys of a MiniMoog during his period in the band Yes, and then on massively successful solo projects, such as the chart-topping *Six Wives of Henry XIII*.

The sequencer played a credible part on Pink Floyd's 1973 epic, *The Dark Side of the Moon*: with its filter-swept sequences, the track "On the Run" still sounds remarkably contemporary.

The early 1970s also saw the synthesizer hitting the pop charts, with Hot Butter's novelty hit "Popcorn" becoming something of an unofficial theme for the instrument. During the same period, a minor British group called Chicory Tip enjoyed

Brian Eno was the founding father of "ambient" music.

The influence of synth star Jean-Michel Jarre can be heard in the much of the dance music of the late 1990s.

a handful of synth-based hits around the world—they remain significant in that their producer was Giorgio Moroder, a figure that would later play such a key role in the development of electro-pop.

THE GIANTS OF ELECTRONIC MUSIC

The two most significant and influential bands in electronic music history both hailed from Germany. In their own unique ways, Tangerine Dream and Kraftwerk had a major impact on the musical landscapes that followed.

Formed as a psychedelic improvisational rock band in 1967, by the early 1970s, Tangerine Dream's music was almost entirely based around synthesizers and other electronic keyboards. Their benchmark album was *Phaedra*, released in 1974. Containing almost nothing in the way of conventional melodies, the album was a soundscape constructed from low-key VCS III sequences and swathes of Mellotron. Although seemingly uncommercial, the "Tangs" sold millions of albums during the 1970s.

Although they may not be a household name, Kraftwerk's influence on the development of electronic pop music is immense. Formed in Düsseldorf, in the center of Germany's industrial heartland, the music of Ralf Hutter and Florian Schneider was unique in that all of it was electronically generated. At this time there were no programmable electronic drum machines on the market—rhythms were created using specially built electronic drum pads. Kraftwerk's music itself contained simple rhythms and melodies, sometimes layered with monotone vocals. Although it was not exactly "pop," the track "Autobahn"— an electronic simulation of a journey along a freeway—was a major international hit in 1974. Albums such as *Radioactivity, Trans-Europe Express* and *Man Machine* provided a template for much of the electronic pop and dance music that followed.

Orbital—the brothers Phil and Paul Hartnoll—are among the most significant electronic bands of the past decade.

ELECTRONICS IN THE MAINSTREAM

Although "classic electronic" bands such as Tangerine Dream were able to sell large quantities of their music during the 1970s, these musicians were cult figures rather than household names. This changed in 1976 when a little-known French keyboard player named Jean-Michel Jarre produced a credible electronic album that had far wider appeal than its forebears. *Oxygene* differed from other electronic music of the time in that rather than creating sound collages it contained a wealth of immediately memorable tunes. It topped the charts the world over.

Commercial electronic keyboard music took another step forward in 1977 when David Bowie, seeking a complete change of direction, collaborated with Brian Eno on the album *Low*. Although the album was not a massive commercial success by Bowie's standards, it introduced Eno's ambient style to a new and mainstream audience.

THE ELECTRO-POP EXPLOSION

Whilst Kraftwerk had made its mark using largely self-designed equipment, the end of the 1970s saw a proliferation of increasingly affordable new technology. Once the preserve of wealthy rock stars, synthesizers were now in the same cost bracket as electric guitars, providing access to interesting sounds for a new generation of young musicians.

The turn of the decade saw the birth of a whole movement of synth-based pop music by bands such as The Human League, Depeche Mode, Yellow Magic Orchestra, Soft Cell and Gary Numan. Most of these artists owed a major debt to Kraftwerk,

the *Low* album and the productions of Georgio Moroder—most notably the disco classic, Donna Summer's "I Feel Love."

LET THERE BE DRUM MACHINES

Also important to the music of this period was the development of the programmable rhythm machine. Although there had been earlier beat boxes, the first to make any great impression was the Roland CR78, launched in 1978. Two years later, the same company unleashed the classic TR-808—used on more hit records over the past two decades than any other drum machine. Both models featured completely analog sounds, and were not terribly "realistic"—a fact that some musicians found off-putting.

Sceptics began to change their views when they first heard the Linn digital drum machine in 1980. Instead of synthesized drum sounds, the Linn triggered digital recordings of real instruments. Widely used during the first half of the 1980s, when properly programmed and recorded it was not always easy to tell that you were not listening to the real thing.

ATLANTIC CROSSING

Until the early 1980s, synth-pop and other forms of electronic music was dominated largely by European bands. Although some of them had crossed over to enjoy success in America, they mainly appealed to young, white college audiences. It was, once again, Kraftwerk who helped alter the course of pop music when they began to reach an audience of young black DJs, musicians and producers. By mixing synth-pop rhythms created using cheap technology with the energy of hard funk, hip-hop began to emerge—indeed, one of hip-hop's first big hits—"Planet

KEYBOARD CLASSICS

- Add N to X—*On the Wires of our Nerves*
- Africa Bambata—*Planet Rock*
- Laurie Anderson—*Weird Science*
- Beaver and Krause—*In a Wild Sanctuary*
- The Blue Nile—*A Walk Across the Rooftops*
- The Blue Nile—*Hats*
- David Bowie—*Low*
- David Bowie—*Heroes*
- Cabaret Voltaire—*Mix Up*
- Cabaret Voltaire—*Three Mantras*
- Depeche Mode—*Speak and Spell*
- Thomas Dolby—*The Age of Wireless*
- 808 State—*Ex:El*
- Brian Eno—*Discreet Music*
- Brian Eno—*Thursday Afternoon*
- Eurythmics—*Savage*
- Future Sound of London—*Future Sound of London*
- Herbie Hancock—*Rockit* (single)
- Paul Hardcastle—*19* (single)
- The Human League—*Dare*
- Jean-Michel Jarre—*Oxygene*
- Jean-Michel Jarre—*Equinoxe*
- Kraftwerk—*Trans-Europe Express*
- Kraftwerk—*Man Machine*
- L. L. Cool J—*Mama Said Knock You Out*
- New Order—*Blue Monday* (single)
- New Order—*State of the Nation* (single)
- The Orb—*Little Fluffy Clouds* (single)
- Orbital—*Chime* (single)
- Pet Shop Boys—*Please*
- Pizzicato Five—*Happy End of the World*
- Public Enemy—*Yo, Bum Rush the Show*
- The Passage—*Pin Drops*
- The Residents—*A Tale of Two Cities*
- Roxy Music—*Roxy Music*
- Run–DMC—*Tougher than Leather*
- Donna Summer—*I Feel Love* (single)
- Tangerine Dream—*Phaedra*
- Throbbing Gristle—*20 Jazz Funk Greats*
- Rick Wakeman—*The Six Wives Of Henry XIII*

Rock" featured Kraftwerk samples. As technology became cheaper, new forms of electro-dance emerged: in the hands of producers Derrick May and Lenny Larkin, the Roland TB-303 Bassline and TR-909 rhythm machines were used to create Acid House during the mid-1980s. One way or another, electronic dance music has dominated the past 15 years, and shows little sign of relaxing its grip.

SAMPLING AND RETRO

The digital sampling keyboard had made a big impact on the music world during the early 1980s. Although extremely expensive, those you could afford access were quick to exploit its power. Producer Trevor Horn was responsible for creations such as Frankie Goes To Hollywood and Art of Noise, all of which could be heard using the characteristic "orchestral stab."

As samplers became cheaper, interest in regular synthesizers began to wane. For the past 15 years, sampling has dominated much of the music scene, with dance producers building rhythm loops taken from existing tracks into their own music. This, in turn, has influenced the independent pop and rock scenes— "non-dance" artists such as Beck basing songs around samples. This "lo-fi" influence has extended even further as increasing numbers of rock and pop bands continue to embrace much of the junked analog technology so beloved of dance world.

Add N To X, one of a new wave of "retro" keyboard bands.

CHAPTER 2
PLAYING KEYBOARDS
WHERE TO START

This chapter presents the broad basics of keyboard playing in ten easy-to-follow lessons. To follow the course you need one essential items: some sort of keyboard. If you have access to an acoustic piano, then you're halfway there. Of course, certain types of electric keyboard have additional needs. Whilst some of the cheaper domestic keyboards have a built-in amplifier and speakers, for more serious professional models you will be expected to provide these independently.

WHAT DO YOU NEED?

The days when no household was complete without a piano in the corner of the living room are now long gone. This means that unlike the distant past, most people who want to learn how to play a keyboard instrument have to buy one.

Choosing a keyboard instrument can be a tough experience for a beginner. The most important decision to start off with is whether to buy a traditional acoustic piano or an electronic keyboard. This will depend both on the type of music you want to play and practical issues, such as whether you have the space to accommodate such an instrument. If you are serious about acquiring a formal musical education, a piano will be more suitable for practice. If you are more interested in informal pop and dance music, an electric keyboard will be better. Whatever direction you choose, though, it always helps if you involve someone who has experience in these matters, especially if you intend buying second-hand.

For your first keyboard instrument, spend as much as you can reasonably afford. You may be able to pick up a broken-down old upright piano for virtually nothing, but if the keys don't work properly and it doesn't stay in tune, then you might as well not bother: even good players will make a terrible sound on such an instrument.

CHECKING A PIANO

Judging the value of a piano is something of a skill, and so if you do decide to follow this route, you really are advised to take someone who at least knows a little about the instrument. Here are a few points that are worth considering:

• You can tell quite a bit from an instrument's external appearance. Whilst a scratched and broken piano will look horrible as a piece of furniture—which is a consideration for most homes—they can also provide you with a clue that the instrument might have been abused.

TEACHING AIMS

A variety of different teaching modes are used throughout this book. Much of the learning can be achieved by following the overhead hand photographs and assorted diagrams. Toward the end of Chapter 2, however, to make the most of the exercises you need to be able to follow the notated music.

The lessons have been devised so that you can learn to read music while you are learning to play keyboards—this is far and away the most effective way of doing it. In fact, by the end of the chapter you should have a reasonable understanding of basic music theory. That said, this is not the primary aim of the book. Whilst we touch on "classical" music in Lesson 10, those wishing to pursue a *bona fide* traditional piano training really need to acquire one-to-one specialized training with a teacher.

The basic goal is to present a broad approach to playing the many different modern musical styles for which the keyboard is a central instrument. Thereafter the player is advised to pursue their own specific interests.

Of course, modern keyboard playing is not only (or necessarily at all) about playing in the conventional sense. Keyboards are the most important of all instruments when it comes to the area of programming sounds and sequences: this also receeives a good deal of attention.

• Play each of the keys independently. They should provide a uniform feel throughout. When you apply different levels of pressure to each key you should be able to detect the volume changing consistently.

• Listen out for rattling and scratching noises when you work through the notes. These can indicate that something is wrong with the hammer mechanisms.

• Try to ascertain if the piano is in tune. You can do this by taking a standard tuning device and testing out the pitch of the note A below Middle C. Pianos rarely go out of tune in a consistent manner, but if a piano has been subjected to extremes of cold and damp, the strings can easily rust, making it impossible to achieving concert tuning.

ELECTRONIC OPTIONS

When deciding to buy an electronic keyboard, one of the hardest things to accept is the rate at which new technology becomes redundant. Unlike guitarists, whose instruments often increase in value, electronic keyboards are more akin to computers in the way their resale value can quickly plummet: a new brand keyboard costing a thousand pounds may well have a market value of a good deal less than half of that amount within a few months. Let's be honest, nobody likes to see their investments so dramatically reduced, but this comes with the territory when you buy the latest in technology.

For this reason alone, novices are advised to start out with a second-hand instrument. If you don't like that idea, there are plenty of new bargains to be found when music stores sell off last year's models at "knock-down" prices.

Since there are so many fundamentally different types of electronic keyboard, the buyer is often spoilt for choice. A good starting point is to buy one of the numerous monthly music technology magazines. Not only do they provide reviews of new equipment, but they will get you accustomed to the sometimes baffling language of music technology. Advertisements are also useful in that they can provide you with a good feel for what kind of instruments and features you can expect for your budget; you can also gauge resale prices by looking at the going rates in the second-hand pages.

You can broadly group the options into four categories: home keyboards; digital pianos; polyphonic "workstation" synths; and monophonic synths. If you are learning to play conventional keyboards you can immediately discount the last of those options since a monophonic keyboard can only play one note at a time.

Home keyboards represent the cheapest option, and although they often seem to have the most to offer, this is not necessarily the best route to follow. A typical home keyboard offers a variety of preset sounds, which are usually cheap synthesized takes on acoustic instruments. They usually also feature a built-in amplifier and speaker. This means that everything you need to make music is in place. However, more often than not, the keys themselves have a cheap plastic feel to them that makes playing anything too demanding an impossibility.

Digital pianos have largely replaced acoustic instruments in the home. They usually contain a limited range of piano-based voices that are created by digital samples—recordings of an acoustic piano. This means they are capable of producing very realistic sounds. Additionally, the best models are built with weighted or wooden keys to give the effect of playing a real piano.

Workstation synthesizers are probably the most useful from an all-round point of view, although they are also the most expensive. Some models feature multiple programmable sounds, digital samples of acoustic instruments and even on-board sequencing facilities.

FUNDAMENTALS OF MUSIC

Any piece of music can be notated using a special language of lines and symbols. If you are completely new to the idea of written music, the next few pages will give you a brief overview of what it's all about. This can seem a bit daunting when you first start, but don't worry—music works in an extremely logical way. *TOTAL KEYBOARD TUTOR* uses several different methods to get across its musical ideas. Most of the exercises are shown using standard music notation (the five-line treble staff). Visual diagrams looking onto the keyboard from above are used as a convenient way of showing chord positions. Photographs are also used to show some examples.

NAMING THE NOTES

Before we start to look at written music we first need to clarify the most basic of principles. Think of a simple song that everyone knows, for example "When The Saints Go Marching In". If you sing the first line of the tune—"Oh, when the saints…" you will notice that it contains four different notes. This is because each note has a different PITCH. Each of these notes can be scientifically defined in terms of the frequency of its soundwaves. This means that the pitch of any note is fixed.

OCTAVE INTERVALS

All music is made up of twelve different notes—that means twelve fixed pitches. These are best viewed as the notes of a piano keyboard (*see below*). Notes increase in pitch as you move from left to right along the keyboard. The white notes on the keyboard are named from A to G. Each of the black notes can have two possible names, depending on their musical context; we'll talk some more about those in a moment.

If you look at the way the notes are named you will see that these sequences repeat themselves. When you get to G, the next white note along the keyboard is once again called A. Although this has the same name, it clearly has a higher pitch than the previous A in the sequence. If you play both notes, one after the other, you will hear that in spite of the different pitches, they are in fact the same note. This special relationship is called an OCTAVE—scientifically speaking, doubling the frequency of any note creates the same note one octave higher in pitch.

SHARPS AND FLATS

The interval between any two adjacent notes is called a HALF STEP. This represents one-twelfth of an octave. In terms of the white keys, B and C are a half step apart, as are E and F. However, the other white keys are two half steps apart. This is usually referred to as a STEP. If you move a half step in either direction from these notes, you will play a black key. These can be given names relative to the notes on either side. For example, the black note between F and G can be called

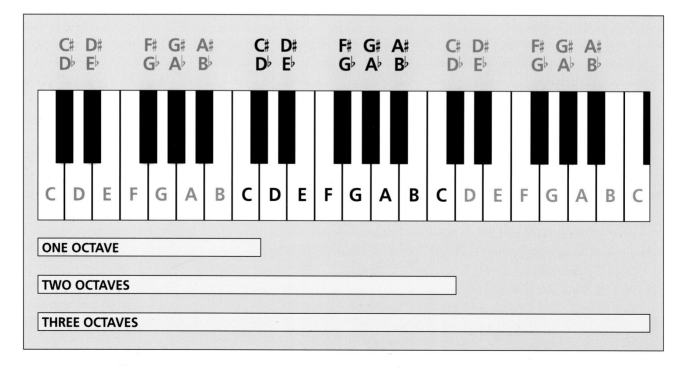

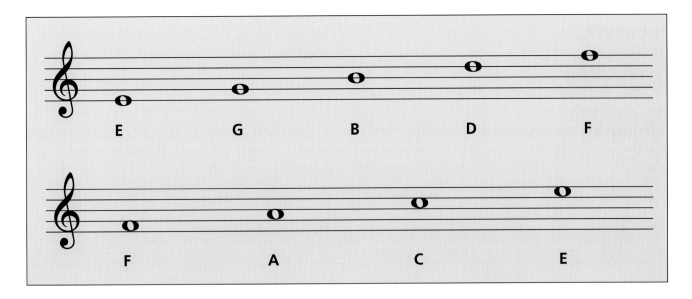

"F sharp" (which is written as F♯) or G flat (notated as G♭). The term "sharp" means to raise the pitch of a note by a half step, thus F♯ is the note F raised by a half step. Similarly, the term flat means to lower a note by a half step—so G♭ is the note G that has been lowered by a half step.

Notes such as these with two possible names are referred to as being ENHARMONIC.

STANDARD MUSIC NOTATION

Music is traditionally written on a five-line grid known as a STAFF (this becomes "staves" in the plural form). A variety of symbols can be positioned on and between the lines of the staff to indicate the pitch and duration of a single note.

Musical instruments such as the piano have a very wide range of notes—a concert grand can encompass over seven octaves. As such, all of these notes cannot be fitted within a single five-line staff. Therefore, a staff can be given a unique range of notes by positioning a symbol at the start of the music. Notes that are predominantly above "Middle C" on a piano are positioned on a "treble" staff, which is prefixed by a treble clef (𝄞); notes predominantly below Middle C are positioned on a staff prefixed by a bass clef (𝄢). For this reason, piano music is invariably written over two concurrent staves.

NOTES ON THE TREBLE CLEF

The clef defines the notes on and between each line on the staff. For a treble clef, the notes on the lines are fixed as E, G, B, D and F. The notes between the lines are F, A, C and E. If you look at the two staves at the top of the page you can see that each of these notes is represented by a circular symbol. You will later discover that the appearance of these symbols will change in accordance with the length of the note, although it

is the position of the circle—the HEAD of the note—on the staff that always defines the pitch of the note.

We can see how the white notes are shown on the staff, but what about the enharmonic black notes? These appear on the line or space after which they are named and are shown with either a flat or sharp symbol to the immediate left of the head of the note.

REMEMBERING THE NOTE POSITIONS

The lines and spaces on the staff are always referred to from bottom to top. In this way, the bottom line of the staff is properly referred to as the first line; similarly, the top line of the staff is known as the fifth line.

Learning the note names on the lines and spaces of the staff is the most fundamental lesson in being able to read music. When you first start, it will take a while for your brain to become used to interpreting the positions of these symbols. Later they will come instinctively to you.

One of the most commonly used aids for memorizing the notes on the lines and spaces of the treble clef is to use a mnemonic phrase. This is an easy-to-remember expression in which the first letter of each word represents the sequence of notes. For the notes on the line you can use the phrase "Eat Good Bread Dear Father." For the spaces in between you can use the word "FACE." Remember that they refer to the note names from the bottom of the staff upwards.

EAT	=	E	F
GOOD	=	G	A
BREAD	=	B	C
DEAR	=	D	E
FATHER	=	F	

THE BASS CLEF

By replacing the treble clef with a bass clef, the notes on the lines and spaces of that staff take on different names and pitches. By definition, the notes on the bass clef are lower in pitch than their treble counterparts: the note E on the third space of the bass clef (*see below*) is exactly one octave below the note E on the first line of the treble clef. You can remember the notes on the lines of the bass clef using the phrase "GOOD BOYS DESERVE FUN ALWAYS," and the spaces with "A COW EATS GRASS."

GOOD	=	G		A	=	A
BOYS	=	B		COW	=	C
DESERVE	=	D		EATS	=	E
FUN	=	F		GRASS	=	G
ALWAYS	=	A				

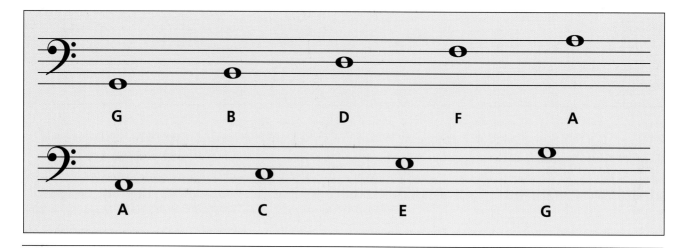

LEDGER LINES

The problem with the staves as you've seen them so far is that they can only represent a range of nine pitches: from E on the bottom line to F on the top line of the treble clef; and from G on the bottom line to A on the top line of the bass clef. Even the simplest music requires notes outside of these ranges.

This problem can be overcome using ledger lines. These allow notes to run "over the edge" of the staff using additional lines that are added for each occurrence.

The two staves below show how notes can be extended above and below the five staff lines to cover a range of more than two octaves. The same principle can also be applied to the notes on the bass clef.

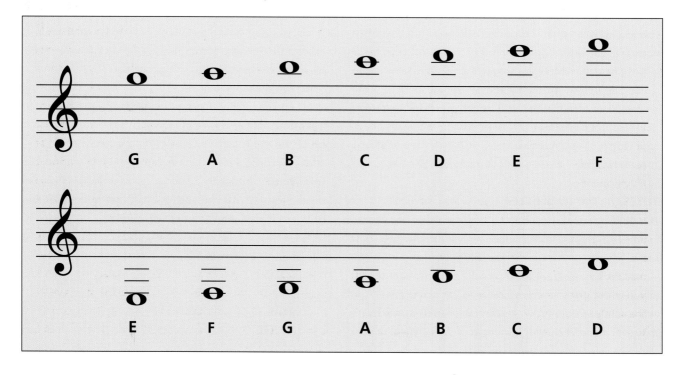

JOINING THE TWO STAVES

Because it has a wider range of notes than any other musical instrument, works composed specifically for the piano or other keyboards are nearly always written over two concurrent staves. The curly bracket shown at the beginning indicates that the two staves are to be played simultaneously.

As a general rule, the left hand is used to play the notes on the bass staff, and the right hand, the notes on the treble staff, although this is by no means always the case.

The example below shows a range of nine notes—from G to A—played over both bass and treble staves. You will notice that there is a crossover point where three of the notes—C, D and E—could be written on either staff. This separation is usually governed by the musical context, which often does come down to a matter of which hand should play the note. The note C in this range is referred to as MIDDLE C.

ALTERNATIVES TO LEDGER LINES

Although ledger lines are useful, if they are used with lengthy sequences of notes, they can become difficult to interpret. One common alternative is to use the *ottava* symbol. This is shown as either **8** or **8va** and is followed by a line marking out the range of notes. If it appears above the notes, they have to be raised by an octave; if it appears below the notes then they should be lowered by an octave.

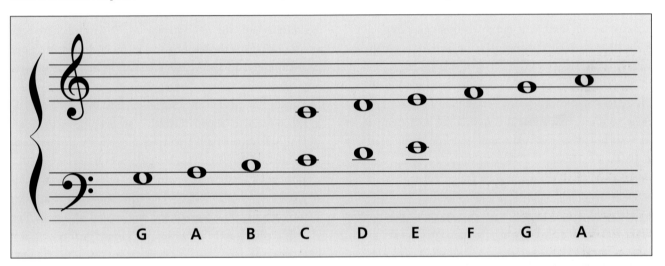

G   A   B   C   D   E   F   G   A

GETTING TO GRIPS WITH MUSIC THEORY

However dull or scary you find the idea of learning music theory, you should at least remain open-minded about it for the moment. For most people, learning how to read music is rather like learning a language that uses an unfamiliar alphabet. When Westerners encounter Russian or Japanese for the first time, they may be able to pick up some basic phrases within a few days, but the skill of being able to recognize those words when they are written down takes much longer.

As you will see when you work through the book, there is nothing essentially difficult about music theory. It doesn't amount to much more than simple arithmetic—indeed Pythagoras, one of the first music theoreticians, considered music to be a branch of mathematics. But however quickly you get to grips with the fundamentals of written music, the ability to sight-read—that means the skill of being able to see a piece of music and immediately sing or play it—will only come with time. And that inevitably means practice. If you want your sight-reading abilities to develop alongside your keyboard playing you will need to take on some additional study.

A sensible methodical approach to using this book is to set yourself a timetable and try to stick to it. Although working through a single lesson may take you very little time, don't try to race your way through the book. Space out your lessons. In between times, try to get hold of some published sheet music and apply the things you have taught yourself to "real" examples of written music.

You'll be surprised how quickly you can develop your sight-reading skills in this way. All it takes is as little as FIVE MINUTES A DAY reading through ANY piece of written music, marking down the note names and their time values, and WITHIN A YEAR you will be able to work through some extremely demanding pieces of music with little difficulty.

LESSON ONE
BEFORE YOU START...

Before we get down to the nitty gritty of making a noise, we'll start with a look at some of things that you'll first need to know about. This includes a detailed view of the basic components of your keyboard, including the connections at the back. If you have an electronic keyboard you also need to know which types of sound are most suitable for the lessons ahead. It's also important that you get into good habits from the start, such as getting used to the best posture for playing any style of keyboards.

GET TO KNOW YOUR KEYBOARD

Things were a good deal simpler when the only realistic way of learning to play keyboards was to take lessons sitting at an acoustic piano. Once you had worked out how to open the piano lid, press down the keys and stand on the foot pedals, you were ready to play.

Nowadays, novices are more likely to learn using some kind of electronic keyboard. Consequently, before doing anything else there's a pretty fundamental need to know something about its sonic capabilities, as well as any other equipment necessary to produce a sound.

Since every electronic keyboard is slightly different it's difficult to make major generalizations about facilities. However, the photograph below—a "workstation" polysynth—shows many of the features that are likely to be common to most keyboards.

The most important components are the playing keys themselves. Although a grand piano can span over seven octaves, most electronic keyboards have a far more limited range, usually around four octaves. The quality of the keys will also make a big difference to the way you play. Many attempts have been made to simulate the feel of a real piano keyboard, but none have unreservedly succeeded. Some of the budget electronic keyboards have a cheap "springy" plastic feel to them, which can make playing with any expression difficult indeed.

Of course, if the sounds themselves are not pleasing to the ear then the instrument will be correspondingly less enjoyable to play. Most of the better polysynth keyboards are capable of a a mixture of traditional synthesizer tones and reasonable approximations of a range of acoustic instruments, such as the piano, strings and brass. At the budget end of the market, sounds are likely to be a little on the "cheesy" side.

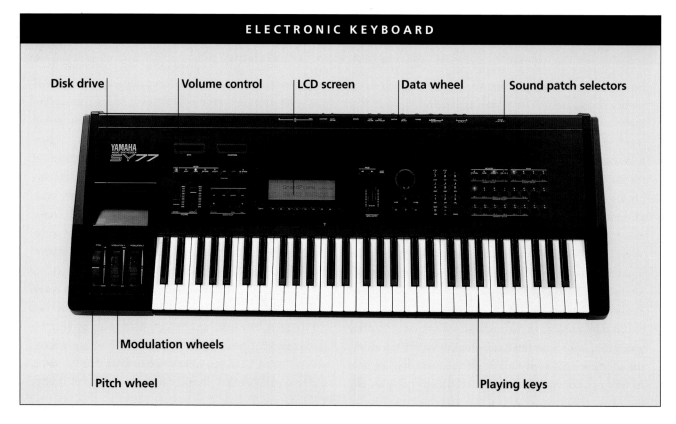

ELECTRONIC KEYBOARD

Disk drive | Volume control | LCD screen | Data wheel | Sound patch selectors

Modulation wheels

Pitch wheel

Playing keys

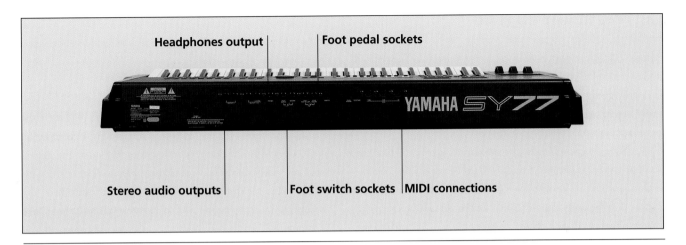

Headphones output — Foot pedal sockets

Stereo audio outputs — Foot switch sockets | MIDI connections

YAMAHA SY77

THE REAR PANEL

In most cases, all of the external connections are found at the back of the keyboard. This typically includes audio outputs, sockets for foot pedals and switches, and MIDI IN, THRU and OUT sockets. Although these all do interesting and useful things, our main area of concern is being able to hear the sounds.

In some cases—and this is especially true of some of the budget keyboards—a basic amplifier and speaker may be built in. Although this will allow you to hear yourself play, it's not likely to sound too great.

Good quality keyboards usually have both audio outputs and connections for headphones. To use the audio outputs you need a separate amplifier and speaker. If you don't have these facilities then a good compromise is to plug the audio outputs into your domestic hi-fi. Most amplifiers have a spare input socket (often labeled "auxiliary") which can be used for this purpose; on older amplifiers an unused turntable input will also work. Alternatively, in desperate cases, you can plug the outputs into the "line" input of a cassette deck. Connections to most electronic musical equipment uses standard "jack" plugs, whereas hi-fi systems are mostly equipped with the smaller "RCA" plugs: to make the connections work you'll need audio cable with a different type of plug on either end.

Of course, you can always use a pair of headphones, which is especially appealing if you don't want others to hear you.

CHOOSING SOUNDS

Every modern electronic keyboard comes equipped with a variety of preset sounds. Most are in some way programmable, meaning that you can edit and modify existing sounds, or create completely new ones and store them in the keyboard's internal memory, or a built-in disk drive. This feature may not be possible on cheaper models. Different sounds—or "patches" as they are sometimes called—are usually accessed by pressing a selection button. Sometimes sounds are grouped into "banks," meaning that the sound selected will depend on which bank number has been chosen. The state-of-the-art modern workstation keyboards are capable of storing thousands of different sounds, which can be recalled at the press of a button.

With all this choice it can sometimes be difficult to know which sounds to use. Although you're certain to find all manner of strange and exotic voices in your keyboard, for the purposes of learning to play it's always a good idea to use a sound that is clean and clear. It's important that you can hear exactly what you are doing: traditional piano and organ sounds will work well for most of the lessons.

Touch sensitivity is another important aspect of sound selection. This is usually termed "velocity sensitivity" and it means simply that the harder you hit the keyboard the louder the note will be, just like on a real piano. This world of dynamics is often overlooked by electronic keyboard players. This is hardly surprising since before the advent of MIDI in 1983, few keyboards were equipped in this way. For this reason, once again, a good piano sound will probably serve you best throughout most of the lessons.

Some sounds—for example, slap bass or synthesized harpsichord—can have a very short "decay" time. This means that if you hold down a note you may only hear the "attack," the rest of the sound will fade out almost instantly. Using these types of voice can be a little misleading when you're learning since it may become difficult to play or sustain notes longer than a couple of beats.

GETTING READY TO PLAY

Before you start to play it's important that you are feeling relaxed and comfortable with your instrument. The posture you choose is largely going to be down to the type of music you play, but there are basically just two possibilities: you either sit down or you stand up.

But before we specifically discuss posture, we should first pay some attention to setting up the keyboard before playing. Unlike a piano, which has a fixed height (3 feet 2 inches in the case of a concert grand), an electronic keyboard can be operated in any position, from a table, chair or sofa to a bed. Although versatile, this is not necessarily a good thing. You should get used to having your keyboard in the same position whenever you play it. This will help your fingers gradually get to know the notes on the fingerboard "by themseleves." To this end, whether you choose to play your keyboard standing up or sitting down, it's a really good idea to acquire a sturdy, purpose-built, adjustable stand.

SITTING COMFORTABLY

There's no question that for most types of formal music, sitting down is the only way to play effectively. It gives maximum control over the hands and fingers, and allows the feet freedom of movement over the pedals. The key to getting into position is in sitting at the correct height in relation to the keyboard.

For the perfect position, when seated with his or her feet flat on the floor, the player's thighs should be in a broadly horizontal position. An adjustable stool is a worthwhile buy for this purpose.

If you have an adjustable keyboard stand, set it up so that when you are sitting down your forearms are in a horizontal position when your fingers touch the keyboard. This is an ideal angle for relaxing the elbows and wrists as well as controlling the movement of the hands.

STANDING UP

Outside of the worlds of classical and jazz music, playing in the standing position is common, especially when performing on stage. Generally speaking, whether standing or sitting down, most keyboard players leave their instruments set up at the same height. This means that when playing while standing, the forearm is naturally higher and so the wrist has to be bent back at an angle. Even though many fine players use this method it can strain the wrist muscles.

Of course it would be possible to raise the overall height of the keyboard or alter its angle so that the keys lean away from the player, but this can look a little unusual or obscure the musicians in a live situation, which is generally of more consideration in pop and rock gigs.

WEARING YOUR KEYBOARD

One other possibility for the live performer is to use a portable keyboard that can be worn on a strap around the neck in the same way as a guitar. These are something of an oddity and although they enjoyed a brief vogue in the mid-1980s they are not used that often these days.

OTHER CONSIDERATIONS

Take care about the kind of clothing you wear when playing keyboards. Bulky or excessively loose clothing can easily restrict your movement. Although rings and other such jewelery shouldn't cause any obstruction, they may create an imbalance in weight among the fingers.

FINGER POSTURE

The exact manner in which the fingers strike the keys is largely a matter of choice. The approach shown at the bottom of page 28 is fairly standard in that the fingers are very slightly clawed but—most important of all—they touch the keys with their pads. The thumb comes into contact with the keyboard with the side of the pad, but still falls short of touching the nail.

The fingers should ideally come into contact with the keyboard at an angle of between 20–30°: if it's less, it can be difficult to control pressure; if it's more, then the fingernails may start rattling against the keys, which is obviously not ideal.

MAKING A NOISE

One thing to consider before you actually get started is the issue of noise. No matter how satisfying or enjoyable you find learning the keyboard, it's going to be a good deal less fun for those around you. So always try to keep your family, neighbors or roommates in mind when you are playing.

One way you can do this is by keeping your practicing to reasonably civilized hours. If you really have to play until the early hours of the morning, make sure you do it on an electronic keyboard with the volume down low, or better still wearing a pair of headphones.

RELAXATION TIME

To get the best of the piano or electronic keyboard it's important to relax the muscles. As the great Frédéric Chopin told his students: "souplesse avant tout"—"suppleness before everything".

It can be tiring sitting at a keyboard for long periods, and consequently very easy to hunch the back and shoulders. Try always to keep your back perfectly straight. Before you begin playing, it's always a good idea to relax your arms and hands before bringing them in position on the keyboard. Here is a simple relaxation exercise:

- **Sit down at your keyboard.**
- **Slowly breathe in through your nose, and then exhale quickly through the mouth. Repeat ten times.**
- **Drop your arms to your side so that they hang loosely from the shoulder.**
- **With your arms still in position, slowly stretch your fingers out as widely as you can and hold them in position for ten seconds before releasing them to their natural positions.**
- **Repeat this exercise ten times.**
- **Now wriggle your hands quite vigorously from your wrists for about ten seconds.**
- **Let your arms hang loosely from the shoulder again for about ten seconds.**

POSTURE POINTERS

Both the piano and electric keyboards make use of different types of foot pedal to add expression to playing.

All pianos have at least two foot pedals. Often these are simply referred to as being "loud" or "soft," but in truth this is not quite accurate.

The most important pedal is the "sustain," which is usually controlled by the right foot. When the pedal is held down, the dampers on the piano strings are lifted up so that the notes are allowed to ring for longer.

The "soft" pedal on a grand piano is technically known as *una corda*, or "one string." When a hammer strikes a note, it is actually playing a number of different strings all tuned to the same pitch. This pedal shifts the entire mechanism of the piano, including the keyboard and hammers, to the right, so that the hammers strike one string less. Although the sound is by definition less loud, the main purpose of this pedal is to alter the tonal quality of the notes being played.

On a concert grand piano, a third pedal is fitted between the other two. This is called the "sostenuto," which is an alternative sustain pedal.

It's important to understand that these pedals are not simple "on-off" switches. They can be used to varying degrees to produce a wide array of very subtle effects.

ELECTRIC KEYBOARDS
Sets of pedals can also be used on electronic keyboards. These are usually crude approximations of the two principal piano foot pedals. Rather than altering volume, the "sustain" pedal simply lets notes linger while the pedal is pressed; at best, the "soft" pedal dulls the tone of sound.

One pedal that is unique to electronic keyboards—most commonly used by electronic organs—is a volume pedal. Rather than simply being activated by pushing the foot down, the volume pedal has a rocking motion that can be fixed in any position by removing the foot.

LESSON TWO
WORKING THOSE FINGERS

With the preliminaries out of the way, it's now time to get down to business. The examples and exercises shown in this lesson aim to get your fingers working, your brain recognizing notes and your keyboard making a noise. Getting your fingers used to moving correctly is essential for playing any type of keyboard music. Taking the easiest route at the start can be a false economy—it may create the illusion of progress but you may well later find that you have to "unlearn" bad habits. That can be easier said than done.

RIGHT-HAND EXERCISES

Let's begin with something very gentle. The diagrams below and across the page show you how to play the notes C, D, E, F and G using the thumb and four fingers of the right hand.

Each box contains a keyboard diagram with a single note highlighted with its name. Beneath the keyboard you can see how the note is written on a the staff alongside the treble clef. The photograph alongside shows you which finger (or thumb) you need to use.

FIVE-FINGER SEQUENCE

This very simple set of exercises illustrates one of the most fundamental aspects of keyboard playing—making use of the most appropriate fingers. The five keyboard diagrams show the notes C to G being played by the thumb and four fingers respectively. Clearly it would be possible to play all of these notes using the same finger. Indeed, rather like novices encountering a computer keyboard, when you are learning you will probably find it more natural to play just using the strongest finger, probably your first (index) finger. However, if you become used to a restricted range of fingers you will later find it difficult to

play fast sequences of notes or chords— groups of three or more notes played simultaneously.

What this exercise is definitely NOT saying is that the note C should always be played by the thumb, D by the first finger, and so forth. The simple practice we're showing is that adjacent notes in a sequence are best played by adjacent fingers: if the

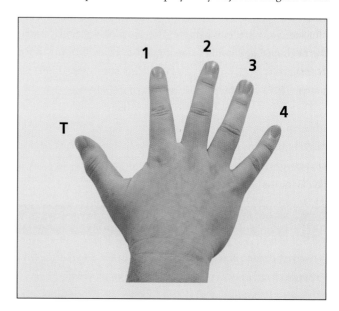

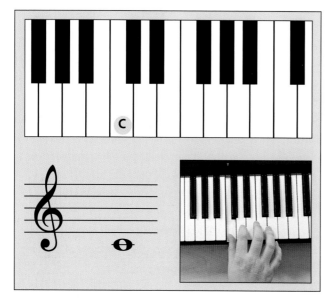

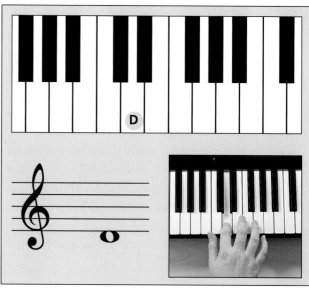

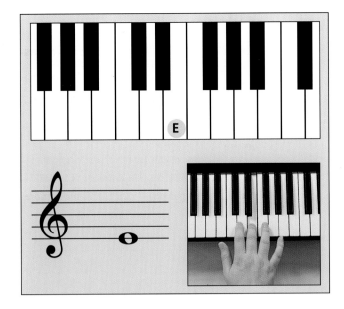

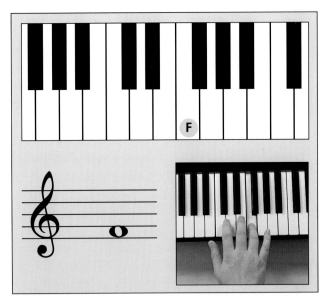

sequence goes C-D-E you should use the thumb and first two fingers; if the sequence is C-E-G then you could use the thumb, second and fourth fingers. As you will see later, this kind of approach to fingering can be adapted to any set of circumstances.

All of the exercises in this lesson are intended for the right hand only—we'll deal with the left hand later. Start off by playing the note C with the thumb. Exert a delicate touch—you don't need to poke at the keyboard, just press down firmly. Repeat this exercise, playing the notes D, E, F and G with the first, second, third and fourth fingers respectively.

As you play, pay special attention to the position of the note on the staff. It may help to think back to those little phrases shown on page 23 telling you how to remember the note names on the staff: <u>E</u>at <u>G</u>ood <u>B</u>read <u>D</u>ear <u>F</u>ather for the lines; <u>FACE</u> for the spaces.

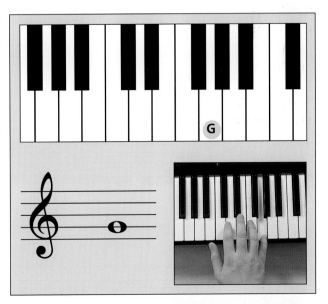

PUTTING IT TOGETHER

When you've played each note through on its own, play the exercise shown below. This is a simple sequence featuring all five notes played one after the other. Throughout this lesson you'll find a number of exercises in this style. In each case, you will see the notated music. Directly beneath, you can see the note names, and the finger you should use to play the note. In each case, "T" represents the thumb, and the four fingers are numbered from "1" to "4."

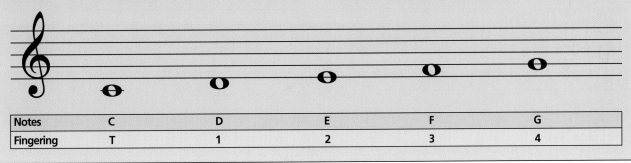

Notes	C	D	E	F	G
Fingering	T	1	2	3	4

GETTING USED TO THE NOTES

Here are four further exercises in the same style as the one shown on the previous page. These are more demanding in that this time the notes are not shown being played in ascending order of pitch, but are randomly selected. Once again, use the thumb and fingers "1" to "4" to play the notes C, D, E, F and G respectively. You can make the exercises even more demanding by covering the panels beneath each staff. This means that you have to work out the notes for yourself.

Since you are probably not yet used to the names of the notes and where they appear on the keyboard, a useful tip is to mark them on your own keyboard. This is not as drastic as it sounds. You can go to any stationery store and buy packs of sticky labels. Simply write the note name on the sticker and fix it to your keyboard. Make sure that you buy the ones that claim to be easily removable otherwise your keyboard may be left with an unpleasant sticky residue.

This exercise is all about familiarization with the note names and working the fingers. It's worth stressing again that we're NOT saying that these combinations of note and finger will always be used together.

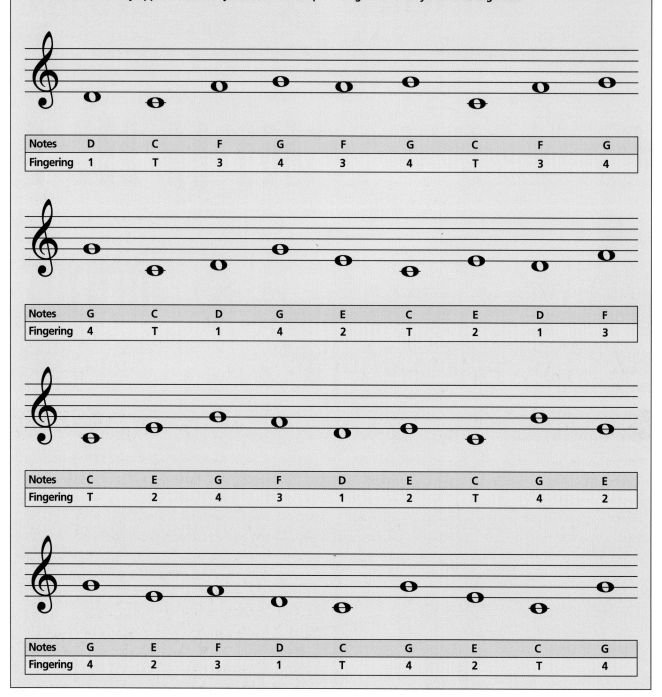

Notes	D	C	F	G	F	G	C	F	G
Fingering	1	T	3	4	3	4	T	3	4

Notes	G	C	D	G	E	C	E	D	F
Fingering	4	T	1	4	2	T	2	1	3

Notes	C	E	G	F	D	E	C	G	E
Fingering	T	2	4	3	1	2	T	4	2

Notes	G	E	F	D	C	G	E	C	G
Fingering	4	2	3	1	T	4	2	T	4

HAND MOVEMENTS

Using the thumb and four fingers to play notes independently is all well and good if you only need to play a range of five notes, such as C to G, but in practice this will never happen. So what do you do when a piece of music calls for you to continue playing the white notes on the keyboard beyond G?

TUCKING THE THUMB (ASCENDING)

The most important aspect in acquiring any reasonable level of dexterity on the keyboard is in having your hand and fingers in the correct position so that they are always ready to play the next note. If you are playing a sequence of successive white notes running from C to A, it's no good playing the penultimate note (G) with the fourth finger because that leaves you without another finger free to play the note A without moving your entire hand. You may not have time for this if the music calls for notes to be played in fast succession.

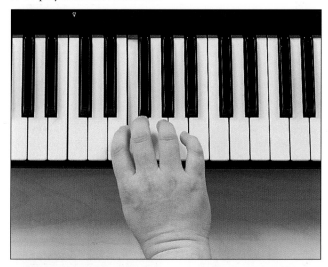

If you place your right hand down on the keyboard, with the thumb on the note C, you have a range of notes that easily covers between C and G without having to spread your fingers too far. If you now move your entire hand to the right, so that the thumb covers the note F, your range of notes has shifted to between F and C. To move smoothly between both ranges you need to use the thumb as a kind of pivot for the whole hand. This can be done when following on from notes played by the first three fingers.

Here is an example of how this can work. If within a piece of music the note E is being played by the second finger, and you know that the next note to be played is F, you have the choice of playing that note with the third finger—as was the case in the previous exercises—OR you can bring your thumb BEHIND the first and second fingers to play the note, as shown in the photograph on the left.

CROSSING THE FINGERS (DESCENDING)

Moving between ranges by tucking the thumb only works when you are playing notes that are ascending in pitch. When you are playing descending notes a similar principle is used, but this time the hand pivots on the first or second fingers and CROSSES OVER the thumb. For example, if the note D is being played by the thumb, and the next note to be played is C, then the first or second finger can be crossed over the thumb to play the note.

LEFT-HAND ISSUES

Although we're not going to concern ourselves with the working left hand until chapter six, it's worth pointing out that the two techniques shown above work in reverse when used with the left hand: when descending, you tuck the thumb; when ascending, you cross the fingers.

ASCENDING AND DESCENDING

Tucking the thumb and crossing the fingers are vitally important parts of keyboard technique. Remember the golden rule: when you are ascending with the right hand, tuck the thumb; when you are descending with the right hand, cross the fingers.

Here is a stage-by-stage example of playing a sequence of notes that ASCENDS between C and A:

- Play C with the thumb.
- Play D with the first finger.
- Play E with the second finger.
- Tuck the thumb behind the fingers to play F.
- Pivot on the thumb and play G with the first finger.
- Play A with the second finger.

Now the same sequence can be played in reverse, from A DESCENDING to C:

- Play A with the fourth finger.
- Play G with the third finger.
- Play F with the second finger.
- Play E with the first finger.
- Play D with the thumb.
- Cross the first finger over the thumb to play C.

PLAYING WITHIN AN OCTAVE

The C that you've been playing so far is a particularly significant note in that it is "Middle C." This is the note that is closest to the center of a piano keyboard, and is often used as a reference source for tuning within an ensemble. On the treble clef, it is shown notated on the first ledger line BELOW the staff; on the bass clef it is shown on the first clef ABOVE the ledger line.

EIGHT-NOTE SEQUENCE

Over the next two pages we'll extend the range of notes up to eight—from Middle C to the next occurrence of C on the keyboard. If you play both C notes, one after the other, you will be able to hear that they are the same note, even though one has a higher pitch than the other. The interval between the two C notes is one octave, or twelve half steps. To see how this works in practice, begin on Middle C and count every note (including the black ones) until you reach the next C; the interval between any two adjacent notes is a half step, so your count should come to twelve.

Before you play the eight-note sequence, take a look at the individual notes that are shown at the bottom of the next two pages. You can see that C, D and E are played with the thumb and first two fingers, but then F, instead of using the third finger, tucks the thumb BENEATH the fingers. Remember, you need to pivot the whole hand around the thumb, moving it to the right, so that the notes F to C can be played as a single run using the thumb and four fingers.

Although we're not concerned with timing for the moment, try to play any of these sequences as smoothly as possible, spending the same amount of time sustaining each note. It's likely that at first you will encounter difficulties with moving the thumb behind the fingers. Don't worry about that too much—you'll soon get used to it. You should also try to get into the habit of applying equal pressure to each note. This is because on a piano or any reasonably good quality electronic keyboard, the volume of the note depends on how hard the key is pressed. Since your fingers will be of different strengths—the thumb and first finger will be much stronger than the fourth finger—it may take you a while to master the art of consistent touch.

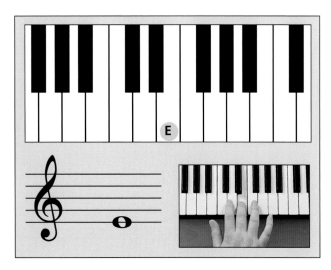

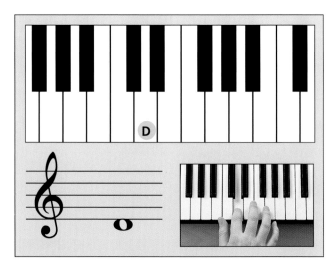

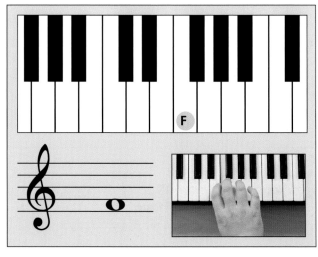

EIGHT-NOTE SCALE

The staff contains all eight notes shown on the previous page and below played as a sequence. As you can see from the finger positions, instead of using the third finger to play F, you bring the thumb underneath and then play the remaining notes with the four fingers.

This sequence of notes will probably sound familiar to you: Indeed, you might have heard this range of notes sung as "Do-Re-Me-Fa-So-La-Ti-Do" (think of that song which begins "Doe, a deer…" from the film *The Sound of Music*).

As you will discover in a few lessons from now, this sequence of notes is called a "major scale." Since this one begins on the the note C, it is known as "C MAJOR."

To work through the sequence in reverse—as a descending scale—play C with the fourth finger, B with the third finger, A with the second finger, G with the first finger and F with the thumb. Now cross the second finger OVER the thumb to play E, pivot the hand on the second finger to play D with the first finger, and C with the thumb.

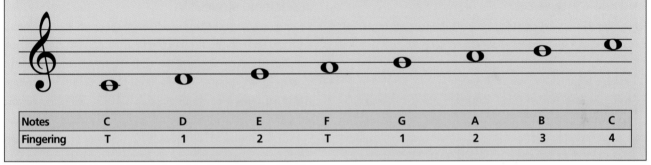

Notes	C	D	E	F	G	A	B	C
Fingering	T	1	2	T	1	2	3	4

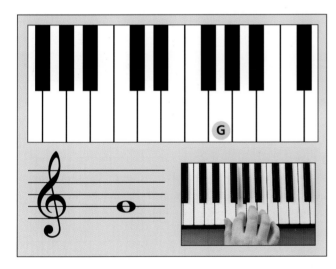

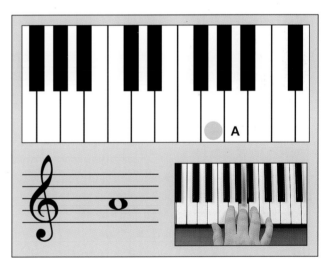

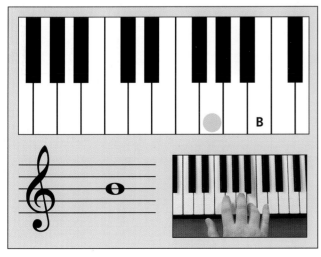

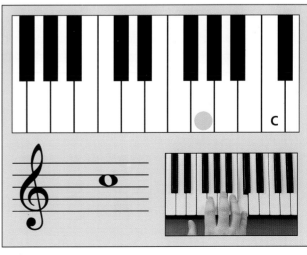

INTEGRATING THE BLACK NOTES

When you are just using the white notes of the keyboard, fingering practice is fairly straightforward. This can change when we start to introduce the "enharmonic" black notes. Because these notes stand back from the white keys, the entire hand has to be moved back and forth as well as from side to side for them to be played. Once again, there are different ways of dealing with such sequences of notes, depending on whether the movements are ascending or descending in pitch.

ASCENDING MOVEMENT

Let's take a look at the music shown at the foot of the page—the sequence of 13 notes between C and octave C.

- Begin by playing C with the thumb.
- Follow it up with the first finger on C♯/D♭.
- The next note you need to play is D, but using the second finger to play this note is a little awkward, especially if the sequence has to be played quickly. The only logical solution is to use the thumb once again, passing it behind the first finger.

- You can then repeat this movement between D and D♯/E♭.
- Now bring the thumb under the first finger once again, this time to play E.
- F can be played with the first finger, and F♯/G♭ with the second finger.
- Since the third finger is not in a comfortable position to play G, you must again revert to the thumb.
- The remaining notes follow the same pattern: play G♯/A♭ using the first finger, A with the thumb, A♯/B♭ with the first finger, B with the thumb and C with the first finger.

DESCENDING MOVEMENT

We can take a similar approach when the pitch is descending. Such movements don't necessarily use adjacent fingers: for example when playing the notes C, B and Bb, the most effective movement is to play C with the third finger, B with the thumb, and cross over the first finger to play A♯/B♭. Continuing the sequence, play A with the thumb, G♯/A♭ with the first finger and G with the thumb. From here, F♯/G♭ needs to be played with the second finger, allowing the first finger to play the consecutive white notes—F and E. The remaining notes are played between the first finger and thumb.

MOVEMENTS OF HALF STEPS WITHIN THE OCTAVE

The finger movements described above are shown along with the note names underneath the staff below. This shows the enharmonic notes as exclusively made up of sharps (♯), meaning that each one takes the name of the adjacent white note to its left. Thus, the second note in the sequence (C♯) is shown as C on the staff with a sharp symbol alongside, indicating that C has been raised by a half step.

Depending on the circumstances in which they are used, these enharmonic notes can equally be labeled as their equivalent flats (♭). The staff on the right shows the same pitches with all of the enharmonic notes described as flats. In this instance, the second note of the sequence (D♭) is shown as D on the staff with the flat symbol alongside, indicating

that it is a D which has been lowered by a half step.

On that same staff, pay attention to the use of the NATURAL symbol (♮). Whenever a note is sharpened or flattened, the symbol only needs showing in the first instance within a bar of music. Thereafter, notes on the same line are assumed to remain at that pitch—the symbol need not be used again. The natural symbol is the instruction that the note should return to its "natural" state—thus the third note has to be given a natural for it to be played as D—if it were left with no symbol it would still be D♭.

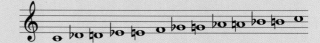

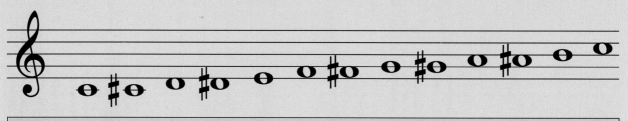

Notes	C	C♯	D	D♯	E	F	F♯	G	G♯	A	A♯	B	C
Fingering	T	1	T	1	T	1	2	T	1	T	1	T	1

NOTE RECOGNITION

It should be stressed at this point that there really are no hard-and-fast rules about these keyboard fingering positions. The movements shown in this lesson represent effective ways of doing the job, but they are by no means definitive—many other possibilities exist.

This final set of exercises features randomly selected notes within the range of the octave from Middle C. Exercises like these are useful for several different reasons. Most significantly, they get your fingers moving around the keyboard. They also aim to familiarize you with the names of the notes as they appear on the staff. Recognizing this new language is at the very heart of acquiring sight-reading skills—the ability to see a piece of music and play it just as if you were reading a book.

Finally, hearing groups of notes played one after the other will help you to hear how these notes sound in relation to one another—this is fundamental to understanding the mechanics of music.

Notes	F	G♯	A	E♭	G♯	D	F♯	B♭
Fingering	2	T	4	T	3	T	3	4

Notes	C	C	B♭	G♯	F♯	G	E	A
Fingering	4	T	4	T	1	2	T	3

Notes	B♭	D	A	E♭	G♯	F♯	G♯	C
Fingering	3	T	3	T	2	1	T	4

Notes	C	E♭	D	F♯	B♭	E	C	A
Fingering	T	2	T	1	3	T	4	2

LESSON THREE
A MATTER OF TIME

Playing in time is a basic art that every musician has to develop. This means being able to play a piece of music (or accompany other musicians) at the right speed, without getting faster or slowing down. This lesson is concerned with the essential basic elements of timing and rhythm. For many beginners these are among the hardest skills to master at first, although, like everything else related to playing a musical instrument, they will improve the more you practice.

RHYTHM AND TEMPO

In music, timing is made up of two distinct and essential elements: tempo and rhythm.

The TEMPO is the speed at which a piece of music is played. It can measured either in terms of a specific number of "beats" per minute (abbreviated as BPM) or a series of written instructions called "tempo marks."

RHYTHM refers to the way in which notes are played or accented. If you listen to any piece of music, irrespective of its genre, you will hear a pulsing effect that seems to be "driving" the music along. This is its rhythm. If you now clap along to the music, you will probably find yourself naturally drawn to a consistent beat. Irrespective of the tempo, the time interval between each clap will be the same value as all of the others.

Most of the music played in the West can be counted out in cycles of four beats. This natural grouping of beats is known in written music as a BAR. The rhythm is created and defined by the length of the notes played within each bar. The most common type of beat you will hear groups together four notes called QUARTER NOTES, each one of which has a value of one beat. A rhythm which is made up of four beats in a bar is said to be in FOUR-FOUR time.

A note that has a value of four beats is called a WHOLE NOTE. The value of any other note is fixed to its relationship to the whole note. The whole note can be subdivided four times by the quarter note—the note value that forms the beat in the vast majority of music. One way or another, every note can be viewed as being a multiple or division of a quarter note. This is an important point to grasp in understanding written music. Each of these multiples or sub-divisions has its own name.

NOTE VALUES

A length of time a note is played can be defined by its value in beats. These are shown on the staff using a number of different symbols. For example, the quarter note is shown as a filled circle with a line attached, known as a "stem." A description for each of the note types is shown below—their relative values are shown in the diagram on the right.

QUARTER-NOTE MULTIPLES

A WHOLE NOTE sustains over four beats. This means that it lasts for the same amount of time it takes to play four quarter notes. A whole note is written as a hollow circle with no stem.

A HALF NOTE sustains over two beats, and lasts for the same amount of time it takes to play two quarter notes.

NOTE APPEARANCE

Notes written down on a staff have a number of attributes, each of which affects the specific value of the note.

The circle is known as the "note head." As you've already seen, its position on the staff defines the pitch of the note. Furthermore, whether the note head is open or filled will determine its length.

The line that you see attached to some types of note head is called the "stem." This will also affect the note's length—a stem attached to an open head is a HALF NOTE, worth two beats; when attached to a closed head it is a QUARTER NOTE, worth one beat. The stem extends upwards unless the note head on the staff is on or above the third line, in which case the stem extends downwards.

The shortest notes are defined by a "tail" (or "flag") attached to the stem. A single tail indicates an EIGHTH NOTE worth half a beat; a double-tail defines a SIXTEENTH NOTE, worth a quarter of a beat; a note with a triple tail is a THIRTY-SECOND NOTE, worth an eighth of a beat.

Groups of quarter notes (and below) can be joined together by "beams." You can see how these work in the diagram across the page, where the bottom three staves contain groups of beamed notes.

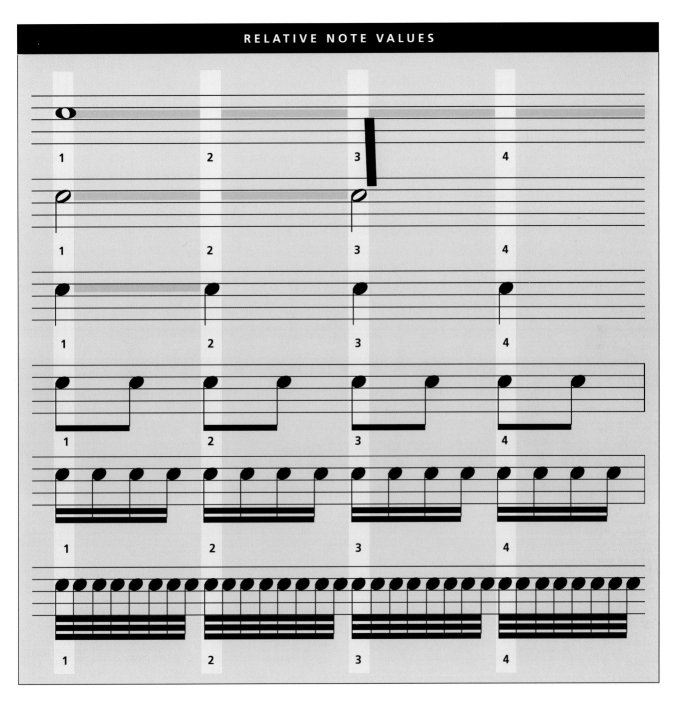

RELATIVE NOTE VALUES

WHOLE NOTE · **HALF NOTE**

Finally, a THIRTY-SECOND NOTE has one-eighth of the value of a quarter note, and therefore also one-eighth of the value of a beat.

QUARTER-NOTE DIVISIONS

Note divisions are named very logically. A QUARTER NOTE sustains over one beat. A note with the value of half of a quarter note is called an EIGHTH NOTE: two eighth notes can be sustained in the time it takes for one quarter note to be played.

A SIXTEENTH NOTE has quarter of the value of a quarter note, and therefore a value of a quarter of a beat.

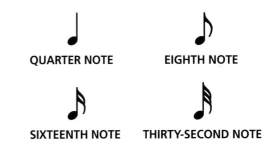

QUARTER NOTE · **EIGHTH NOTE**

SIXTEENTH NOTE · **THIRTY-SECOND NOTE**

MIXING UP NOTE VALUES

In any piece of written music, the notes are grouped into bars: these are shown as vertical lines dividing the staff. The specific number of beats in a bar of music is defined by what is known as the TIME SIGNATURE. This is indicated by the two numbers that you see at the beginning of a piece of music. You already know that four quarter-note beats in a bar is called "four-four time"—this is an example of a time signature.

Music takes its rhythm from the way the notes are grouped or accented within a bar. To create more interesting rhythms, notes of different time values are combined within the same bar. However they must be arranged so that the value of the notes in a bar remains consistent with the time signature. This means that in a bar of "four-four," whatever the value of the individual notes, they must add up to a total of four beats.

Look at the two staves shown below. The first bar consists of two quarter notes and a half note: since a quarter note is worth one beat and a half note two, that makes a total of four beats. The same is true of the other seven bars.

Let's now see how to go about counting out rhythms created using mixed notes. Begin by working out the note values on every beat as shown beneath each note. Now play the first staff —to make things easier, the pitch has been fixed throughout. In the first line, all of the notes are either quarter notes (one beat), half notes (two beats) or whole notes (four beats). Follow the count shown beneath the staff. The second staff line includes eighth notes and sixteenth notes. To count out these you have to split the beat—a common way of counting eighth notes is to insert "AND" between beats.

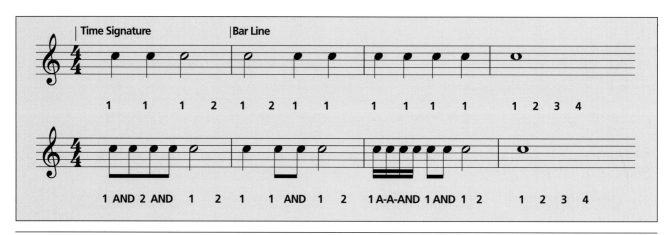

TIES AND DOTS

The note values you've just been using are all based around continually halving whole notes and their subdivisions. But this provides you with a fairly limited palette from which to draw. What for example, do you do if you want to play a note that lasts for THREE beats? Or what if you want to sustain a note across the bar line? The answer is to use TIES and DOTS.

TIES

A tie is a curved line that is used to link together notes of different values, creating a single note with the value of the two notes combined. Look at the first and second bars in the staff below. As you can see, the two half notes either side of the bar line are linked with a tie. This effectively gives the first half note a value of four beats (two beats + two beats). In this case, the first half note is played on the third beat of the first bar and sustains into the first two beats of the following bar. THE SECOND HALF NOTE IS NOT PLAYED. This is a crucial point to remember: the second note in a tied pair is NEVER played, its value is merely added to that of the first tied note.

When ties are written they always join the notes at the head. If the stem points downward the tie is above the note; if the stem points upward, the tie begins below the note.

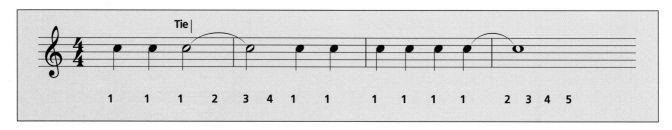

DOTS

By adding a dot to any of the standard note types, it becomes possible to increase their value by half. For example, a half note followed by a dot has a value of three quarter-note beats. This is referred to as a DOTTED HALF NOTE. Similarly, a DOTTED QUARTER NOTE has a value of one-and-a-half quarter-note beats.

DOTTED HALF NOTE = 3 QUARTER-NOTE BEATS

DOTTED QUARTER NOTE = 1 ½ QUARTER-NOTE BEATS

The first bar of the example below begins with two dotted quarter notes. The first dotted quarter note plays on the first beat; the second comes in halfway between the second and third beats; the final quarter note plays on the fourth beat. Notice that whatever alterations are made to the notes, the total value remains consistent with the time signature (1½ beats + 1½ beats + 1 beat = 4 beats).

The third bar is a little trickier to follow in that it features dotted eighth notes. Although each pair of notes is of a different value, they are easier to read if they are beamed. The dotted eighth note is worth three-quarters of a beat; since the second note has a beam and a "broken" beam, it can be interpreted as effectively having two "flags" (*see page 38*) and is thus a sixteenth note, and has a value of a quarter of a beat. Work through all four bars carefully counting out the rhythms.

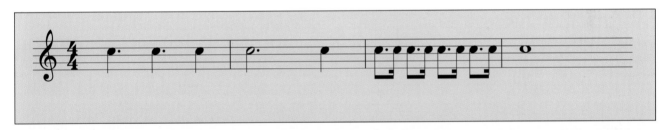

RESTS

Silence is a crucially important part of all music. Without it, all you would hear is a continuous sound. Musical notation has instructions showing periods of silence, or RESTS. Each of the standard note types has its own associated rest. The most commonly used rests are shown on the right.

In the first bar, nothing is played on the fourth beat. In the second bar, nothing is played on the third or fourth beats. The third bar is a trickier proposition in that the four quarter notes are played between the beats.

In practice, a rest can sometimes be quite difficult to perceive, especially below the value of an eighth note, where the difference between a rest and the natural pause that occurs when moving from one note to another may be hard to discern.

WHOLE NOTE

EIGHTH NOTE

HALF NOTE

SIXTEENTH NOTE

QUARTER NOTE

THIRTY-SECOND NOTE

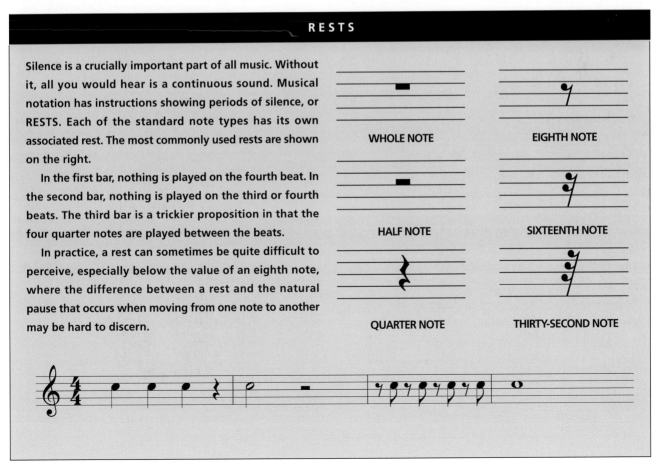

TIME SIGNATURES

As you already know, the time signature is defined by the two numbers that appear at the beginning of every piece of music. The number at the top tells you how many beats there are in the bar. The number at the bottom indicates the time value of each of those beats. If the bottom number is two, the beat is shown as half notes; if it is four the beat is shown as quarter notes; if it is eight, the beat is shown as eighth notes.

A four-four beat is the most commonly used time signature, so much so that it's often referred to as COMMON TIME. However, there are many other possible time signatures.

SIMPLE TIME

The three bars shown below are written in time signatures of two-four, three-four, and four-four. These three time signatures are known as SIMPLE TIME. In each case, when counting through the beats, the natural emphasis always falls on the first beat. It is this emphasis that creates the mood of the piece of music.

Indicates the number of beats in the bar.

Indicates the note value of each beat: "4" means that they are quarter notes.

After four-four time, three-four time is the most commonly used time signature. This is sometimes also referred to as "waltz time." If you count out the time in groups of three (again, emphasizing the first beat), you will hear the unmistakable flavor of the waltz rhythm.

The distinction between two-four and four-four is a little less obvious, since it is clearly possible to count out two bars of two-four as a single bar of four-four. The difference is best illustrated when you understand that most military marching music is in two-four time: imagine soldiers on parade marching to the order "LEFT-RIGHT-LEFT-RIGHT." In each case, the first beat "LEFT" is emphasized.

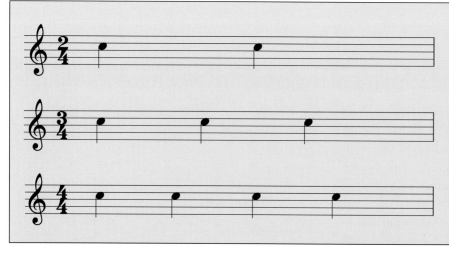

The first example, in two-four, repeats the count ONE-TWO; the second example, in three-four, repeats the count ONE-TWO-THREE. You can think of four-four time as having two accents, the strongest on ONE and the weakest on THREE. Since the tempo is the same in each case, if it were not for these accents the three time signatures would sound the same.

COMPOUND AND ASYMMETRIC TIME

Each of the "simple" time signatures shown above have beats that are divisible by two. A different type of time signature is possible where the beats are divisible by three. This is known as COMPOUND TIME.

A two-beat bar in simple time can be played as two groups of eighth notes. In compound time, a two-beat bar with a time signature of six-eight would be played as two groups of three eighth notes. Similarly, a three-beat bar can be played as three groups of eighth notes in a time signature of nine-eight, and a four-beat bar can be played

as four groups of eighth notes in a time signature of twelve-eight.

A number of less commonly used time signatures feature numbers not divisible by two or three. These are ASYMMETRIC time signatures. These most frequently count in fives and sevens, however bars of eleven and thirteen are also sometimes used. As "unnatural" as some of these may sound, even the toughest asymmetric time signature can be viewed more easily as a combination of groups of two, three or four beats.

EXERCISE IN FOUR-FOUR TIME

Now, for the first time, we can combine the different note values shown during this lesson with notes of different pitches to play a simple tune. The first example is the nursery rhyme "This Old Man." To keep things simple, it's written out below in the key of C. This means that it can be played using just the white notes of the keyboard.

Here is a good way of approaching the task. Begin by working out the pitch of each note. Refer back to page 23 if you need a reminder of the phrases that will help you remember the names of the notes on the lines and spaces. If you like, you can write them down underneath each staff.

Once you have the pitches worked out, take a look at the time values of each note. One approach is to write down the beat value of each note. For example, in the first bar, two quarter notes are followed by a half note: that's two notes each worth one beat followed by one note worth two beats. Tapping out the rhythm can also help. When you're ready you can put the tune and rhythm together.

EXERCISE IN THREE-FOUR TIME

The second example uses three-four time and slightly more complex note values, notably dotted eighth notes and sixteenth notes. You may recognize the tune as "Clementine."

One approach to working out the rhythm for songs that use such small note values is to give the smallest note a count value of one, and multiply the larger counts accordingly. In this case, a sixteenth note takes a value of "one," a dotted quarter note of "three" and a quarter note "four." If you count out the note values in this way (always emphasizing the first beat on which the note is played) you'll be able to hear clearly the rhythm created by the notes. You'll see that they are shown on the first staff of the music below.

Don't get this count confused with the natural three-four beat, though. That's still repeating "ONE-TWO-THREE" every bar—all you are doing is subdividing each beat into four so that it becomes easier to work out the rhythm.

A final point to note is in the content of the first and last bars. As this song is in three-four time, each bar should have a combined value of three quarter notes. However, the first bar contains a dotted eighth note (three-quarters of a beat) and a sixteenth note (a quarter of a beat)—a combined value of one beat. Similarly, the final bar only contains a half note, worth two beats. The reason for this is that the song is written to be sung with many verses. If you count along with the tune, the notes of the first bar would begin on the third beat. When the song reaches the end of its first verse (after the half note has been played for the first two beats) the song returns to the first bar to play the dotted eighth note on the third beat again. In this way, when the notes of the first and final bars are combined, they produce the correct number of beats—three.

LESSON FOUR
SCALES AND KEYS

A scale is sequence that begins with a set note called the TONIC and moves through to the octave of that same note. Although there are many different types of scale, each one can be identified by the pattern of intervals—the distance in steps or half steps between each note—that exists between the root and the octave. Each scale has a key that it takes from the name of the tonic note. The major scale—which is the most commonly used—and the minor series of scales are shown in this lesson.

INTRODUCING THE MAJOR SCALE

On page 35, when you played all of the white notes for the octave starting on Middle C, you were, in fact, playing a C major scale. Each of the notes of this scale can be given a name and a Roman numeral "degree" based on its position within the scale. They are: TONIC (I); SUPERTONIC (II); MEDIANT (III); SUBDOMINANT (IV); DOMINANT (V); SUBMEDIANT (VI); and LEADING NOTE (VII). The diagram below shows the names each of these degrees on the keyboard.

Each degree of the major scale also has a special relationship to the tonic (or root note). The gap between any two notes is referred to as an INTERVAL. The names of the intervals between the tonic and each degree are: MAJOR 2ND (C-D); MAJOR 3RD (C-E); PERFECT 4TH (C-F); PERFECT 5TH (C-G); MAJOR 6TH (C-A); MAJOR 7TH (C-B); and OCTAVE (C-C).

The smallest possible interval on a keyboard is a HALF STEP, which is the distance between any two adjacent notes. Some degrees of the major scale also have intervals of two half steps. This is referred to as a STEP.

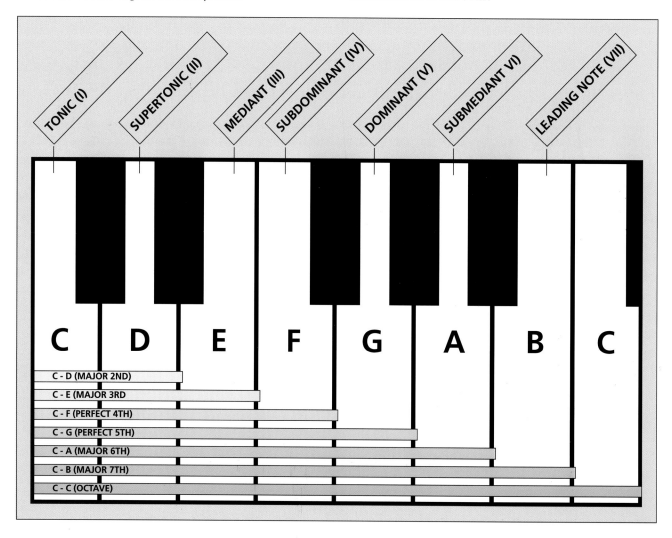

MAJOR-SCALE INTERVALS

Let's now take a closer look at the intervals between each of the degrees of the major scale. The pattern of intervals between each of the notes that make up the scale are shown below. They are STEP (C-D), STEP (D-E), HALF STEP (E-F), STEP (F-G), STEP (G-A), STEP (A-B) and HALF STEP (B-C).

An important point to understand is that it is NOT the note names themselves that define this as being a major scale, but the intervals between each note. Any scale that does NOT have those exact intervals between each of the degrees CANNOT be called a major scale. A scale can be played in ascending or descending order, but the intervals between the notes must always remain the same.

Try playing the scale below using the fingering shown at the end of Chapter 2. Here is a reminder of those finger positions: play C, D and E using the thumb and first two fingers respectively, bring the thumb under the two fingers to play F, and then use the four fingers to play the notes G, A, B and C. For this exercise, also count out beats as you play, making sure that each new note is played on the beat. This kind of exercise will help to improve your skills in keeping time.

Once you've done that, you can play the same notes in descending sequence. Play C with the fourth finger, B with the third finger, A with the second finger, G with the first finger and F with the thumb. Cross the second finger over the thumb to play E, before finally playing D with the first finger and C with the thumb.

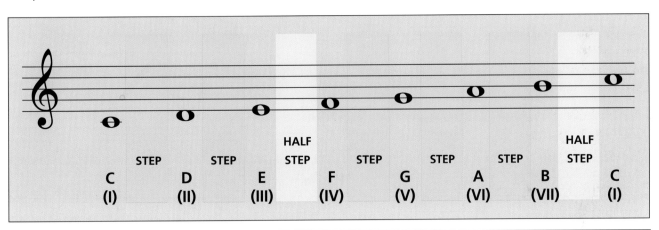

G MAJOR SCALE

Including both black and white keys, there are twelve different notes within an octave. It is possible to create major scales using any of these notes as the root.

If the tonic is moved up to the note G, the same set of step and half-step intervals can be used to produce a G major scale. In this case, as you can see from the staff below, the interval between the sixth and seventh degrees means that we must use a black note to make the correct scale: if the note were left as F, the interval between the sixth and seventh degrees would only be a half step, and thus the scale would not be correct. In the key of G, the black note MUST be named F♯, even though it has the same pitch as G♭. This is so that a note appears on every line or space in the sequence of the scale—if it were called G♭ there would be two Gs on the staff.

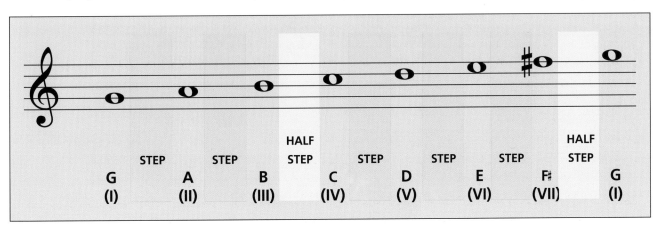

TRANSPOSITION

In the previous exercise, you took the set of intervals that make up the C major scale and repeated them with a different root note. In this way, the C major scale became a G major scale. This process is called TRANSPOSITION. Any sequence of notes can be moved in this way. By transposing the scale from C major to G major, each of the notes had its pitch raised by an interval of a perfect 5th—that's the interval between C and G. By applying that rule consistently, the intervals between the notes always remain exactly the same—the only difference is that they are in a different key.

Transposition is such an important concept in music. For example, if you have a song in a specific key that happens to be outside a vocalist's range, the ability to transpose allows you to rework the music in a different key.

Here is a final major scale for you to look at. Transposing the C major scale by a perfect 4th creates the scale of F major. As you can see from the diagram below, the intervals have remained the same.

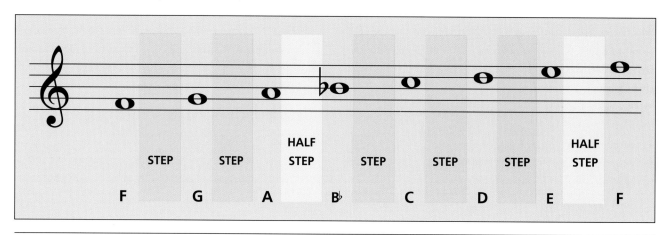

KEY SIGNATURES

So far you have seen the major scales built on a tonic of C, G and F. These notes represent the KEY SIGNATURES for each of those scales. A key signature is indicated at the start of a piece of music by a series of sharps or flats that can be seen between the clef and time signature. This doesn't happen in the key of C, which uses no sharps or flats. For all the other major keys, however, the sharps or flats are positioned on the staff in accordance with their use within that scale. To see how this works, let's look at an example in the key of G.

The G major scale consists of the notes G, A, B, C, D, E and F♯. To indicate this, music "in G major" is shown with a sharp symbol on the top line of the staff, directly following the treble clef. What this means in practice is that, unless otherwise shown (by the use of the "natural" symbol), the note names given to each space and letter on the staff are to be used throughout the piece. Thus, in G major, each time a note appears on the top line of the staff it has to be played as F♯ rather than F, since F is not a part of the G major scale.

Although a little confusing at first, this idea will soon become so familiar that you will immediately know that any piece of music with one sharp after the clef has a key signature of G, and that all references to F should be played as F♯. This is the reason why the note MUST be called F♯ rather than G♭: if it were not, the staff would have no Fs, but two Gs (G and G♭) which could only be distinguished if every single occurrence of G was either as marked as a flat or a natural. This would make the written music appear terribly confusing.

The same is true for the key of F, which uses the notes F, G, A, B♭, C, D and E. Any piece of music written for the key of F major will appear with a single flat on the third line of the staff. This indicates that all the notes that appear on this line must be played as B♭ rather than B natural.

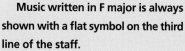

Music written in the key of G major also has a key signature of G major. This is shown with a sharp on the top line of the staff and indicates that in all instances, unless otherwise shown, the note should be played as F♯. For the note F to be played during the piece would require a natural symbol to be used (♮).

Music written in F major is always shown with a flat symbol on the third line of the staff.

Key of G

Key of F

IDENTIFYING KEY SIGNATURES

As you've seen, the keys of G major and F major can be identified by the positioning of either one sharp (G) or one flat (F) at the start of the music. In fact, key signatures for ALL of the major scales can be recognized simply from the number of sharps or flats shown at the beginning of the staff. The number and position of sharps and flats on each new scale follows a very specific simple mathematical pattern.

F is the fourth degree of the C major scale. Building a new major scale from the fourth degree creates the F major scale, which is recognizable by the fact that it features a single flat —the note B♭. If you continue this process, building new scales from the fourth degree, an interesting mathematical pattern emerges. Let's see how this works.

Projecting the same pattern of intervals from B♭ (which is the fourth degree of the F major scale) creates a B♭ major scale. This comprises the notes B♭, C, D, E♭, F, G and A. As you can see, this scale and key signature has TWO flats. If we take it to the next stage, you will see the pattern beginning to emerge.

The fourth degree of B♭ major is E♭. If we build a major scale with this note as the root, it comprises the notes E♭, F, G, A♭, B♭, C and D. As you can see, this time signature features THREE flats. If you continue this process, building a new major scale from the fourth degree of an existing major scale, the new scale will always require the use of one extra flat. In this way, it is ALWAYS possible to recognize a key signature simply by counting the number of flats shown at the start of the music. This set of relationships is shown in the left-hand column below.

A similar kind of principle can be applied to those key signatures that use sharps. If you build a scale from the FIFTH degree of an existing major scale, the resultant scale ALWAYS adds a sharp to the seventh degree. For example, G is the fifth degree of C major: if you build a major scale from G major, the seventh degree requires a sharp (F♯). If you now build a major scale from the fifth degree of G (D), you will see that the original sharp (F♯) remains, and a new one (C♯) is added to the seventh degree. This means that it is also always possible to recognize a key signature by the number of sharps it uses.

F MAJOR (ONE FLAT)   **G MAJOR (ONE SHARP)**

B♭ MAJOR (TWO FLATS)   **D MAJOR (TWO SHARPS)**

E♭ MAJOR (THREE FLATS)   **A MAJOR (THREE SHARPS)**

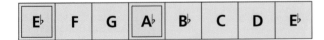

A♭ MAJOR (FOUR FLATS)   **E MAJOR (FOUR SHARPS)**

D♭ MAJOR (FIVE FLATS)   **B MAJOR (FIVE SHARPS)**

CIRCLE OF FIFTHS

We can summarize the relationship between the key signatures using a diagram known as the CIRCLE OF FIFTHS. The twelve segments of the circle are laid out so that moving clockwise, the notes change by a perfect 5th. This also represents scales built on the fifth degree of the previous major scale.

Starting with key of C at the top of the circle, each step you count clockwise adds a sharp to the key signature of that note. Moreover, the additional sharp is always on the seventh degree of the new scale.

The principle works for additional flats if you move in an anticlockwise direction, where each subsequent key signature is a perfect 5th DOWN from the root note of the previous scale. In practice, this makes the root for each new scale the same as the fourth degree of the previous scale. Thus by starting at the top of the circle, each step you count anticlockwise adds a FLAT to the key signature for that note.

The circle of fifths is useful in memorizing the patterns that create key signatures. It's worth taking some time out to learn these key signatures by heart. And it's an absolute necessity if you are planning to be able to sight-read effectively.

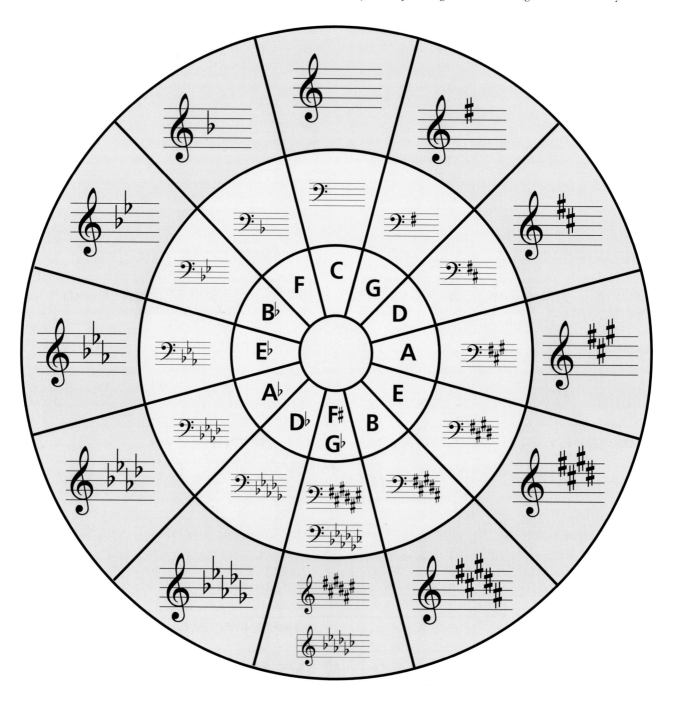

SIGHT-READING

Although the contents of this lesson provide practical tuition for the piano and other keyboards, it is essentially concerned with necessary music theory. As such, all of this can be applied to any other musical instrument. In fact, much of this content is aimed at developing or improving sight-reading skills—this means the ability to be able to read a piece of music just as easily as you can pick out words in a book.

Although many well-known keyboard players cannot read music well, it is a useful skill to develop, especially when playing with other musicians. Even though a good deal of modern music is sufficiently simple to "play by ear," if you want to work your way through complex classical or jazz pieces, sight-reading skills are essential.

SIGHT-READING CHECKLIST

Here is a brief list of useful pointers that will help you gain sight-reading skills:

• **Get used to reading unfamiliar music. Go to a music library and take out any examples of written music. If you spend as little as five minutes a day just working out time signatures, key signatures, note names and rhythms, within a year you should be able to comprehend even the most complex pieces of written music.**

• **When you tackle a new piece of music, begin by checking out the time signature. Remember that the top number tells you how many beats in the bar; the bottom number tells you what kind of beats they are.**

• **Study the key signature. Look at how many sharps or flats there are at the beginning of the staff—these tell you the sharp or flat notes you have to play.**

• **Look out for unfamiliar notes or symbols. In particular watch out for the "accidentals"—sharps, flats and naturals—and their effect.**

• **A lot of written music revolves around repeating patterns of notes or rhythms. Look out for where these occur since this will make your task easier.**

• **When playing a new piece of music, begin with a steady tempo. Give yourself a one-bar count-in before you start, but keep counting the beats out in your head while playing.**

TIPS FOR PRACTICE

This is a convenient point to raise the thorny issue of practice. Although it can be boring working your way through scales and other such exercises, or simple tunes that reflect your current capabilities, practice is essential. To be honest, there is no other way of getting to be a good keyboard player.

Here are some key tips to help you put together a useful practice session:

• Try to work out a practice routine for the week ahead and stick with it. As a rule, it's a good idea to practice frequently but for short periods, rather than having one long session. It will help retain your interest and make it easier to remember lesson content.

• Make sure you feel ready to practice, which means being alert and ready to concentrate.

• Make sure that you can do your practice without being interrupted.

• Regularly check your posture—make sure that your forearms are in a horizontal position.

• Start off by playing a familiar piece. This will help to "warm up" your fingers.

• When approaching a new tune, start off by tapping out the rhythm of the notes—this will get you accustomed to the sounds of certain combinations of note types.

• Learn new tunes slowly at first so as to avoid making mistakes. If you do make a mistake, don't stop, carry on playing to the end of the piece.

• If you encounter a difficult section, practice it over and over again before trying to play the whole piece from the beginning.

• A varied practice regime is always a good idea. Whilst it's always more fun trying to play a piece of music, don't ignore technical exercises, such as practicing scales. You can buy books that only contain scales in a variety of different keys—this can be useful.

THE THREE MINOR SCALES

The major scale, as you should now be aware, is constructed from a fixed pattern of seven intervals from the tonic to the octave. Although the major scale is much the most common type of scale used in Western music, it is by no means the only one. Also in common use is the MINOR SCALE.

WHAT IS A MINOR SCALE?

As a piece of music written in a major key has an easily identifiable characteristic flavor, so too does music written in a minor key. Although the comparison may be a little superficial, you can think of the difference between music written in major and minor keys as being rather like the difference between a sound that is happy and one that is sad. Generally speaking, music with a mournful or melancholic flavour will have been written in a minor key.

Perhaps a good symbolic example of this difference can be heard in the contrast between the joyful "Wedding March," which is played in a major key, and the mournful "Funeral March," which is played in a minor key.

There are three principal types of minor scale, each of which—like any other type of scale—can be defined by a fixed set of intervals from the tonic to the octave.

THE NATURAL MINOR SCALE

Unlike the major scale, in which the pattern of intervals always remains the same, there are three different types of minor scale, each of which has its own subtly different characteristics. The three minor scales are the NATURAL MINOR (which is sometimes also known as the RELATIVE MINOR), the HARMONIC MINOR and the MELODIC MINOR.

All three minor scales have one common difference from a major scale in that the third degree is always flattened by a half step. The differences among the three minor scales revolve around movements of the sixth and seventh degrees.

The pattern of intervals between the notes that make up the NATURAL MINOR scale are shown below for the key of C. The intervals are STEP (C-D), HALF STEP (D-E♭), STEP (E♭-F), STEP (F-G), HALF STEP (G-A♭), STEP, A♭-B♭), STEP (B♭-C).

PLAYING THE MINOR SCALE

To form a natural minor scale from a major scale, the third, sixth and seventh degrees are each lowered by a half step. Play the scale in ascending sequence (as shown on the staff below) and then in descending sequence.

The fingering for the ascending scale can be played in the following way. You'll probably find it particularly demanding spreading the second, third and fourth fingers to move between A♭, B♭ and C, but the more you practice movements such as these, the easier they'll become.

- Play C with the thumb.
- Play D with the first finger.
- Play E♭ with the second finger.
- Bring the thumb underneath the fingers to play F.
- Play G with the first finger.
- Play A♭ with the second finger.
- Play B♭ with the third finger.
- Play C with the fourth finger.

To play the descending scale:

- Play C to G using the fourth, third, second and first fingers.
- Play F with the thumb.
- Bring the second finger over the thumb to play E♭.
- Play D with the first finger.
- Play C with the thumb.

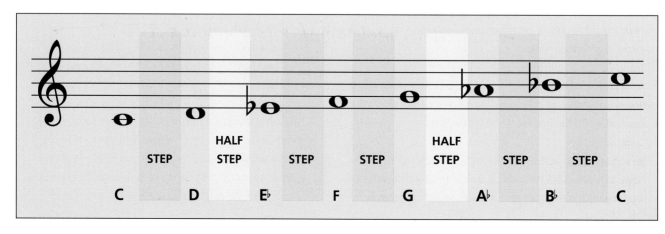

RELATIVE MAJORS AND RELATIVE MINORS

If you play a C major scale followed by its natural minor counterpart, it will be self-evident that the two scales are different. This is because the pattern of intervals used by a major and natural minor scale are not the same.

However, an interesting relationship between these two types of scale can be heard when you build a natural minor scale from the sixth degree of a major scale.

In the two examples shown below, the first staff contains the notes of the C major scale; the second staff shows the natural minor scale in the key of A. The choice of keys here is significant in that A is the sixth degree of the C major scale.

As you can see by looking at both staves together, the C major scale and the A natural minor scale actually use the same set of notes, even though they start from different roots. But if you play the two scales alongside one another you will hear that they have very different characteristics.

This significant relationship between the C major scale and the A natural minor scale can be described in two different ways. the A minor scale can be called the RELATIVE MINOR of the C major scale. Equally, the C major scale can be referred to as the RELATIVE MAJOR of the A minor scale.

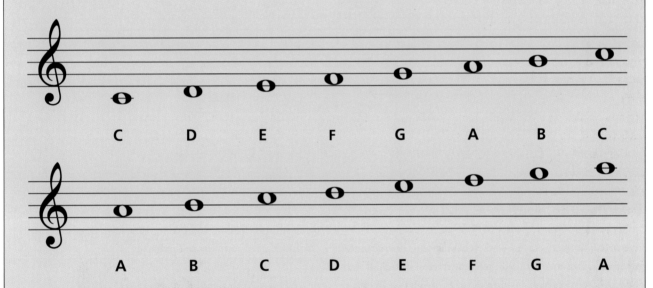

The relationships between the two scales shown above are very important to understand. Since both are played without sharps or flats, the key signatures appear to be the same.

You've already seen that it's possible to tell the key of a piece of music by counting the number of sharps and flats between the clef and the time signature. The mutual relationship described above means that the same observations can also be made for music written in a minor key.

If you turn to page 99, you will see that the key signature for Bach's *Minuet in G Major* is—unsurprisingly —G, and that the characteristic "one sharp" is shown at the beginning of the staff. If you now turn to page 103, you will see that *Partita in E Minor* appears to have the same key signature. This is because E minor is the relative minor of G major, and the notes used in each scale are the same.

Below you can see a list of the most commonly used major key signatures along with their relative minors.

RELATIVE MAJOR		RELATIVE MINOR	
C MAJOR	=	A MINOR	
G MAJOR	=	E MINOR	(1 sharp)
D MAJOR	=	B MINOR	(2 sharps)
A MAJOR	=	F♯ MINOR	(3 sharps)
E MAJOR	=	C♯ MINOR	(4 sharps)
B MAJOR	=	G♯ MINOR	(5 sharps)
F♯ MAJOR	=	D♯ MINOR	(6 sharps)
F MAJOR	=	D MINOR	(1 flat)
B♭ MAJOR	=	G MINOR	(2 flats)
E♭ MAJOR	=	C MINOR	(3 flats)
A♭ MAJOR	=	F MINOR	(4 flats)
D♭ MAJOR	=	B♭ MINOR	(5 flats)
G♭ MAJOR	=	E♭ MINOR	(6 flats)

THE HARMONIC MINOR SCALE

The HARMONIC MINOR scale differs from the natural minor scale in that the seventh degree is sharpened—it is raised by a half step. Thus, the pattern of intervals required to create the scale are STEP (C-D), HALF STEP (D-E♭), STEP (E♭-F), STEP (F-G), HALF STEP (G-A♭), STEP PLUS HALF STEP (A♭-B) and HALF STEP B-C). Notice that by sharpening the seventh degree, the interval between the sixth and seventh degrees is now three half steps.

Play the harmonic minor scale for the key of C shown below in ascending and descending order. The same kind of fingering can be used here as for the natural minor scale, although the step-plus-half-step jump between the sixth and seventh notes may make this alternative more suitable:

- Play C with the first finger.
- Play D with the second finger.
- Play E♭ with the third finger.
- Bring the thumb underneath the fingers to play F.
- Play G with the first finger.
- Play A♭ with the second finger.
- Bring the thumb underneath to play B.
- Play C with the first finger.

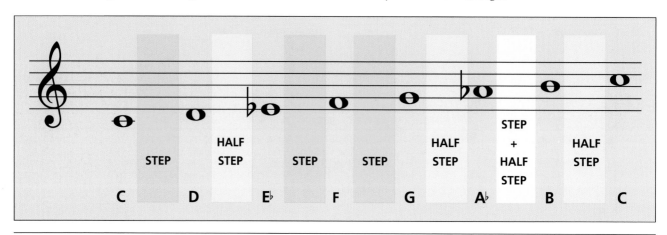

THE MELODIC MINOR SCALE

One of the problems faced when working with the harmonic minor scale is in the "difficult" pitch interval of three half steps between the sixth and seventh degrees. To make this more musically palatable, the submediant (that's the sixth degree — check back to page 44 for the names of each degree) can be raised by a half step to create what is called a MELODIC MINOR scale.

The pattern of intervals that defines a melodic minor scale are STEP (C-D), HALF STEP (D-E♭), STEP (E♭-F), STEP (F-G), STEP (G-A), STEP (A-B), HALF STEP(B-C).

Play the melodic minor scale shown below to hear the smoothing effect of "sharpening" the sixth degree of the scale. You can use the following fingering:

- Play C with the first finger.
- Play D with the second finger.
- Play E♭ with the third finger.
- Bring the thumb underneath the fingers to play F.
- Play G with the first finger.
- Play A♭ with the second finger.
- Play B with the third finger.
- Play C with the fourth finger.

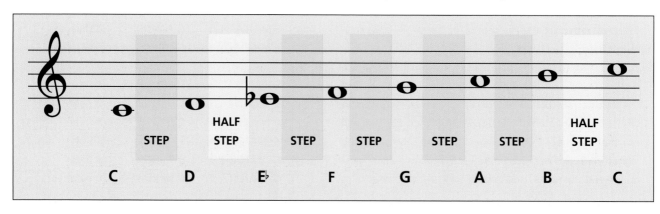

DESCENDING THE MELODIC MINOR SCALE

You can only use the melodic minor intervals shown on the previous page for playing the ascending melodic minor scale. When descending the scale, the sharpened sixth and seventh notes often sound rather awkward.

To resolve the problem, when descending the melodic minor scale you will find that playing the UNSHARPENED sixth and seventh notes will sound more pleasant. This means that when descending the melodic minor scale you revert to the notes of the NATURAL MINOR scale. It is extremely important that you understand the distinction between these two scales.

The pattern of intervals for the descending melodic minor scale are STEP (C-B♭), STEP (B♭-A♭), HALF STEP (A♭-G), STEP (G-F), STEP (F-E♭), HALF STEP (E♭-D), STEP (D-C).

- Play C with the fourth finger.
- Play B♭ with the third finger.
- Play A♭ with the second finger.
- Play G with the first finger.
- Play F with the thumb.
- Bring the third finger over the thumb to play E♭.
- Play D with the second finger.
- Play C with the first finger.

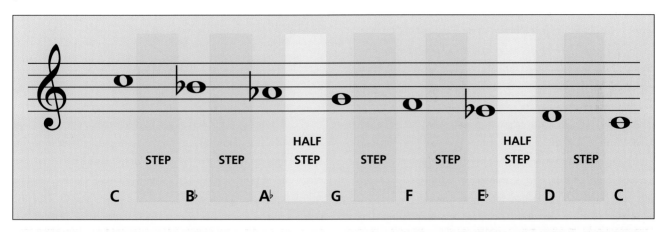

		HALF			HALF	
STEP	STEP	STEP	STEP	STEP	STEP	STEP
C	B♭	A♭	G	F	E♭	D	C

DOUBLE SHARPS AND FLATS

By now you will be familiar with the idea of sharps raising a pitch by a half step, flats lowering a pitch by a half step, and naturals, which revert a sharp or flat to its original pitch. These symbols are all examples of what are known as ACCIDENTALS.

In some situations, however, such as the creation of certain minor scales, it becomes necessary to sharpen a note that has already been sharpened, or flatten a note that has already been flattened. To achieve this you use either a DOUBLE FLAT or a DOUBLE SHARP.

The double flat is shown in written music using the symbol "♭♭." This has the effect of reducing the pitch of the note by two half steps. A note named B♭♭ has the same pitch value as the note A, although it would be

wrong to call it "A" in this context. Similarly, The double sharp—shown either as "x" or the musical symbol "x" —has the effect of raising the pitch by two half steps.

The staff below shows the notes of an ascending G♯ melodic minor scale. The key signature of G♯ minor already features a sharpened F. However, this scale requires the seventh degree (F♯) to be sharpened. Thus the note is shown as F✕.

Although this note has the same pitch as G, the key signature of G♯, the "G" space that sits on the top line of the staff, is already a G♯ by default.

To restore the note to its original pitch you have to replace the "double" symbol with either a single sharp or a single flat.

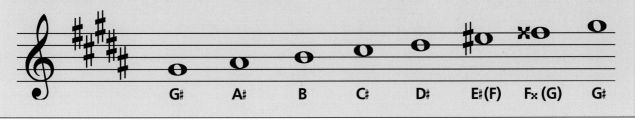

| | G♯ | A♯ | B | C♯ | D♯ | E♯(F) | F✕ (G) | G♯ |

LESSON FIVE
UNDERSTANDING CHORDS

Music is sometimes informally broken into three components: rhythm, harmony and melody. You already know a little about rhythm. You've also worked your way through a couple of simple tunes—these are examples of melodies. Harmony, however, deals with notes of different pitches that are played at the same time. When three or more different notes sound together the resulting effect is a CHORD.

THE IMPORTANCE OF INTERVALS

Before we look at chords, let's spend a few moments on the subject of intervals, since a good understanding of the way they work provides important clues as to how chords are built.

An INTERVAL is the distance between any two notes. You've already been introduced to this idea on page 44, where you saw how to name the intervals between the tonic and each degree of the major scale.

Any pair of notes played at the same time can be called a HARMONIC INTERVAL. Sometimes you will hear harmonic intervals referred to as a type of chord. Although they can be used to create chordal effects, technically a chord requires three different pitches. The staff on the right shows the notes C and G played at the same time. This is a harmonic interval of a perfect 5th. Play it now to get yourself accustomed to the sound.

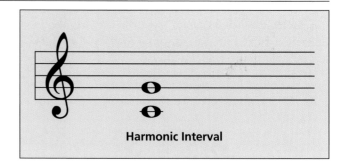
Harmonic Interval

If the notes of the interval are played separately it is called a MELODIC INTERVAL. If the the second note rises in pitch, it becomes an ASCENDING MELODIC INTERVAL; if the pitch falls it is a DESCENDING MELODIC INTERVAL. The staves in the panel below also use the notes C and G. The one on the left shows a descending melodic interval of a perfect 5th; alongside it, an ascending melodic interval of a perfect 5th.

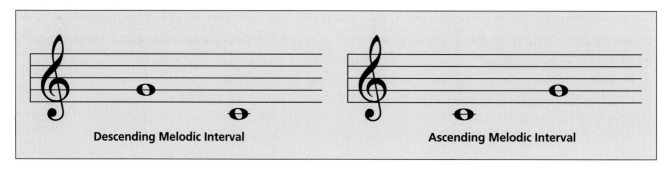
Descending Melodic Interval   **Ascending Melodic Interval**

NAMING AND NUMBERING THE INTERVALS

It's not only the intervals within a major scale that we can name. In fact, ANY note can be named in relation to any other note. In any scale, these intervals can be given an identifying number by counting from the lowest-pitched note through each degree of the scale until you reach the highest-pitched note.

Here is a practical example. The interval between the notes C and D is a known as a SECOND, because D is the second degree of the C major scale. Similarly, the interval between C and E is a THIRD, and so on.

However, labeling intervals numerically doesn't create a unique description. For example, the notes that make up an interval of a 3rd in a C major scale are C and E, but in a

C minor scale they are C and E♭. The situation can be clarified unequivocally by adding a prefix to describe the "quality" of the relationship between the notes.

In a major scale, because of their harmonic importance, the term PERFECT is used to describe the 4th and 5th degrees of the scale; the other degrees are prefixed with MAJOR. Thus, C to F is a described as a perfect 4th, whereas C to A is called a major 6th.

In a minor scale, the notes that have been flattened to distinguish them from the major scale are called MINOR intervals. In this way, the interval between C and E♭ is a minor 3rd; between C and B♭ it is a minor 7th.

MAJOR SCALE MELODIC INTERVALS

To help you appreciate the way these intervals sound, the staff below shows all of the notes of the C major scale presented as ascending melodic intervals. Play through each pair of intervals and listen out for the unique charcteristics of each one. Try the same exercise using a different key—G major and F major, for example—and see if you can spot the similarities between the same intervals in different keys.

After a while you will be able to identify intervals instinctively. This will come in very handy when you are dealing with chords, allowing you to distinguish three or more notes when played together. For this reason, understanding intervals is fundamental to the art of arranging music.

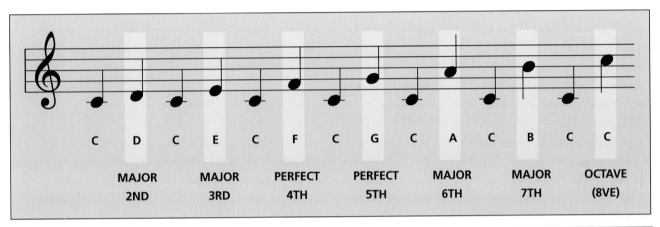

THE MINOR SCALES

The major scale and three minor scales are often referred to as being DIATONIC scales. The first, second, fourth, fifth and eighth degrees are the same for all of the diatonic scales. In all of the minor keys, the third degree is always flattened (as are the sixth and seventh degrees depending on the type of minor scale being used). Therefore, to name the intervals on the minor scales, three new labels are required. The flattened third, sixth and seventh degrees become MINOR 3RD, MINOR 6TH and MINOR 7TH intervals respectively.

The staff below shows a full set of diatonic intervals. The major intervals are named below the staff and the minor intervals are named above.

The exercises you have tried out so far have been concerned with playing single notes, grouping them into rhythms and playing melodies. Since you are not yet accustomed to hearing notes of different pitches played at the same time it can be a little difficult to predict how any two notes will sound together. Study the staff below and play each of the intervals, paying special attention to the effect of each set of notes when they are played as a pair.

It is useful to be able to make a connection between how the same set of intervals sound when played both melodically and harmonically. To reinforce this point, play the same set of intervals again, only this time follow each harmonic pair with a melodic interval (both ascending and descending) using the same two notes.

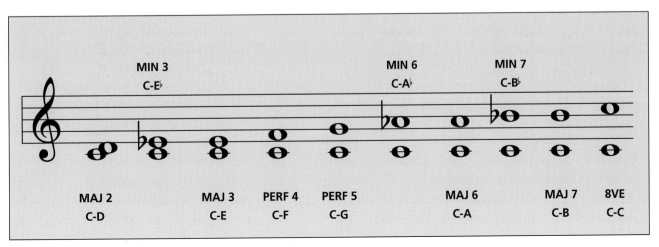

FILLING IN THE GAPS

All intervals that are not diatonic—meaning those that are not part of the major or minor series of scales—can be termed CHROMATIC. If you take a look at the diagram at the foot of page 55, you will see that there are two possible intervals not shown on the staff. These intervals—C to D♭ and C to F♯—do not form part of a major or minor scale in the key of C, and so are chromatic.

Now look at the first of those chromatic intervals—C to D♭. Since the interval of C to D is a major 2nd, by flattening the D you create an interval of a MINOR 2ND.

However, this raises a further question: if the upper note used its enharmonic equivalent to D♭ (which is, of course, C♯) would the interval still be a minor 2nd? After all, the number of half steps separating the two notes is the same.

AUGMENTED INTERVALS

In spite of the two notes being identical in pitch, the interval would take on a new name. Since C♯ is C raised by a half step, we need a new description to reflect this state. In such cases, the prefix AUGMENTED is used.

To see how the numbering works in this instance we first need to discuss the relationship between two identical notes. Rather than calling the interval between C and C when the pitch is identical a "1st" (as would be logically consistent with the other labels), it is instead referred to as a UNISON.

Therefore, although the the intervals between C and D♭, and C and C♯ sound identical in pitch, they take two different names depending on their use: C to D♭ is a MINOR 2ND; C to C♯ is a UNISON AUGMENTED. It is possible for any other interval to be augmented in this way.

The interval between C and C♯ can also be described as a CHROMATIC HALF STEP since it is not used in any diatonic scale; C to D♭, on the other hand, whilst a chromatic interval in the context of the key of C major, does appear in other keys (A♭ major or F natural and harmonic minors, for example). In such a situation, this interval can be called a DIATONIC HALF STEP.

DIMINISHED INTERVALS

The opposite effect of an augmented note is one that is DIMINISHED. This flattens the upper note, lowering it in pitch by a half step. Like its augmented counterpart, any interval can be diminished.

THE FIVE QUALITIES

We now have the full set of "qualities" used to describe intervals between any two degrees of any type of scale. They are: perfect, major, minor, augmented and diminished.

Intervals with a numeric value of a 2nd, 3rd, 6th and 7th can be diminished, minor, major or augmented; intervals of a unison, 4th, 5th and 8ve can only be diminished, perfect or augmented.

CONSONANCE AND DISSONANCE

As you have been working through this lesson, you will no doubt have become aware of the fact that some of these harmonic intervals seem to "work" better than others. The musical terms to describe this kind of effect are CONCORD and DISCORD. Although these words are sometimes used very loosely to describe whether a piece of music is pleasing to the ears, they also have very specific meanings.

All intervals can be described in terms of being either consonant or dissonant. There are two distinct categories of consonance. <u>PERFECT</u> concords are the "perfect" intervals: unison, perfect 4th, perfect 5th and octave. The <u>IMPERFECT</u> concords are the minor 3rd and minor 6th intervals. All other intervals, including those that are augmented or diminished, are deemed to be dissonant. Concords and discords are often discussed in terms of their musical "stability", which can be complicated for the

perfect 4th, which can in some contexts be deemed as dissonant, and the augmented 4th/perfect 5th (also called a "Tritone") which has an ambiguous nature.

C-C	OPEN CONSONANCE
C-D♭	SHARP CONSONANCE
C-D	MILD DISSONANCE
C-E♭	SOFT CONSONANCE
C-E	SOFT CONSONANCE
C-F	CONSONANCE OR DISSONANCE
C-F♯/G♭	NEUTRAL OR "RESTLESS"
C-G	OPEN CONSONANCE
C-G♯/A♭	SOFT CONSONANCE
C-A/B♭♭	SOFT CONSONANCE
C-B♭	MILD DISSONANCE
C-B	SHARP CONSONANCE
C-C	OPEN CONSONANCE

THE FULL SET OF INTERVALS

A full set of the intervals from C are shown below. Notice that when perfect intervals are flattened, the results are diminished intervals. Where major intervals are flattened, the results are minor intervals; a diminished major interval has to be "double-flattened"—reduced in pitch by two half steps.

All of these possible intervals can also be notated in shorthand using a variety of different symbols. A major or perfect interval can be shown as upper-case roman numerals—a major 7th can be notated as "VII."

Minor equivalents are always shown in lower-case Roman numerals. In this way, a minor 2nd can be notated as "ii."

Augmented intervals are indicated with a "plus" sign and diminished intervals with a "degree" symbol. Thus, "V+" signifies an augmented 5th and "V°" denotes a diminished 5th.

RANGE	ABBREVIATION	INTERVAL
C-C♭	I°	DIMINISHED UNISON
C-C	I	UNISON
C-C♯	I+	AUGMENTED UNISON
C-D♭♭	II°	DIMINISHED 2ND
C-D♭	ii	MINOR 2ND
C-D	II	MAJOR 2ND
C-D♯	II+	AUGMENTED 2ND
C-E♭♭	III°	DIMINISHED 3RD
C-E♭	iii	MINOR 3RD
C-E	III	MAJOR 3RD
C-E♯	III+	AUGMENTED 3RD
C-F♭	IV°	DIMINISHED 4TH
C-F	IV	PERFECT 4TH
C-F♯	IV+	AUGMENTED 4TH
C-G♭	V°	DIMINISHED 5TH
C-G	V	PERFECT 5TH
C-G♯	V+	AUGMENTED 5TH
C-A♭♭	VI°	DIMINISHED 6TH
C-A♭	vi	MINOR 6TH
C-A	VI	MAJOR 6TH
C-A♯	VI+	AUGMENTED 6TH
C-B♭♭	VII°	DIMINISHED 7TH
C-B♭	vii	MINOR 7TH
C-B	VII	MAJOR 7TH
C-B♯	VII+	AUGMENTED 7TH
C-C♭	VIII°	DIMINISHED OCTAVE
C-C	VIII	OCTAVE
C-C♯	VIII+	AUGMENTED OCTAVE

NAMING EXERCISE

Some of you might have found the last couple of pages slightly heavy going—if not downright dull. Hang on in there—it really is useful information.

Comprehending intervals goes right to the heart of understanding the way every kind of music works—from the most formal of classical compositions to the noisiest of thrash metal. When you understand intervals you will know which combinations of notes sound better than others, and how they can be used to create emotional impact.

So before we move onto creating chords, let's finish off with a little exercise. Below you will see twenty different ranges of notes. Your task is to work out the name of each interval. This will test your understanding of both scales and intervals.

You can use the list on the left as a template for keys other than C. The answers are shown below, so cover them up while you're working through the exercise. Watch out for the enharmonic notes, remembering that they take different names depending on their use.

1. G TO A	2. B TO F♯
3. F♯ TO A	4. B♭ TO G♭
5. D♭ TO C	6. G TO D♯
7. D♭ TO A	8. F TO G♭♭
9. C TO A♭	10. A♭ TO D♭
11. D♭ TO A♭	12. G♭ TO C
13. C TO G♯	14. B♭ TO D♭
15. E♭ TO C	16. A TO B
17. D TO F	18. B TO F
19. F TO B	20. A TO A♭

ANSWERS

1. Major 2nd.	2. Perfect 5th.
3. Minor 3rd.	4. Minor 6th.
5. Major 7th.	6. Augmented 5th.
7. Augmented 5th.	8. Diminished 2nd.
9. Minor 6th.	10. Perfect 4th.
11. Perfect 5th.	12. Augmented 4th.
13. Augmented 5th.	14. Minor 3rd.
15. Major 6th.	16. Major 2nd.
17. Minor 3rd.	18. Diminished 5th.
19. Augmented 4th.	20. Diminished octave.

INTRODUCING CHORDS

When three or more notes are played at the same time, the resulting musical effect is called a CHORD. The simplest form of chord is called a TRIAD, which, as the name suggests, is a type of a chord made up from three notes.

Triads are built from a ROOT NOTE and follow a specific set of intervals. The three notes are always the root, the 3rd and the 5th. Since there can be a number of different types of 3rd and 5th note, it follows that there are a number of different types of triad. There are, in fact, four different kinds of triad, each of which uses 3rds and 5ths of differing "qualities."

The MAJOR TRIAD consists of the root, major 3rd and perfect 5th. In the key of C, as shown below, the notes C, E and G are used. This combination of notes is commonly referred to as C MAJOR. Play the chord as shown, using the thumb, first and second fingers to play the three notes.

The MINOR TRIAD consists of the root, minor 3rd and perfect 5th. In the key of C it uses the notes C, E♭ and G. This chord is often known simply as C MINOR.

The AUGMENTED TRIAD (*see bottom left*) comprises the root, major 3rd and augmented 5th intervals. In the key of C the notes required are C, E and G♯.

Finally, the DIMINISHED TRIAD (*see bottom right*) is made up from the root, minor 3rd and diminished 5th intervals. In the key of C the notes used are C, E♭ and G♭.

If you play all four triads one after the other in the sequence shown below you will appreciate the different sounds they create. Making a distinction between the major and minor triads is especially important to grasp.

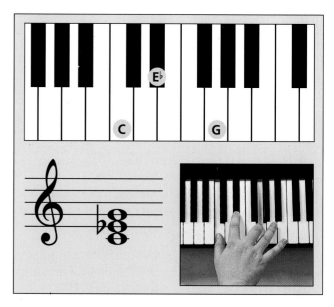

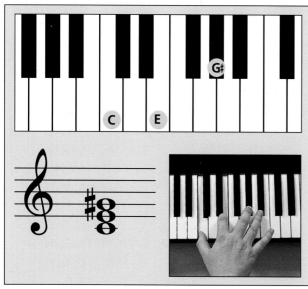

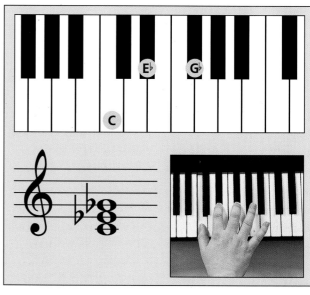

TRIADS ON THE MAJOR SCALE

The most fundamentally significant aspect of harmonic theory is the way in which chordal effects sound when played alongside one another. This is, after all, the basis on which all song structures stand or fall.

You already know how the notes of a diatonic scale relate to each other, so the most effective way of showing similar relationships for chords is by building a series of triads from the major and minor scales. The staff below shows triads built from the C major scale. It is, in effect,

a scale of chords. But although it is a major scale, you will see that it is not only made up from major triads: the second, third and sixth degrees require a minor triad; the seventh degree uses a diminished triad.

Play through this sequence using the fingering decribed on the opposite page. Listen to the smooth manner in which the triads flow into one another, and notice in particular how satisfactorily the B diminished triad "resolves" back to C major.

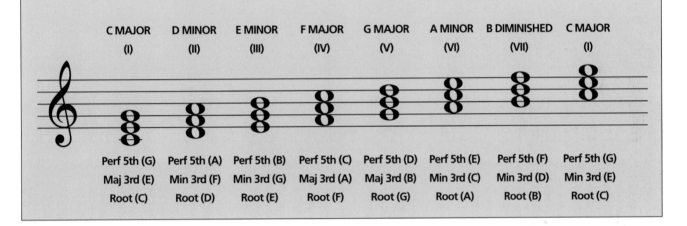

C MAJOR (I)	D MINOR (II)	E MINOR (III)	F MAJOR (IV)	G MAJOR (V)	A MINOR (VI)	B DIMINISHED (VII)	C MAJOR (I)
Perf 5th (G)	Perf 5th (A)	Perf 5th (B)	Perf 5th (C)	Perf 5th (D)	Perf 5th (E)	Perf 5th (F)	Perf 5th (G)
Maj 3rd (E)	Min 3rd (F)	Min 3rd (G)	Maj 3rd (A)	Maj 3rd (B)	Min 3rd (C)	Min 3rd (D)	Min 3rd (E)
Root (C)	Root (D)	Root (E)	Root (F)	Root (G)	Root (A)	Root (B)	Root (C)

TRIAD RELATIONSHIPS

Just as each degree of the major scale has its own "degree" and name, so too have the triads shown on the staff above. In fact, they are named after the degrees on which they are constructed. The triad on the first degree of the scale can be referred to as the TONIC TRIAD. Similarly, the chord on the second degree may be called the SUPERTONIC triad. You can use this naming system right up to the octave.

Although this is still basic music theory, the idea has practical value in that the degrees themselves can also be used as a kind of musical shorthand description. In the key of C major, for example, the DOMINANT TRIAD (G major) could also be called the "five" chord because it is built from the 5th degree. In such cases it would be written down as a "V" chord.

This approach is sometimes used within informal musical settings (especially jazz) where chord charts may be used instead of notated music. For example, a "one-four-five in G" would describe a chord sequence revolving around the chord progression G major ("I"), C major ("IV") and D major ("V").

As you will increasingly discover, there is a special musical relationship between chords and notes built on the first, fourth

and fifth degrees of a diatonic scale. In fact, the "I", "IV" and "V" triads are also known as the PRIMARY TRIADS.

MINOR TRIADS

You can also build triads from each degree of the minor scale. However, because of the differences between the natural, melodic and harmonic minor scales, the triads used are variable. An example is shown below for the key of C.

I	C Minor	(C, E♭, G)
II	D Diminished	(D, F, A♭)
	D Minor	(D, F, A)
III	E♭ Major	(E♭, G, B♭)
	E♭ Augmented	(E♭, G, B)
IV	F Minor	(F, A♭, C)
	F Major	(F, A, C)
V	G Minor	(G, B♭, D)
	G Major	(G, B, D)
VI	A♭ Major	(A♭, C, E♭)
	A Diminished	(A, C, E♭)
VII	B♭ Major	(B♭, D, F)
	B Diminished	(B, D, F)

INVERSION

The triads you have just seen have all been built from notes played in order of pitch from the root. That means the 1st, 3rd and 5th notes have all been successively higher in pitch. However, this need not be the case.

In the staff below, you can see three triads. The first chord is C major, using the notes C (root), E, (major 3rd) and G (perfect 5th). But what happens if you move the root note (C) ABOVE the 3rd and the 5th notes, as shown in the middle chord below. If you work out the notes from the bottom up, you can see that the lowest note is now E. So does this make it a chord in the key of E? Before we answer that question, play the two triads, one after the other. You will hear that they clearly have a different emphasis in their sound, and yet they somehow still have a "sameness" to them. This is because they ARE the same chord. The process of altering the order of notes is called INVERSION. In fact, a triad in which the 3rd note is the lowest in pitch is called a FIRST INVERSION. That same triad can be further rearranged so that the 5th is the lowest in pitch. This is known as a SECOND INVERSION.

COMPARING INVERSIONS

You can compare the sounds created by the original C major triad (ROOT POSITION), and the first and second inversions by playing them as shown below.

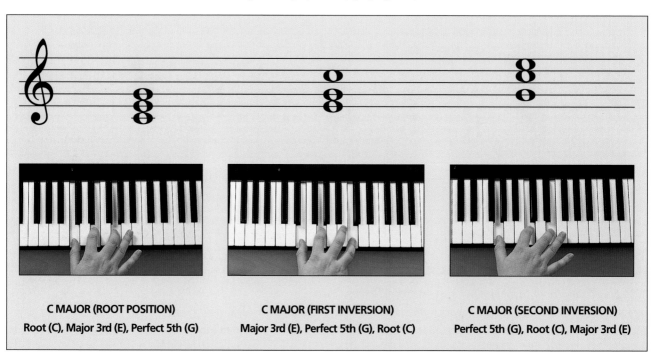

C MAJOR (ROOT POSITION)
Root (C), Major 3rd (E), Perfect 5th (G)

C MAJOR (FIRST INVERSION)
Major 3rd (E), Perfect 5th (G), Root (C)

C MAJOR (SECOND INVERSION)
Perfect 5th (G), Root (C), Major 3rd (E)

NAMING THE INVERSIONS

The abbreviated names given to the triads formed on a a major or minor scale (*see page 59*) can be further extended to cover inversions. Each of the Roman numeral degree positions can be suffixed with a lower-case letter denoting their construction.

The letter "a" following the degree indicates that the chord should be played in its root position; "b" is used to indicate the first inversion of a chord; and "c" indicates a second inversion.

For example, "IIa" ("two a") in the key of C major indicates a root-position supertonic triad—the chord D minor, played (in pitch sequence) D, F, and A.

Similarly, "IVb" ("four b") in the key of G major indicates the FIRST INVERSION of the subdominant triad—that's the chord C major, played E (major 3rd), G (perfect 5th) and C (root) where (E) is the lowest-pitched note.

Finally, a "Vc" ("five C") in the key of F is the SECOND INVERSION of the leading note triad. This is the chord C major played G (perfect 5th), C (root) and E (major 3rd).

There are a number of other types of inversion to cover chords that use more than three notes.

Learning to get the best out of inversions is really important for keyboard players in any genre. It really can give a whole new dimension to your playing.

MOVING INVERTED TRIADS

This next exercise teaches you movement among the different inversions. Each of the eight bars represents one of the chords on the major scale from the TONIC TRIAD to the OCTAVE TRIAD.

Within each bar, triads are played as quarter notes—that's one chord on every beat—moving from the root position to the first inversion, second inversion and back to the root position, which this time is played one octave above the starting chord. Play the eight bars slowly, giving yourself sufficient time to change chords without making mistakes.

Since the fingering for each chord always remains the same, every time you play a new chord you need to move the entire right hand.

Another effective exercise that you can try using the chords below is to play each one as a BROKEN CHORD. This means playing each triad as a sequence of separate notes. To do this, you need to dispense with the time signature shown below, and instead play them as quarter notes within a bar of three-four time. Thus, the first four bars would play the notes C-E-G (1) E-G-C (2) G-C-E (3) C-E-G (4).

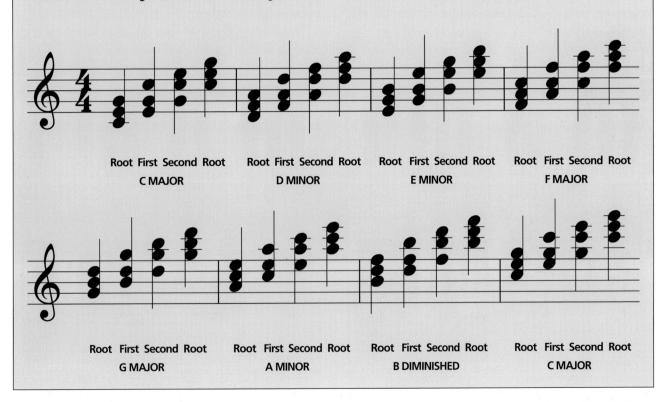

Root First Second Root
C MAJOR

Root First Second Root
D MINOR

Root First Second Root
E MINOR

Root First Second Root
F MAJOR

Root First Second Root
G MAJOR

Root First Second Root
A MINOR

Root First Second Root
B DIMINISHED

Root First Second Root
C MAJOR

THE OPEN AND CLOSE POSITIONS

All of the triads shown above have their notes grouped as closely as possible to one another. Chords played this way are referred to as being in the CLOSE POSITION.

However, notes within a triad can also be grouped in what is called the OPEN POSITION. This is where the notes are spaced out so that there is an interval of more than an octave between the highest and lowest notes.

Let's look at an example of a G major triad. If we take this chord in the root position and raise the perfect 5th (D) by an octave, the sound and character of the triad will be altered greatly. However, since the order of notes from the root is unchanged, this movement does not constitute an inversion: it could be described as a root triad played in the open position.

Similarly, triads with first and second inversions can also be created in the open position. For example, you could play a first inversion of G major in the open position using the notes B, G (a 6th above B) and D (a perfect 5th above G). In the same way, you could play a second inversion of G major in the open position using the notes D, B (a major 6th above D) and G (a 6th above B).

THE PIANO AND INVERSIONS

The wide range of notes available on a piano or other keyboard makes it possible to create a great many number of rich and varied inversions. The greatest composers, arrangers or improvisational keyboard players are invariably masters of manipulating inversions.

INTRODUCING SEVENTH CHORDS

Moving around the notes of a triad can provide endless fascinating variations. However, why should we restrict ourselves to a harmonic palette of three notes when there are another nine different notes from which we can choose? There's no reason at all. In fact, if polyphony—the sound of more than one pitch being played at the same time—was restricted to three notes, hardly any of the music with which we are so familiar would be possible.

Adding notes from outside the triad allows for the creation of a greater range of harmonic texture. Although there are numerous possible notes from which to choose, by far the most common addition is that of the leading note—the seventh. Adding a seventh to any type of triad creates what is called a SEVENTH CHORD.

However, as you have already learned, a seventh note does not in itself describe a strict pitch within a key. For example, in the key of C major, the MINOR 7TH is B♭, the MAJOR 7TH is B, the DIMINISHED 7th is B♭♭ (which has the same pitch as A) and the AUGMENTED 7TH is B♯ (which has the same pitch as C). Thus, depending on context, it is possible to produce a number of different types of 7th chord.

The four most commonly used seventh chords are shown below. The first is called the DOMINANT SEVENTH and is formed by adding a minor seventh to a major triad. It is shown below, top left. The chord C dominant seventh uses the notes C, E, G and B♭. Dominant seventh chords are often known simply as "sevenths."

The second type of seventh chord we'll look at is the MINOR SEVENTH, which is made up from a minor triad with an added minor seventh. The chord C minor seventh

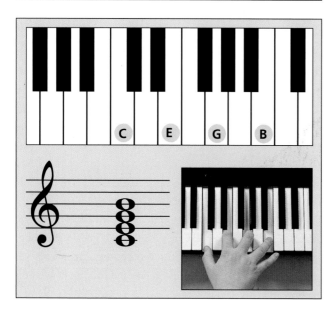

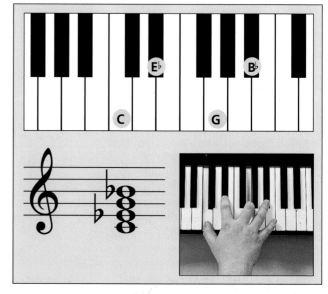

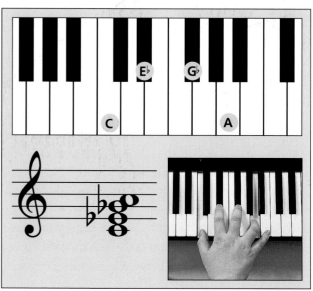

(*shown across the page, top right*) therefore consists of the notes C, E♭, G and B♭.

The third type of seventh chord we'll look at is called the MAJOR SEVENTH. This is a major triad with the addition of a major seventh note. On the opposite page (*bottom left*) you can see the chord C major seventh, which consists of the notes C, E, G and B.

The final seventh chord we're going to look at is the DIMINISHED SEVENTH. This is a diminished triad with the addition of the diminished seventh. C diminished seventh is shown across the page (*bottom right*) and consists of the notes C, E♭, G♭ and B♭♭ (shown as A).

CONTRASTING CHORDS

The eight-bar sequence shown below puts together most of the chord types you have so far met, again in the key of C major. As you play it through you will not only be able to contrast the way the four seventh chords sound, but the effect they create when played alongside one another.

There are many other types of seventh chord, some of which you can find listed in the Chord Dictionary (*see pages 110–135*). These other sevenths vary in their usefulness—some of them, it has to be said, are so obscure that you probably won't come into contact with them outside of the realms of abstract classical or jazz forms.

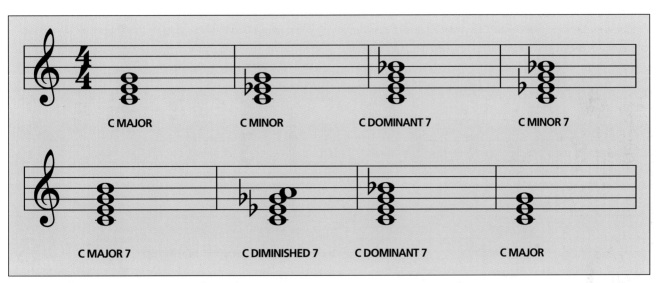

C MAJOR   C MINOR   C DOMINANT 7   C MINOR 7

C MAJOR 7   C DIMINISHED 7   C DOMINANT 7   C MAJOR

SUSPENDED CHORDS

Taking a major triad and moving the major third up or down by a half step creates what are called SUSPENDED chords. The two most common suspended chords take their names from the repositioning of the major third: they are the SUSPENDED FOURTH and the SUSPENDED SECOND.

The suspended fourth chord consists of the root, perfect 4th and perfect 5th. Thus, C suspended fourth is made up from the notes C, F and G. These chords are commonly used and are often referred to as "sus fours." The replacement of the major 3rd by the perfect 4th can also be used with seventh chords, creating a SEVENTH SUSPENDED FOURTH, or "seven sus four."

Suspended fourth chords are widely used in all forms of music. One particularly common movement sees the suspended fourth resolving to the major chord at the end of a piece of music.

The SUSPENDED SECOND works in much the same way. This time, the major 3rd is replaced by the major 2nd. For example, C suspended second used the notes C, D and G.

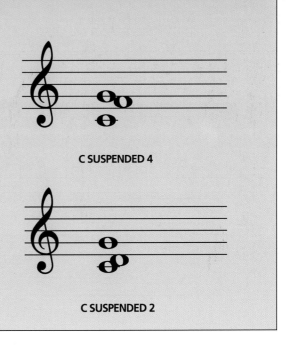

C SUSPENDED 4

C SUSPENDED 2

USING INVERSIONS TO CREATE MELODY

When you played the inversion exercise on page 61 all you were doing was simply moving through inversions of the same chord. However, one of the things you will have noticed was how the tonal balance of a chord altered with each movement. This effect can be used in music to create an "implied" melody. This works because when you change chords, the movement between the highest pitched notes creates a melodic effect.

To illustrate this in practice, work your way through the piece of music below. As you will quickly begin to hear, it is not just a set of chords, but creates the effect of playing a tune—in this case, the song "Clementine," the rhythm and melody of which you'll have already worked out on page 43.

If you look at the make-up of each chord, you will see that the song is constructed from inversions from four

chords: C major, F major, G major and G dominant seventh. Seventh chords can be inverted in exactly the same way as triads: if the seventh note of the chord is the lowest in pitch, the result is a THIRD INVERSION.

If you look at the first four chords, you can see that if you only play the highest notes, they are C, C, C and G. If you check back to the melody shown on page 43, you will see that they are exactly the same notes. If you continue in the same way through the entire song leaving out the lowest two notes, you will hear yourself playing the familiar melody.

You might find it easier playing this sequence if you use the thumb, first and fourth fingers to play each chord. This will minimize the stretching that is necessary between some of the chords.

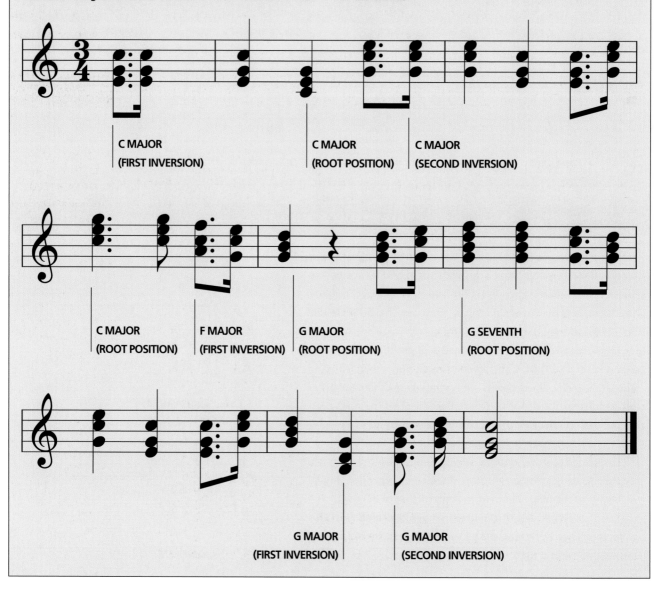

C MAJOR
(FIRST INVERSION)

C MAJOR
(ROOT POSITION)

C MAJOR
(SECOND INVERSION)

C MAJOR
(ROOT POSITION)

F MAJOR
(FIRST INVERSION)

G MAJOR
(ROOT POSITION)

G SEVENTH
(ROOT POSITION)

G MAJOR
(FIRST INVERSION)

G MAJOR
(SECOND INVERSION)

COMPLETING THE SET

Until now we have created chords that use each degree of the major scale with the exception of the sixth degree. Indeed, even the major 6th can be added to a major triad to create a SIXTH chord. By adding the same note to a minor triad it's also possible to create a MINOR SIXTH chord.

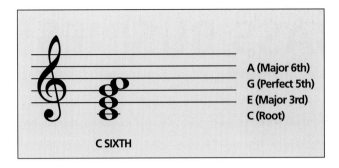

A (Major 6th)
G (Perfect 5th)
E (Major 3rd)
C (Root)

C SIXTH

PLAYING WITH CHORDS

Having a vast vocabulary of chords with their inversions, and the ability to use them intelligently is one of the most useful facilities a keyboard player can acquire. Although the "Clementine" example across the page might have been a less than thrilling experience to play, exercises like this are valuable in that they will gradually make your playing instinctive. Pretty well any other basic tune can be adapted in the same way—being simple by definition, children's nursery rhymes are especially well-suited to this idea.

If you want a challenge, take one of your favourite songs and try to work it out just using the basic chords. You'll be surprised at how much of the popular music of the past fifty years is based around relatively simple chord progressions.

The most difficult starting point is in finding the key of the song. It's relatively rare these days for a pop song to be written in an enharmonic key, so you can do a lot worse than play through the chords on the C major scale until you get one that fits.

One clue is that the opening chord will often provide you with the key. When you've sussed that out, watch out for the relationships between chords on the root, fourth and fifth degrees of the scale—you'll be surprised at how many songs use little more than these chords alone.

EXTENDED CHORDS

Some chords are created by adding notes that go beyond the octave of their root. An interval of beyond an octave is called a COMPOUND INTERVAL. The notes are named and numbered as continuations of the scale from the root. This means that in the key of C major, the interval between C and D beyond the octave is called a NINTH—this is the same as the note on the second degree only one octave higher.

The most common compound intervals used in chords are the NINTH (one octave above the 2nd), the ELEVENTH (one octave above the 4th) and the THIRTEENTH (one octave beyond the 6th). Chords using these intervals are called EXTENDED CHORDS.

On the right you can see a set of ninth, eleventh and thirteenth chords in the key of C. The dominant ninth is created by adding the major 9th to a dominant seventh chord. Thus, C dominant ninth (usually just called "C9") uses the notes C, E, G, B♭, and D.

The dominant eleventh adds the perfect 11th to the dominant ninth chord. In the key of C it uses the notes C, E, G, B♭, D and F).

The dominant thirteenth adds the major 13th to the dominant eleventh chord. In the key of C it uses the notes C, E, G, B♭, D, F and A).

Minor and major equivalents of these chords can be created by adding the same notes to minor seventh and major seventh chords respectively.

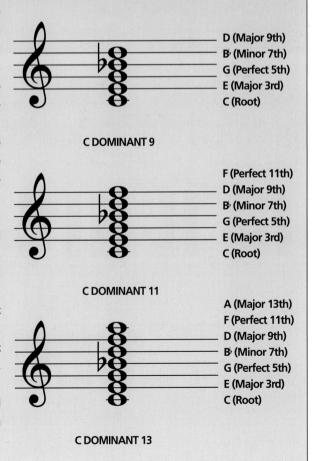

D (Major 9th)
B♭ (Minor 7th)
G (Perfect 5th)
E (Major 3rd)
C (Root)

C DOMINANT 9

F (Perfect 11th)
D (Major 9th)
B♭ (Minor 7th)
G (Perfect 5th)
E (Major 3rd)
C (Root)

C DOMINANT 11

A (Major 13th)
F (Perfect 11th)
D (Major 9th)
B♭ (Minor 7th)
G (Perfect 5th)
E (Major 3rd)
C (Root)

C DOMINANT 13

LESSON SIX
BASS BUSINESS

One of the reasons why the piano and other types of keyboard are so great is the fact that if you use both the left and right hand it becomes possible to play ten notes simultaneously. This degree of polyphony allows for the creation of extremely sophisticated music, and is simply not possible with any other musical instrument. However, for most novice keyboard players—especially those who are naturally right-handed—getting the left hand working can be a demanding and frustrating experience.

WORKING THE LEFT HAND

In the vast majority of notated piano music, the left hand is used to play the bass notes. These can be found on a second adjoining staff beneath the treble notes. To indicate that they are lower in pitch, the staff containing the left-hand notes is headed by a BASS CLEF. You may remember from the introductory chapter that the names of the notes on the lines and spaces on a staff that uses a bass clef are not the same as for a treble clef. The lines are (from bottom-to-top) G, B, D, F, A (think of the phrase <u>G</u>ood <u>B</u>oys <u>D</u>eserve <u>F</u>un <u>A</u>lways; the spaces are A, C, E, G (or <u>A</u> <u>C</u>ow <u>E</u>ats <u>G</u>rass, if you like).

USING FOUR FINGERS AND THE THUMB

Getting the left hand working for the first time can be a tricky business. For most people, the left hand gets less use, so is weaker and more difficult to control than the right. This is especially so for movements between the third and fourth fingers.

To begin with, we'll simply get the different fingers playing notes, echoing the right-hand lesson on page 30. Start by playing the note C with the fourth finger as shown below. Pay special attention to the notation. Notice how the bass clef redefines the

names of the notes so that, in this instance, C is represented on the second space of the staff. You should be aware, though, that this is NOT the Middle C that you have been using up until now. Middle C on the bass clef would appear on the first ledger line ABOVE the staff, which means that the C you are playing with the fourth finger is one octave BELOW Middle C.

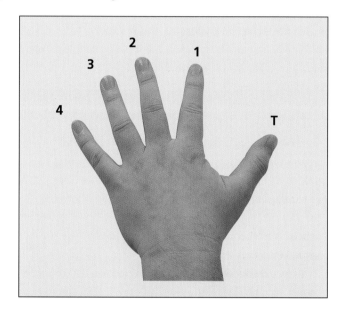

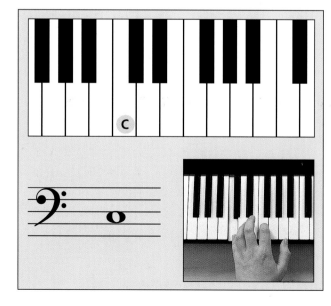

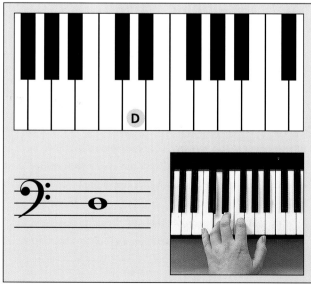

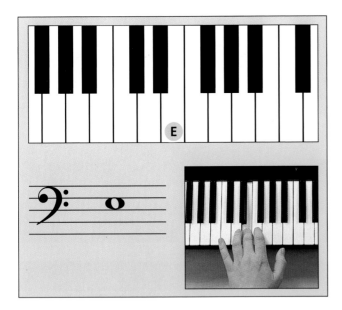

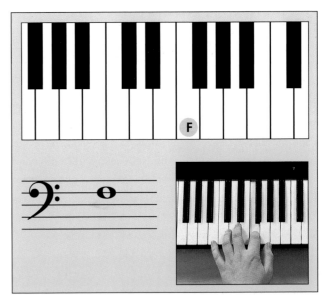

Continue through the exercise, playing the contents of each new box as you go. This means that D is played by the third finger, E by the second finger, F by the first finger and G by the thumb.

Once you've played the sequence of all five notes in ascending order, play them in reverse, starting with the thumb on the note G and working back down to C with the fourth finger.

Here is a further exercise you can try out that will help to improve co-ordination between the fingers. It takes the form of a series of brief ascending and descending sequences:

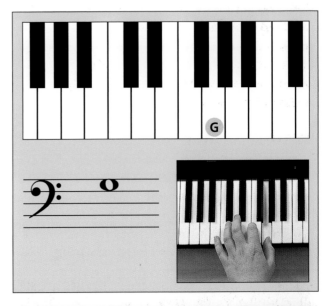

- **Begin with C–D–C.**
- **Now play C–D–E–D–C.**
- **Follow this with C–D–E–F–E–D–C.**
- **End with C–D–E–F–G–F–E–D–C.**

BASS NOTES

Listen to any modern pop music and you will hear that the overall sound is underpinned by a line of low-pitched notes. This is the bass line, which is usually played by a bass guitar—an instrument with strings tuned to one octave below the bottom four strings on a regular guitar.

However, since the widespread use of the synthesizer, bass parts are increasingly played (or programmed) on a keyboard. More than ever, modern keyboard players are expected to have an understanding of the way bass lines work with the other parts of an arrangement.

A traditional approach to bass playing (which is effectively the mindset the keyboard player has to adopt

in this role) is to write down the chords of the song and coincide the root note with each chord. Although this is a very safe approach—it's impossible to do anything that sounds "wrong" when you play in this way—the results can sometimes be rather dull.

Some of the best bass lines have been approached from a melodic angle, creating an identifiable repeating sequence (or "riff") that underpins the sound, fits in with the harmonic structure of the song and helps to define the rhythm. Listen to the bass playing on classic soul music recorded in the 1960s, and hear how fundamental it was to the classsic Motown and Stax sounds.

CROSSING THE FINGERS AND TUCKING THE THUMB

You're already familiar with the idea of moving the fingers so that they can extend beyond the range of five notes. This uses the idea of tucking the thumb beneath the fingers or crossing the first or second fingers over the thumb to move beyond the range. The same principle applies to the left hand, but—since the thumb and fingers of the left hand are mirror images of the right hand—they are used in reverse order. This means that when DESCENDING in pitch, the thumb is tucked beneath the fingers to extend the range of notes; when ASCENDING in pitch, the first or second fingers can be crossed over the thumb.

ASCENDING AND DESCENDING THE MAJOR SCALE

The two staves below show a C major scale played on the bass clef. The first staff is an ascending scale, the second is descending scale. The notes on the staves are an octave lower than the C major scales you have played on the treble clef—using the right hand. In these example, the highest note—the one on the first ledger line above the staff—is MIDDLE C. Here is the fingering for the ascending scale:

- Play C with the fourth finger.
- Play D with the third finger.
- Play E with the second finger.
- Play F with the first finger.
- Play G with the thumb.
- Cross the second finger over the thumb to play A.
- Play B with the first finger.
- Play C with the thumb.

If you pay careful attention you will see that that the fingering for the ASCENDING C major scale played with the left hand is identical to the DESCENDING C major scale when played with the right hand.

Here is the fingering you need to use to play the descending C major scale with the left hand.

- Play C with the thumb.
- Play B with the first finger.
- Play A with the second finger.
- Tuck the thumb beneath the fingers
- Play G with the thumb
- Play F with the first finger.
- Play E with the second finger.
- Play D with the third finger.
- Play C with the thumb.

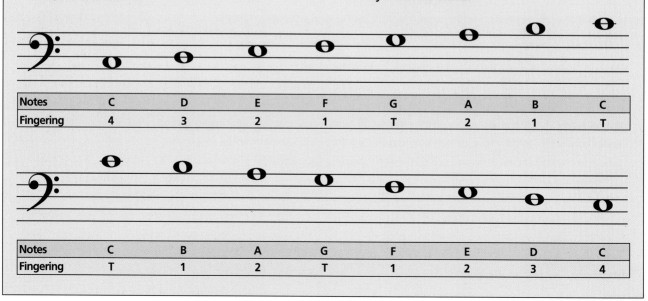

Notes	C	D	E	F	G	A	B	C
Fingering	4	3	2	1	T	2	1	T

Notes	C	B	A	G	F	E	D	C
Fingering	T	1	2	T	1	2	3	4

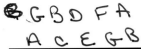

EXERCISING THE LEFT HAND

The six exercises shown below are simple musical sequences. Your task is to play the notes in the correct order and using the correct fingers. The first two staves use just the notes from C to G with fingering to match; the remaining notes draw from the C major scale that ends with Middle C on the first ledger line above the staff.

Notes	C	E	G	F	D	E	C	G	E
Fingering	4	2	T	1	3	2	4	T	2

Notes	G	C	D	G	E	C	E	D	F
Fingering	T	4	3	T	2	4	2	3	1

Notes	C	F	B	F	A	G	C	G	B
Fingering	4	1	T	1	T	1	T	2	1

Notes	B	A	G	C	F	A	C	B	E
Fingering	T	1	2	4	1	T	4	T	2

Notes	A	C	E	G	B	D	E	C	E
Fingering	1	4	T	1	T	4	3	T	3

Notes	E	F	A	C	B	C	B	A	C
Fingering	4	3	2	T	3	4	3	2	4

BASS POLYPHONY

Here is an example of a very simple bass accompaniment for our old friend "Clementine." As you can see, irrespective of the main melody, all of the activity takes place on the beat.

The idea shown on the staff is that the basic triads you used to play the song on page 64 have been transposed for the bass clef and the notes separated out. Take, for example, the second bar. The notes used are C, E and G—in other words the C major triad. However, they have been separated out so that the C is played on the first beat, and intervals of E and G are played

on the second and third beats. This idea carries on throughout the entire song.

The best fingering to adopt for this bass part is to use the fourth finger to play the single note on the first beat, and the first finger and thumb to play the intervals on the second and third beats. In each case, the song is underpinned by having the root note of the chord played on the first beat. Although it is only written to be played for a single beat, if you sustained the note for all three beats, the full impact of the chord could be heard. However, this would require a slightly complex notation that you won't meet until the final chapter.

BASS RHYTHMS

Although often overlooked, or viewed as an afterthought, the bass part of any song plays a crucial part in creating the overall rhythmic effect. This is even more true of modern dance music, which often largely revolves around a synthesized bass line.

On the opposite page you can see an ascending C major scale presented as a set of three alternative rhythms. In each case, the rhythm is the same for each bar, but when played as a whole it will still provide the flavour of the original scale.

In the top example, the rhythm is created by breaking down the four-four beat into a dotted quarter note followed by an eighth note and then a half note. If you want to get a feel for the rhythm, give each eighth note a count of "one." The count will therefore be "ONE-two-three-ONE-ONE-two-three-four." Remember, though, that since you are counting out eighth-note

beats, you need to count at twice the speed to be consistent with the true beat of the rhythm, which counts on the quarter note. This idea is simply a way of working out a tricky rhythm—once you've done that you need to translate it back to the correct count. Below you can see how that eighth-note count sits over the true four-four count, which is in quarter notes.

<u>ONE</u>	two	three	<u>ONE</u>	<u>ONE</u>	two	three	four
<u>ONE</u>		<u>TWO</u>		<u>THREE</u>		<u>FOUR</u>	

In the third example, you can see that a second note is used in each bar. The interval between the two notes in each case reflects those for the first two notes of the chord created on each degree of the scale. This means that in bars 1, 4, 5 and 8 the interval is always a major 3rd; in bars 2, 3, 6 and 7 it is a minor 3rd. In this way the flavor of chord progression is retained.

BASS LINES

Although the bass lines shown below can be played on a piano, they will sound better using an electronic bass sound and played over a drum beat. Rhythms like these are often programmed into a MIDI sequencer. When you play each example, stick to the fingering that you've been using throughout the lesson. Some keyboard programmers would "tap out" the whole thing using the thumb or first finger of the right hand, but getting used to playing rhythms with the left hand is crucial if you want to attain any degree of versatility.

To get the rhythm for the second example, use an eighth-note count. This time, the rhythm is <u>ONE</u>-<u>ONE</u>-two-<u>ONE</u>-two-<u>ONE</u>-<u>ONE</u>-two. This is an example of SYNCOPATION, which means that the pulse of the rhythm doesn't fall on the beat: since it starts with an eighth note, the second and third notes fall on the half-beat, creating a characteristic effect.

The final example is a very simple eighth-note rhythm—the sort found on many "synth-pop" or dance tracks. The use of the second note in each bar creates a flavor of the chords built on the C major scale.

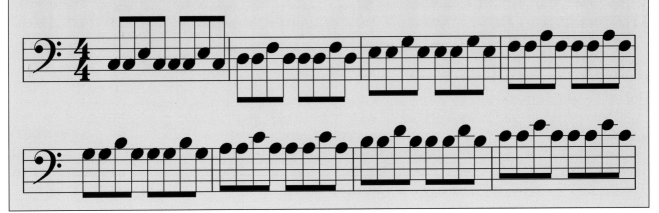

LESSON SEVEN
BOTH HANDS WORKING

As a musical instrument, the piano offers the greatest degree of polyphonic potential in that if you use both hands at the same time it becomes possible to play up to ten different notes. You've already worked separately on both your left and right hands, so now is the time to put them together. The toughest aspect of this lesson is the difficulty in concentrating on both hands at once. This barrier is an important one to overcome for it signals the fact that your fingers are beginning to "think" for themselves.

BASS ROOTS

In a lot of modern music, the role of the left hand for many keyboard players involves little more than playing the root note of the chord being played in full by the right hand. If you try playing the C major chord shown at the bottom of the page you will hear that this is an effective device that neatly emphasizes the key of the chord.

However, it's possible to create a great deal more interplay between the bass and treble parts. Indeed, any music with a degree of sophistication will involve a good deal of independence between the two hands.

The exercises shown throughout this lesson are aimed at gradually getting your hands used to the idea of working apart from one another. Take each exercise slowly, aiming for accuracy rather than speed.

BRACKETS

When notes are played over two staves, one with the left hand and one with the right hand, they are shown as being joined together by a "curly" bracket.

The photograph below shows a C major chord. The triad is played by the right hand, and the bass root note with the left hand. The music can be seen notated over two staves.

Although in most cases the treble staff is played by the right hand and the bass staff by the left, some pieces are written for either hand to cross over the other during the course of a performance.

FOLLOWING THE CHORDS

The two exercises below are relatively simple. The right hand plays the chord progression built on the notes of the C major scale. In the first example, the left hand simply follows those chords along the scale. You can play the triads using the thumb, first and third fingers on the right hand; for the bass line, use the standard major-scale fingering with the left hand.

The second example sees the bass note doubled on the octave. This places even greater emphasis on the root note. This time you can't play the bass line as a regular scale because the octave stretch can only be played using the fourth finger and thumb. Moving along the keyboard in this way is a good test of accuracy for your left hand.

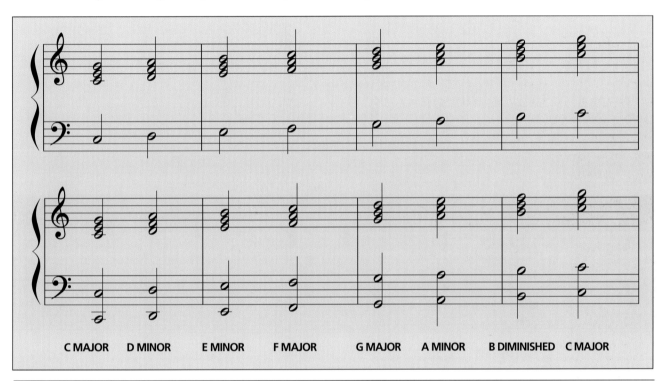

C MAJOR   D MINOR   E MINOR   F MAJOR   G MAJOR   A MINOR   B DIMINISHED   C MAJOR

DOUBLING THE SCALE

In this exercise, both hands play a C major scale simultaneously. Although that may sound simple enough, when you first try it out you might be surprised at how easily you get your fingers in a tangle.

Since the scale is ascending, the left hand must cross OVER the thumb to play it correctly; this means that the right hand must tuck the thumb UNDER the fingers for the scale to work. When you reach the fourth note (F) and the right hand moves the thumb behind the fingers, your natural inclination will be to move your left hand in the same way.

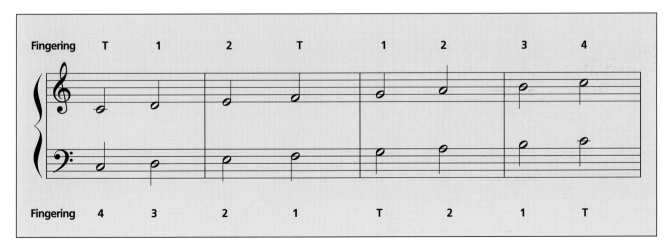

FURTHER TWO-HANDED EXERCISES

Here are another eight two-handed exercises for you to work on before moving on to play a "proper" tune.

The four sets of staves shown below all show a variety of chordal movements played by both hands. In each case, the chords used are those built on each degree of the major scale.

On the opposite page you can see a further set of four exercises. Three of them are based around the idea of both hands playing a single-note run, although not necessarily the same notes. The third and fourth pieces may be especially demanding since different parts of the same scale are being played at the same time, creating a series of harmonic intervals. The fingering is shown in each case.

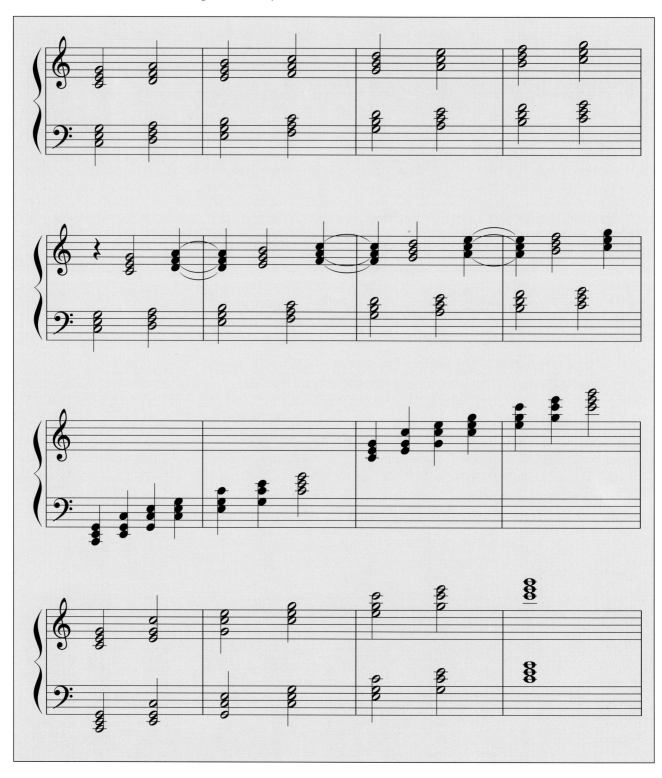

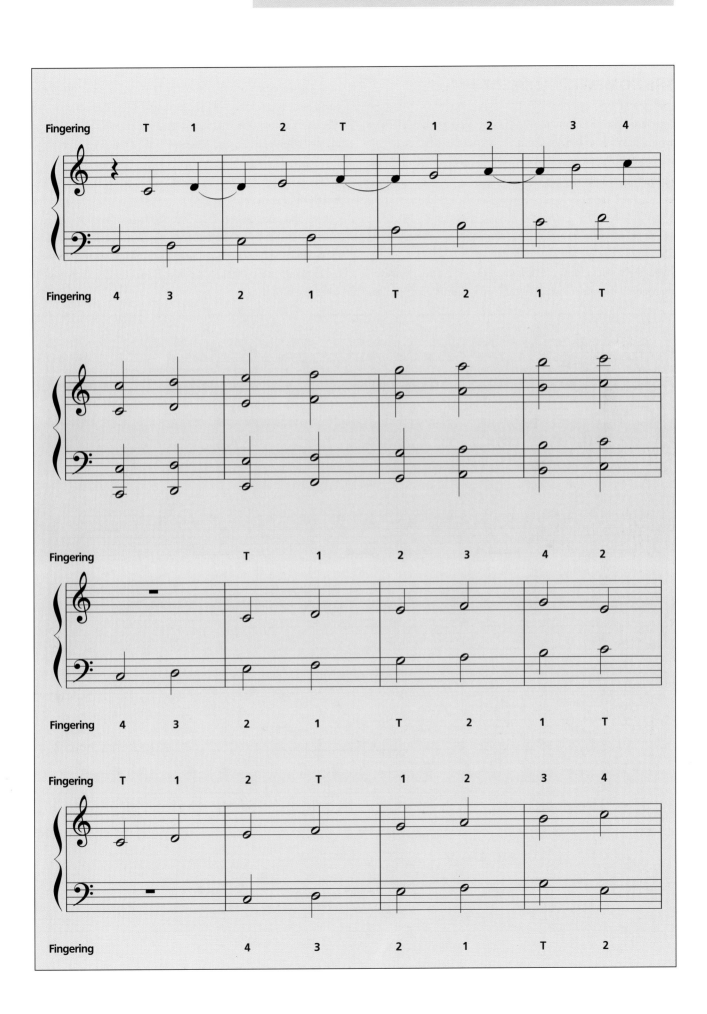

THE COMPLETE "CLEMENTINE"

The three exercises shown over the next two pages provide us with a final look at "Clementine." In each case, the melody is played in the same way, but the bass parts gradually increase in sophistication and difficulty.

EXERCISE 1

In this exercise, the bass part plays simple chords. Each one has a value of a dotted half note, or three quarter-note beats. Only two chords are used: C major and G major. Notice, however, the smooth movement between these two chords. Even though they are a perfect 5th apart, there is minimal shifting of the hand necessary. This is because G major is played as a first inversion: the thumb remains on the note G, which is common to both chords, but C and E shift down by a step to play B and D respectively.

EXERCISE 2

The second exercise breaks the chords so that the root is played on the first beat and the remaining two notes are played on the second and third beats. Notice, however, how in this example the G major chord includes the note F, making it a G dominant seventh chord.

EXERCISE 3

The final exercise has the most demanding bass part that you will so far have had to play. Once again, the root note is played out on the first beat. This time, however, it's "doubled up" with the addition of the same note played an octave lower. This effect is commonly used in all kinds of music, giving the extra emphasis to the beat.

Instead of separating out the notes, as you did in the previous example, full chords are played on the second and third beats. Before you begin playing, take a look at both sets of chords. This time, instead of a root position C triad, a first inversion is used. In the fifth bar you will find a full G dominant seventh chord (as

opposed to the notes F and G which were used to create the dominant seventh effect in the previous example).

When you play the piece below you will undoubtedly find the fingering demanding. If you look at bar 2 you will see that your left hand has to cover a two-octave range of notes. This means playing the upper and lower C on the first beat using the fourth finger and thumb, and then moving the hand so that the fourth finger, second finger and thumb play the notes E, G and C on the second and third beats.

The movement on the G dominant seventh chord is even trickier since your fingers have to find four notes on the second and third beats.

ARPEGGIOS

What we didn't mention in the previous example was the jagged line alongside the chord in the final bar of the piece. This is called an ARPEGGIO and it indicates that instead of playing the notes simultaneously as a chord they are instead played as a quick succession of sustained single notes.

They are written in this way since attributing time values to each note would simply be confusing. In the example above, the six notes affected are played from the lowest pitch to the highest pitch, one after the other, in the space of less than a sixteenth note. Each note when played has to sustain for the remainder of the first two beats, which is defined by the fact that the chord is made up of half notes. This means that the first note played—C on the bass clef—is the

only one that is actually played as a half note: even though all of the notes are written out as half note, each subsequent note has a shorter value.

Arpeggios are used to create a kind of "rolling" effect: the technique takes its name from the Italian word for a harp. Like other types of performance mark (some of which are shown in Lesson 10), arpeggios are not really precise in their instruction, but are largely a matter for the discretion of the player—although this will often be dictated by the context of the music. In the example above, some musicians may roll the notes as quickly as possible; at the other extreme, some may informally divide the six notes equally over the two beats, creating what are called triplet eighth notes.

ALTERING THE BASS NOTES

If you invert the notes of any chord or triad you alter its balance and hence the way it sounds. This can be taken further by extending inversions to cover the notes on the bass clef.

The staves below show how the sound of a simple triad can be changed by playing bass notes other than the root. In the first instance, the C major has a bass note of C (the root).

In the second example, the C major triad is played over a bass note of E (major 3rd); the bottom example has C major played over G (perfect 5th). Listen to those chords played one after the other and hear the harmonic effect of moving the bass line.

Although the chords represent open position inversions they are often written down with the chord name followed by a stroke and then the bass note—for example "C/G." This is described as "C over G."

C MAJOR TRIAD WITH C BASS NOTE

C MAJOR TRIAD WITH E BASS NOTE (C/E)

C MAJOR TRIAD WITH G BASS NOTE (C/G)

UNDERSTANDING CHORD CONSTRUCTION

The naming system for the chords you have used so far is relatively self-evident once you've learned a few simple rules. You know, for example, that by adding a minor 7th to a triad you can create a range of seventh chords, or by adding a major 7th, you can create major seventh chords.

As you will discover when you look at the Chord Dictionary (*see pages 110–135*), there are a great many other chord types—even the 27 shown for each key represents but a small proportion of the possibilities.

All of these chords are logically named, based around the notes they contain. To name any chord—or work out the notes that are contained by any named chord—all you need is the root note and knowledge of the names of the notes in the chromatic scale for that note (the chromatic scale refers to every half-step interval from the tonic to the octave).

Let's look at an example of a chord comprising the notes C, E G♭ and B♭. Here are the interval names: C (root); E (major 3rd); G♭ (diminished 5th); B♭ (minor 7th). The B♭ flat makes it a C seventh type of chord, but the fifth note is flattened. This makes the chord name C seventh diminished fifth, or "C seven flat five." It can be notated as C7-5.

If we see a chord called C maj 7+5 ("C major seven sharp five"), we can easily work out the notes. The first half of the name tells us that it is a C major 7, which uses the notes C (root), E (major 3rd), G (perfect 5th) and B (major 7th). However the "+5" tells us that the fifth note is sharpened and is thus played as an augmented 5th. This means that the notes that make up C maj 7+5 are C, E, G♯ and B.

POLYTONAL EFFECTS

When two different chord types are played at the same time, the result is called a POLYTONAL CHORD (or alternatively a "polychord"). For example, if you take a C major triad (C-E-G) and play it with a G major triad (G-B-D), the result is the combination of C-E-G-B-D, which is the C ninth chord.

One of the simplest ways to illustrate polytonal effects is to play a major triad and then add a bass note from outside that triad. This is an extremely widely used effect in most types of music.

The staff below contains five simple major triads. In each case the bass note comes from outside of that triad. To make comparison easier, the bass note remains the same in each case (C) but is always different in relation to notes of each successive triad. Once again, for convenience, these chords are widely labelled as a triad "over" a bass note.

However, these chords could also be given new names based on the three notes of the triad in relation to the bass notes. Take the first example, which has D major (D, F♯ and A) played over C: it could also be viewed as a chord in the key of C major that uses the notes C (root), D (major 2nd/9th), F♯ (augmented 4th) and A (major 6th). Such a chord *could* technically therefore be termed as a C 6/9+4. Since a relatively small number of musicians have such a wide chord vocabulary as to be able to interpret immediately this kind of naming, it's hardly surprising that "D over C" remains a more popular way of describing the chord.

Let's see how the second example can be named in the key of C: E/C uses the notes C (root), E (major 3rd), G♯ (augmented 5th) and B (major 7th) and so could also be called C major 7+5.

Similarly, F♯/C uses the same notes as C7-5-9; G/C has the same notes as C major 9th; B♭/C contains notes within C eleventh.

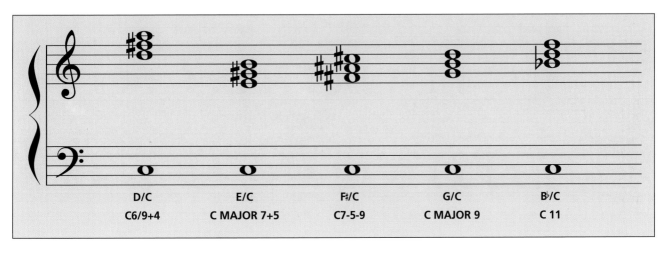

D/C	E/C	F♯/C	G/C	B♭/C
C6/9+4	C MAJOR 7+5	C7-5-9	C MAJOR 9	C 11

LESSON EIGHT
GETTING INTO STYLE

The whole of this lesson is dedicated to letting you put into practice some of things you've previously learned. This section concentrates on providing tips for playing keyboards in a variety of different styles, including dance, reggae, rock and blues, jazz, boogie-woogie and Latin. Each version is based around a simple backing track. In each case you can see the chords to the backing in the form of a chord chart along with musical suggestions to play over the backing.

DANCE BACKING

Each of the four chords is played as a series of whole notes on the first beat of the bar, and so sustains for four beats—the full length of each bar. The chords can be played typically using an organ, or piano or synthesizer voice.

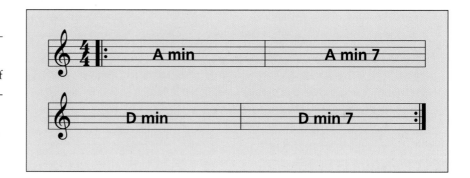

SINGLE-HAND VAMPING

In the first three exercises shown below, each of the chords are played on the beat. In every case, minor seventh chords are used—these will work well over the minor chords of the backing track (the three notes of the basic triads are also used in the minor seventh chord).

The first exercise shows the root position minor seventh chords being played. This means that the notes making up the chord are played in order of their pitch. The chord change "works", but sounds a little clumsy. To improve this, an inversion of D minor seventh is used in the second exercise. The two highest notes of the chord—A and C—have been dropped below the root note.

This makes the chord change sound more natural: in the movement between bars two and three, the intervals between each note have been reduced. This also makes the chord-change easier to play since the hand can remain broadly in the same position.

Exercise three inverts the A minor seventh chord as well, creating a more musically sophisticated sound.

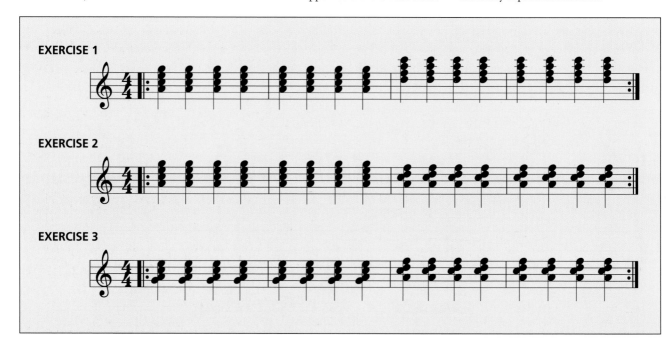

ALTERING THE RHYTHM

In the remaining exercises, the same chords are used, this time played with different note values, creating a more interesting rhythm. If you have a problem working out these note values, try quadrupling the count, breaking each bar down into eighth-note divisions. In this way, a quarter note can take a value of four, an eighth-note a value of two, and a dotted eighth note a value of three.

In exercise four, you can get the rhythm by counting out aloud in the following way, emphasizing the number "one" each time. Remember that you are counting four times faster than the time signature indicates: ONE-two-three-four-ONE-two-three-ONE-two-three-ONE-two-ONE-two-ONE-two.

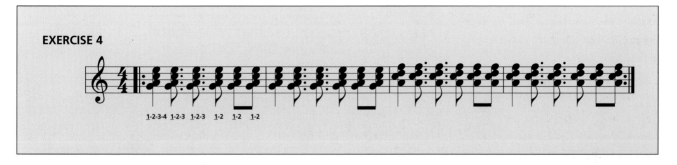

ADDING THE BASS NOTES

The final exercises introduce the left hand, creating rhythmic syncopation between the bass notes (played by the left hand) and the chords (played by the right hand). Syncopation is a rhythm that runs against the prevailing pulse or meter, thereby accentuating "off-beats." You can hear this effect clearly in exercise five, where the syncopated rhythm is played with the right hand; at the same time, the left hand is playing octave root notes on each beat of the bar.

Exercise six breaks the rhythm further between the left and right hands. It also modifies the chords to a minor ninth in bars one and three. Whilst it would just about be possible to play all five notes of a ninth chord using the right hand, a more usual approach is to use the left hand to play the root note. This leaves the right hand to play the remaining four notes. You can use the method above to count out the rhythm, but don't emphasizing the first beat of the count for each rest because no notes are played there. Notice that the notes change in bars two and four, creating variations on the minor ninths played in the other two.

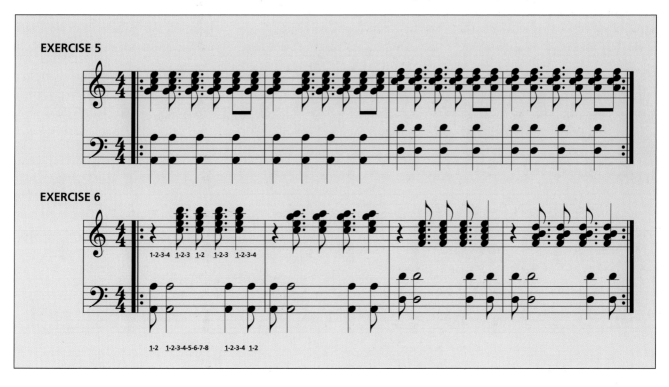

REGGAE BACKING

Reggae music originated in the West Indies and gradually spread throughout the world during the late 1960s. It's two principal centres of activity are Jamaica and London.

There are a number of related reggae forms, such as the faster "ska" style, or the electro-dance "ragga" that emerged in the 1990s.

This particular backing uses the chords A minor, E minor and D minor.

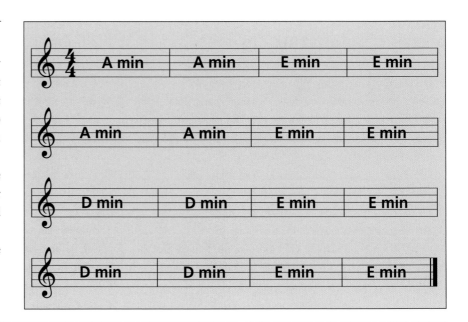

REGGAE RHYTHM

The defining characteristic of reggae music is the way in which the emphasis shifts to the so-called "off-beat." In practice, since reggae music is pretty well always in four-four time, the second and fourth beats are always heavily accented.

You can see the way this works from the music shown on the staves below. In each case, there is a quarter-note rest on the first and third beats; the chords are only played on the second and fourth beats. You should be able play these triads using the thumb, first finger and fourth finger each time.

This is just about as simple as a reggae rhythm part can be, but it is nonetheless effective, creating the "ska" sound that characterizes this type of music.

Once you have worked through the example below, you can try adding some extra notes to create a fuller sound. One effective way of doing this is to add the octave note on top of each chord you play. This means when you are playing an A minor chord, you need to use the thumb to play A, the first finger to play C, the second finger to play E and the fourth finger

to play octave A.

A second alternative is to "convert" each of the minor chords to minor sevenths. This means that instead of playing the octave with the fourth finger, you instead use it to play the minor seventh note – for A minor, this means adding the note G; for E minor, the note D; and for D minor, the note C.

A third possibility is to add a ninth note (for A minor, this means the note B above the octave). To play in this way, you can drop the root note and play the 3rd, 5th, minor 7th and 9th notes with the thumb and first three fingers respectively.

FULLY SYNCOPATED REGGAE RHYTHM

This second example provides a more sophisticated approach to the basic reggae rhythm. Although the treble part played by the right hand is identical to the exercise on the previous page, the left hand is used to play syncopated eighth notes, creating a totally different rhythmic effect.

To work out what at first seems a slightly complex rhythm, start an eighth-note count on the bass notes. The easiest way to do this is to double the tempo of the basic four-four rhythm, and the double the number of beats in the bar. Count from one to eight, and then tap out the rhythm with your left hand on each of the accented beats: "one-<u>TWO</u>-three-<u>FOUR</u>-five-<u>SIX</u>-seven <u>EIGHT</u>."

While you are still counting and tapping out a consistent beat with the left hand, prepare to tap out the right-hand rhythm:

"one-two-<u>THREE</u>-four-five-six <u>SEVEN</u>-eight." It's only when you get both hands working together that you will hear how simple this rhythm really is. Now play the same rhythm using the chords shown below. As you can see, the chords played on the treble staff are the same as those played on the bass staff, only they are one octave higher. There are a great number of alternative possibilities using this fundamental rhythm.

Once again, this part is most likely to be played by an organ or piano sound. In practice, to create this uniform "stabbing" sound, the time values of the chords on both staves are likely to be unified: the crotchets on the treble staff are more likely to be played as quavers. As you will see on page 101, this can be achieved by playing "staccato"—by positioning a dot above or below a note or chord. It then has to be played as half its value followed by a rest of the same value.

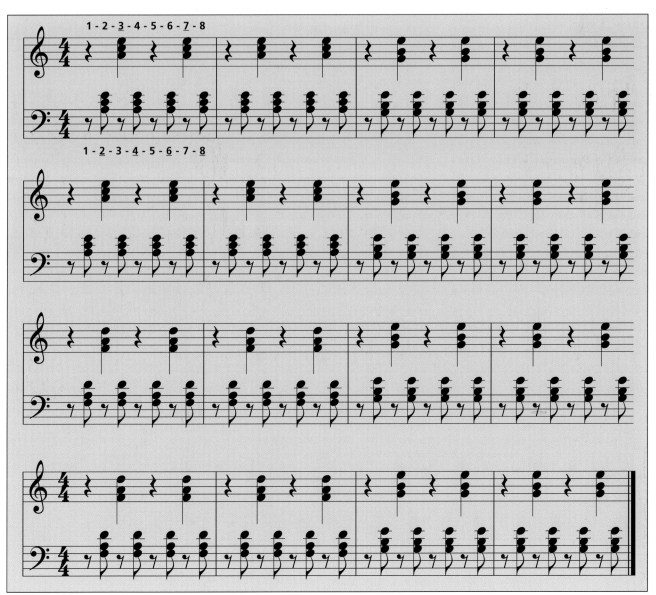

THE BLUES

The chord sequence shown on the right represents a typical twelve-bar blues pattern in the key of C. Although it is most often performed using the most basic major chords, it is also commonly played using minors, sevenths and ninths.

This example on the right uses only dominant ninth chords.

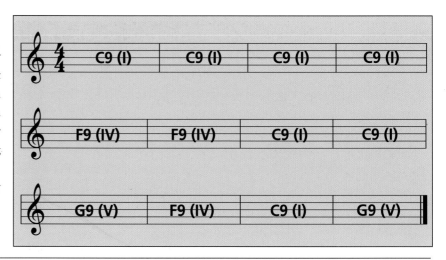

THE 12-BAR SYSTEM

Blues music evolved out of the experiences of Black Americans whose ancestors were transported from their homes in Africa to work as slave labor in America's Deep South. By the beginning of the 20th century it had become a uniquely American folk form. Much of the music of the past century—jazz and R&B as well as rock and roll and other forms of rock and pop—has either evolved from or been strongly influenced by blues music.

Much of the music of the early blues musicians was fairly loose in terms of its chord structuring. It was in the hands of the Chicago bluesmen from the 1930s that the familiar "twelve-bar" structure became the norm. This twelve-bar repeating "turnaround" is based on chords built on the first, fourth and fifth degrees of the major scale. The structure of this type of chord sequence is shown above for the key of C, which therefore uses chords in the key of C (I), F (IV) and G (V). Indeed, this kind of sequence is often referred to as a "one-four-five" (I-IV-V). The exercises over the next two pages are basic examples of a "jazz" blues style that is particularly well suited to a Hammond organ type of sound.

This particular example of a blues structure uses "ninth" chords. To refresh your memory, this means adding a major second ABOVE the octave to a dominant seventh chord. A full ninth chord uses five different notes, but, as you can see in the example below, each of the chords only contains four notes. Look at the first chord: although it's supposed to be in the key of C, only the notes B♭, D, E and G are shown on the staff. There's a perfectly good reason for this. Although the chord you are playing appears to be "rootless," it doesn't matter because in the context of playing with the backing music, the bass guitar is providing the root note.

Knowing which notes can and can't be omitted from a chord is a very useful skill to acquire when you play with other musicians. Think about it for a moment: if every member of the band played exactly the same notes, the effect would be rather dull. Color and sophistication is added to music when different instruments or sounds are used to build up chords.

The example below uses tied notes: the whole-note chord you play on the first beat of the first bar is sustained over the next four bars. The chord on the fifth bar sustains for two bars, as does the chord on the seventh bar.

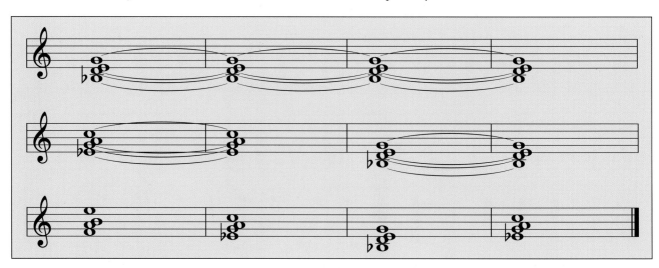

COMPOUND TIME IN PRACTICE

This is an appropriate moment to show a practical example of how compound time (*see page 42*) may be used. You probably already noticed that the music at the foot of this page seems to be peppered with the number "3." This example is in "simple" four-four time. However, to get the rhythm working correctly, the quarter notes need to be subdivided into three equal measures. The music could equally be given a compound time of "twelve-eight," meaning that each bar was made up from twelve eighth notes.

Both methods of notation are equally valid, although the twelve-eight time signature would arguably make the music easier to comprehend.

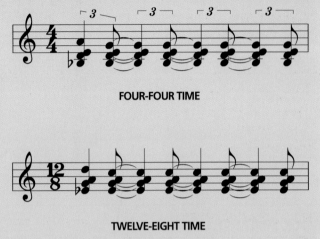

FOUR-FOUR TIME

TWELVE-EIGHT TIME

BLUES TRIPLETS

This is a pretty challenging rhythm accompaniment written, once again, with a Hammond organ in mind. The four-four rhythm is played as a set of eighth-note triplets, which means that each quarter-note beat of the bar is subdivided into three eighth notes—this is shown by the bracketed number three.

To master this rhythm, it's necessary for you to count out each of the quaver triplets. A good way of combining these triplets with the four-four beat is to count out loud "<u>ONE</u>-two-three-<u>TWO</u>-two-three-<u>THREE</u>-two-three-<u>FOUR</u>-two three."

Let's work out the rhythm, starting with the first two triplets. The quarter note when bracketed as a part of a triplet is effectively worth two-thirds of a beat. That fits in nicely with your count, meaning that the first chord is played on "one" and the second on "three." Since the first two triplets are tied, the second chord is effectively worth a count of three—the third chord is not sounded until the third beat of the second triplet. That means that the rhythm for the first bar can be counted like this (with chords played on the emphasized beat): <u>ONE</u>-two-<u>THREE</u>-two-two-<u>THREE</u>-three-two-<u>THREE</u>-four-two-<u>THREE</u>. Notice that the chord also changes on the first beat of the bar.

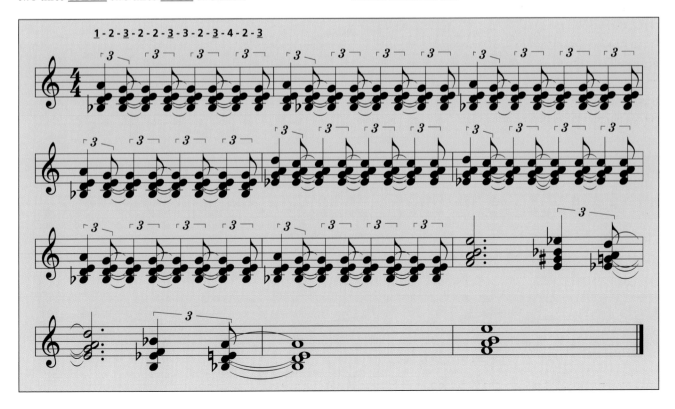

ROCKING BOOGIE

Here is a second blues-oriented backing with which you can play along. This time the twelve-bar structure is written for the key of G.

The exercise over the next two pages are more oriented towards the piano, with some traditional rock and roll and a touch of blues "boogie-woogie."

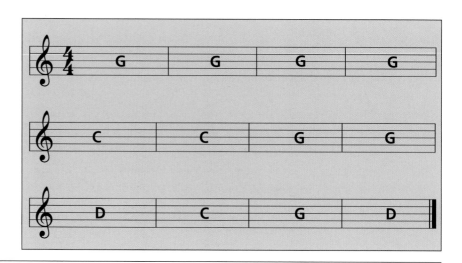

ROCK AND ROLL

This next exercise provides you with a touch of piano rock and roll, the sort of thing that might have been played by the likes of Little Richard or Jerry Lee Lewis in the 1950s.

Approach the piece in two halves, starting off with the bass line. This is a sequence of swift eighth notes which consist of intervals a perfect 4th, perfect 5th and minor 7th from the root note. If you just play this over the backing track it will sound pretty good without any contribution from the right hand.

The rhythm on the treble staff works in repeating two-bar cycles. The notes are largely played on the beat, except for the crossing between the first and second bar. At this point an odd thing happens: the chord that would seem to be intended for the first beat of the second bar is "pulled" back by a half a beat into the first bar. It is then tied, sustaining across the first beat of the second bar. This is a common rhythmic trick that creates an impression of urgency called "anticipation".

When you've mastered both hands independently, you can try to play the two parts together.

BOOGIE-WOOGIE

Here is a neat alternative bass part to the rock and roll piano sequence across the page. This kind of walking bass line, called a "boogie-woogie," first became popular among jazz musicians during the 1930s.

The rhythm pattern is very simple: the first beat is emphasized with a crotchet and then followed by a slick run of eighth notes. Getting the fingers working properly, however, might well be a tougher proposition.

One of the difficulties is that for the fingers to get into a position where they can execute each run, the root note on the first beat has to be played by the fourth—and weakest—finger. This can be tiring, but will also help to build up the strength and maneuverbility of the third and fourth fingers.

For a reasonable fingering, play the first four notes with the fourth, third, second and first fingers respectively, and then alternate the last three notes between the thumb and first finger. Although it is an antiquated form, boogie-woogie can be dazzling when performed by an expert.

OCTAVE BASS LINE

For a real challenge, try this bass part. Although it's based around the boogie-woogie shown above, the octave stretches are even more demanding of the left hand: these occur between the first two eighth notes and the last two eighth notes .

As would normally be the case, the octave spans need to be performed by the fourth finger and thumb. The four-note run in between these two octave jumps can be neatly played by the third, second and first fingers, and thumb. The curves above each bar (slurs) indicate that the notes within have to be played *legato* —with no pauses between them.

SIMPLE JAZZ PIANO

The ability to play unaccompanied jazz piano is one of the most demanding skills any keyboard player can acquire.

It's clearly only possible to give a flavor of something as wide-ranging as jazz in the space of a few pages. Here, then, is a simple but effective little jazz sequence. You'll notice that although it's rhythmically very straightforward, it makes use of some unusual types of chord, such as "six/nines," minor ninths, minor elevenths, seventh augmented fifths and seventh flattened fifths.

Although these chords may be unfamiliar to you right now, you can see how they are formed for any key by using the Chord Dictionary (*see pages 110–135*).

LATIN SOUNDS

The final piece in this lesson is a type of Latin-American music called *bossa nova*, which came out of Brazil in the late 1950s.

The defining characteristic of this type of music is the syncopated interplay between the bass and treble note.

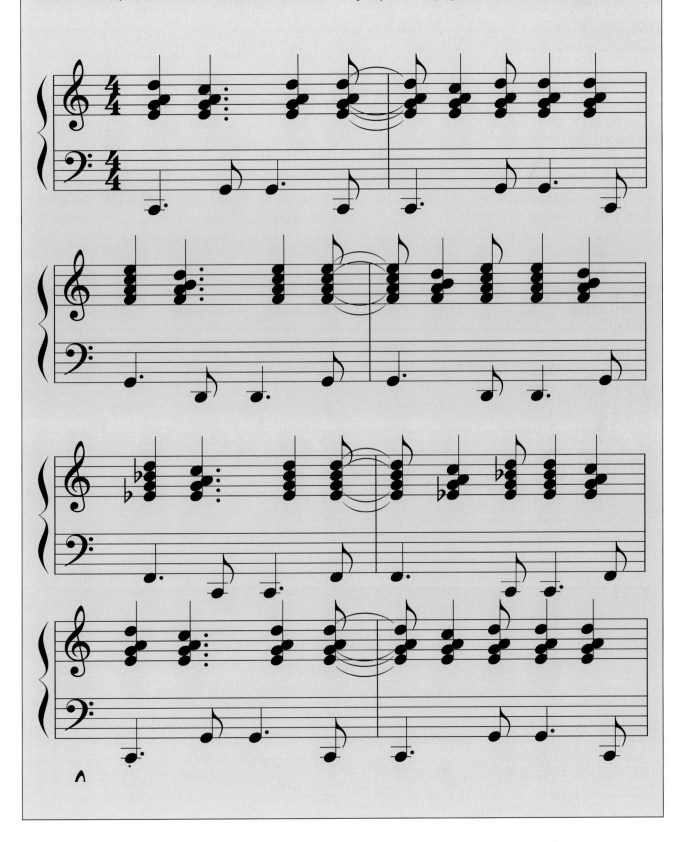

LESSON NINE
DOING YOUR OWN THING

One of the most important aspects of becoming a "total" musician is in having a thorough understanding of the way chords and notes are related to one another. This knowledge can be so valuable in so many different areas of music. If it is ultimately your intention to compose your own pieces, it provides an immediate understanding of what should and shouldn't work, and also the reasons why. A good working knowledge of the mechanics of harmony and melody will also help you to make better decisions when improvising.

WHY IS IT THAT SOME CHORD PATTERNS JUST "WORK"?

You may have already discovered for yourself that there are certain types of chord sequence or intervals of notes that seem to work more harmoniously than others.

You've played the chords on the major scale in a number of different ways (*see below*), and you can tell that they all sound very pleasant when played together. Similarly, the notes on the major and minor scales also sound "correct" when played together in sequence.

There is a particularly strong relationship between the chords formed on the root, fourth and fifth degrees of any diatonic scale. This can be heard in the vast majority of popular songs written over the past century. If you play these chord sequences, you will hear that they create a familiar effect:

C major (I) – F major (IV) – G major (V) – C major (I)
F major (I) – B♭ major (IV) – C major (V) – F major (I)
G major (I) – C major (IV) – D major (V) – G major (I)

Notice how smoothly each chord moves into the next, irrespective of the key. Now try this experiment. Sing the root note of the first chord all the way through each sequence. In the first example, that means singing the note C, even when you are playing the F and G chords. You will hear that even when the chords change, the note you're singing still seems to fit. Why should that be?

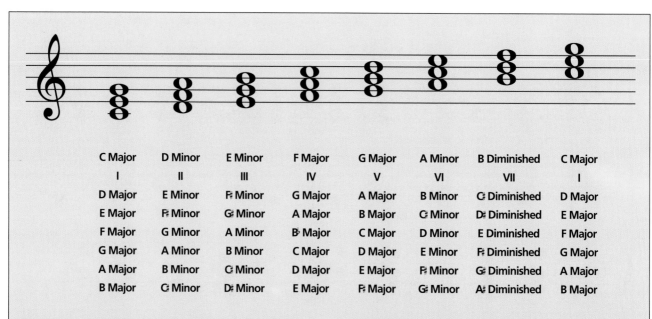

C Major	D Minor	E Minor	F Major	G Major	A Minor	B Diminished	C Major
I	II	III	IV	V	VI	VII	I
D Major	E Minor	F♯ Minor	G Major	A Major	B Minor	C♯ Diminished	D Major
E Major	F♯ Minor	G♯ Minor	A Major	B Major	C♯ Minor	D♯ Diminished	E Major
F Major	G Minor	A Minor	B♭ Major	C Major	D Minor	E Diminished	F Major
G Major	A Minor	B Minor	C Major	D Major	E Minor	F♯ Diminished	G Major
A Major	B Minor	C♯ Minor	D Major	E Major	F♯ Minor	G♯ Diminished	A Major
B Major	C♯ Minor	D♯ Minor	E Major	F♯ Major	G♯ Minor	A♯ Diminished	B Major

By now you should be pretty familiar with the sequence above which shows the chords built on the major scale. Beneath it you'll see the same set of chords transposed to the other most commonly used keys.

A good playing exercise is to work through this chord sequence in other keys. Even though the chords you play will be totally different, you will still recognize the characteristic sound. If you can't work out the full set of chords in each key, turn to the Chord Dictionary (*pages 110-135*) and you'll see the correct fingering.

As you'll see, understanding this set of chords is also extremely useful if you want to try your hand at songwriting.

The reason for this is because the note C appears in the major scale for all three chords. In fact, if you look at the notes of each scale, you will see precisely how closely the three are related. Indeed, F major and G major each have only one different note to the C major scale.

C – D – E – F – G – A – B – C
F – G – A – B♭ – C – D – E – F
G – A – B – C – D – E – F♯ – G

SONG CONSTRUCTION EXERCISE

Because the chords built on the major scale (as shown across the page) are related, there's a good chance that if you create your own structure using chords taken from this sequence they will sound pleasant when played together.

Try this exercise out for yourself. Start off by looking at the left-hand column below. Each of the boxes represent a I-IV-V-I (named after the scale degree) chord progression in the most common keys. Play the sequences through, treating each chord as a bar in its own right. You should play them as whole notes, so that they sustain the length of each bar, or as eighth notes played on the half beat.

After that, look at the boxes on the right. Each one of these contains a different four-bar progression. In each case the chords are drawn from and named after those built on the major scale. For example, the fifth sequence (I-III-VI-V) in the key of C uses the chords C major, E minor, A minor and G major. Work through them all, trying them out in a variety of different keys. You might well even recognize some songs you know from these simple progressions.

I	IV	V	I
C Major	F Major	G Major	C Major
D Major	G Major	A Major	D Major
E Major	A Major	B Major	E Major
F Major	B♭ Major	C Major	F Major
G Major	C Major	D Major	G Major
A Major	D Major	E Major	A Major
B Major	E Major	F♯ Major	C Major

I	V	IV	V
I	II	IV	V
I	II	III	IV
I	VI	II	VII
I	III	VI	V
I	IV	V	III
I	II	VI	V
I	VI	IV	V

DEVELOPING IDEAS

There are numerous approaches that can be taken to creating a composition from scratch. Any of the basic components—rhythm, harmony (chord structure) and melody—can be developed on their own or evolve from one another.

For example, some composers or songwriters just sit down at a piano and play around with chord sequences until something they like emerges; musicians who write together sometimes just "jam" around, letting their ideas interact until something interesting happens.

A common method of working for modern solo MIDI-based musicians is to begin with the rhythm, either provided by drum programming or (given its importance in electronic dance music) the bass line.

The example below shows a bass line in the key of C. The second staff shows a slightly refined version that evolved from the original bass line.

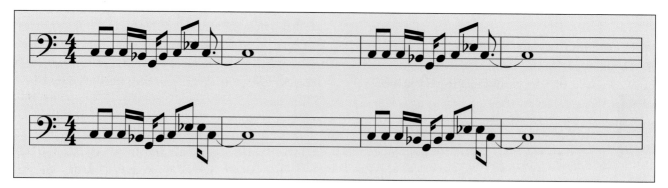

ADDING CHORDS

Look at the bass notes you've just played. The tonic is clearly the note C—the whole riff revolves around this note. But what of the remaining notes, B♭, G and E♭? These are all part of the C natural minor scale. This tells you immediately that a C minor triad will "fit" over the bass line. Since B♭ is also part of the same scale, you can add this note to the chord, making C minor seventh.

This particular bass line has been designed so that it plays through the entire song. So to make its sound more interesting, we'll alter the chords. A good starting point is to consider the C natural minor scale, since the chords built from the scale are guaranteed to work on a musical level (although there's no certainty that it will create the effect you are looking for).

In the example below, we move from C minor 7 to a chord built from the third degree of the scale, which is E♭. Notice in

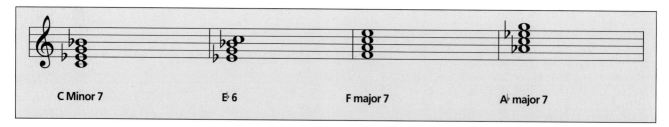

| C Minor 7 | E♭ 6 | F major 7 | A♭ major 7 |

CHOOSING SOUNDS

When arranging a song for electronic keyboards, the sounds you choose can have a dramatic effect on the way the music works. This is especially true of chords.

The sequence shown above has been designed to work with a string or orchestral sound. Since the notes are all semibreves, they should be sustained across the entire bar, retaining their volume throughout. If you instead use an "attack" sound, one in which the voice immediately begins to fade after the note is played—for example, a piano or

harpsichord—the effect would not be the same. This is, of course, not to say that it would be necessarily bad or wrong.

Similarly, voices that are programmed with a vibrato sound can also be problematic in that they can create a "detuning" effect which is not always pleasant or suitable.

There's no reason why you should be predictable in the sounds you choose or program: your keyboard may have a wide array of bass-type sounds, but you may find that playing the part using the bass end of a piano works better.

this case since the bass line will still be playing the note C, we can add the note C to the E♭ triad, making E♭6.

The next chord is based around the note F. In this case, we've made the chord F major seventh, which creates a slightly unusual effect. This is because the major seventh in F is E, which "clashes" with the E♭ used in the bass line. The interval between E♭ and E creates a sharp dissonance. In spite of this, the progression still "works."

When working out arrangements in this way, if you are in any doubt, it's always useful to break the chord down into its constituent notes and play each one over the line that has already been written. You can then hear the effect of the different intervals with greater clarity.

The final chord is A♭ major seventh—since this uses the notes A♭, C, E♭ and G♭ it fits smoothly over the bass line.

MELODY

Like the bass line, the melody written out below also repeats throughout the song. Once again, it uses notes from the C natural minor scale (G, F and E♭). This sequence also creates the same dissonance in the third bar, where E♭ is played over E.

Although the effect is unsettling, it nonetheless works. This dissonance could be smoothed by raising each occurrence of E♭ in the third bar by a half step, to play E instead.

HOW USEFUL IS ALL THIS, REALLY?

Although we are dissecting this arrangement in a rather stolid technical way, it isn't to say that composers view their slowly evolving pieces of work in the same manner. Let's be honest, many of the greatest pop songs of the last century have been written by musicians who know little or nothing of even the simplest harmonic theory. They simply play some chords that they like, hum a tune and then give it some words. End of story.

Songwriting is more likely to be an instinctive process. Judging whether a sequence of chords or a melody sounds good is more a result of the music that we've spent our lives listening to, than understanding the musical reasoning that backs it up. Knowing this basic theory is more likely to be useful when composing or arranging more complex material. It can also help out when the compositional process gets "stuck," for example, resolving the end of a verse so that it "dovetails" neatly back to the starting chords.

PUT IT ALL TOGETHER

You can see the three different parts written down on the staff together. This is a very brief example of what is called a "SCORE."

Although each part is played by a different instrument, the three staves are joined together at the bar lines. The score gives you an at-a-glance view of the music as a whole.

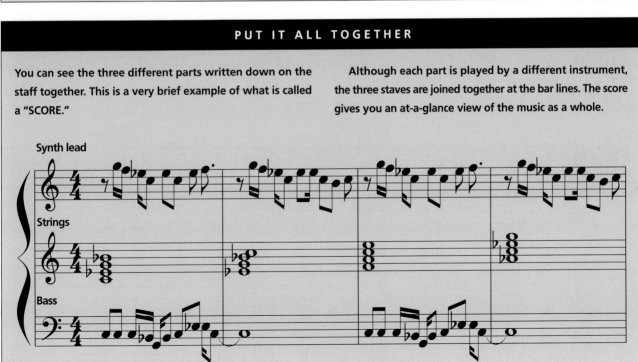

IMPROVISING TECHNIQUES

A reference-book definition of improvisation would be something along the lines of "the creation of new music during the course of a performance." In practical terms, it tends to be viewed as extemporization around an existing melody or an appropriate scale. Indeed, the vast majority of soloing is based on moving around and extending the notes of a scale. After all, if you play the notes of a C major scale over a chord of C major, every note and interval will work to some degree.

Although improvisation can't really be taught as such, a good way of introducing the idea to the novice is to try to get the maximum number of variations from within a very limited musical spectrum. There is no more extreme example of this than playing the same sequence of notes, but using different rhythms or emphases.

Over the next two pages you will see a series of two-bar staves that show a C major scale played over a single octave. In

each case the notes are played in sequence. As you'll hear, even within the realms of using just the same eight notes, the possibilities for variation are quite endless.

EXAMPLES ONE TO FOUR

In the first three examples you can play the same major-scale fingering (T-1-2-T-1-2-3-4). However, this isn't really feasible for the fourth example, which begins with four fast sixteenth notes. These notes (C, D, E and F) really need to played by the thumb and first three fingers in quick succession—the thumb then tucks under the fourth finger to play G, followed by the first, second and third fingers, which play A, B and C respectively.

EXAMPLES FIVE TO EIGHT

The examples on the opposite page can all be performed using standard fingering, although the first two—both featuring swiftly executed sixteenth notes—you are likely to find particularly demanding.

APPROACHES TO IMPROVISATION

Improvisation can mean different things to different players. Take a traditional approach to an improvised jazz solo: at first the melody is predefined; the soloist then moves away from the melody, but still largely bases the solo around the notes used in the melody. This all rather begs the question of what actually constitutes improvisation, and in some cases are we simply confusing artistic inspiration with a well-developed musical vocabulary?

"Free" improvising musicians often take a more radical and responsive line, priding themselves on their flexibility and open-mindedness—although this doesn't always make for the easiest of listening experiences for an audience. But the best improvising musicians are those who can listen and respond quickly, are prepared to take risks and responsibility for their own limits.

Although it may sound like something of an oxymoron, it is possible to practice improvisation. The facility you develop to improvise will—as much as anything else—be down to your attitude as much as your technical capability. However, the very act of improvisation constitutes practice for future improvisation. It's simple: the more you do it, the better you become.

In fact, the discipline of improvising within a very tight musical framework—as shown in the exercises on these two pages—teaches you how to try to draw out as much as possible from very little. Such exercises are worth integrating with your regular scale and chord practice.

Although improvising alone is clearly quite possible, the act of integrating with other musicians is a far more challenging and satisfying experience.

LESSON TEN

CLASSICAL STYLE

The final lesson of this chapter is concerned with working through some classical examples. Here you will find four complete pieces composed in the early 18th century by Johann Sebastian Bach. These have been chosen not because they are easy to play, but because the written music is straightforward to follow. The lesson also illustrates a number of other important aspects of written music, such as use of repeat symbols, dynamics and ornamentations, such as trills and appoggiaturas. These can all be found in the four compositions.

REPETITION IN WRITTEN MUSIC

Whatever style of music you care to play, a great deal of its content revolves around repetition. If a piece of music was notated in full, in many cases you would find that huge segments were almost identical—and the sheet music could be three or four times as long. Fortunately this isn't necessary because using a variety of symbols it is possible to repeat individual notes, bars and whole sections of music.

REPEATING BARS

The "forward slash" symbol (/) is the standard musical shorthand for repeating notes or chords from within a bar. These can also be used effectively in informal chord charts where only the names of the chords are written out: one or more oblique slashes following a chord within a bar is an instruction to repeat that chord on any beats on which there is a slash.

An entire bar, or series of bars, can be repeated in a similar fashion using a slash symbol with dots either side (✗). Whenever this symbol is used, the previous bar with notated music is repeated until further instruction.

REPEATING SECTIONS OF MUSIC

There are a number of ways in which whole segments of music can be repeated. One of the most common is the use of the repeat symbols that can be found at the start and end of bar lines. The "end repeat" bar line (:‖)is a one-time instruction to return and play from a bar marked with the "start repeat" symbol (‖:)—if one doesn't exist then the music should be repeated from the start. A number of other commonly used repeat symbols are shown on the opposite page.

REPEATS IN PRACTICE

On the opposite page you can see all of the most commonly used repeat symbols in context. At the foot of the page you will find a complete exercise that makes use of each type of repeat. Try to work out the playing sequence for all ten bars. The correct sequence is shown below:

- Play bars A, B, C, D and E.
- The end repeat symbol instructs you either to return to the previous start repeat or, if one can't be found, the beginning of the piece.
- Play bars A, B, C, D and E.
- This time, ignore the first end repeat and go on to play bars F and G.
- The end repeat instructs you to look for the previous start repeat, which is at the beginning of bar F.
- Play bars F and G.
- Ignore the end repeat on bar G; play bar H.
- The D.S. (Dal Segno) sign tells you to return to the Segno symbol, which is at the beginning of bar B.

- Play bars B, C, D and E.
- Ignore the end repeat symbol.
- Play bars F and G.
- Ignore the end repeat symbol.
- Play bar H.
- Ignore the D.S. symbol.
- Play bar I.
- The D.C. (Da Capo) symbol instructs you to return to the start of the music.
- Play bars A, B, C, D and E.
- Ignore the end repeat.
- Play bars F and G.
- Ignore the end repeat.
- Play bar H.
- Ignore the D.S. symbol
- The "first time ending" tells you to ignore bar I and go on to the "second time ending", which is bar J.
- The "fine" sign marks the end of the piece.

REPEAT SIGNS

The staff below illustrates the use of the repeat symbols. They can be interpreted in the following way:

- Play bars 1 and 2.
- The "end repeat" symbol at the end of bar 2 instructs you to return to the start of the piece; repeat bars 1 and 2.

- This time around, ignore the "end repeat" at the end of bar 2 and play on through bars 3 and 4.
- The "end repeat" symbol at the end of bar 4 is an instruction to return to the previous "start repeat," which is at the beginning of bar 3; repeat bars 3 and 4.

BAR 1   BAR 2   BAR 3   BAR 4

DA CAPO (shown using the letters *D.C.*) literally means "from the head." This is a one-time instruction to return to the start of the music.

DAL SEGNO (shown using the letters *D.S.*) literally means "from the sign." This instructs the player to repeat the music from the *SEGNO* symbol.

THE *DA CAPO* SYMBOL   THE *DAL SEGNO* SYMBOL   THE *SEGNO* SYMBOL

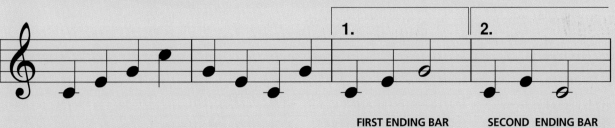

FIRST ENDING BAR   SECOND ENDING BAR

EXAMPLE USING ALL COMMON REPEAT SYMBOLS

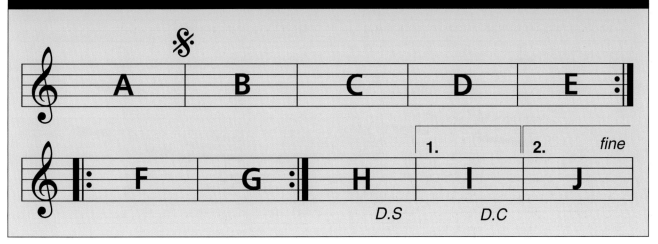

ORNAMENTATION

On the opposite page you can see your first complete piece of music—Bach's *Minuet In G Major*.

Before you prepare to play it, there are a couple of aspects of the notation you need to check out. You will see that bars 8 and 11 are marked "appoggiatura" and "trill." These are two forms of ORNAMENTATION. This refers to the slight modification of a piece of music to make a phrase sound more pleasant or effective. This usually occurs through the addition of note or dynamic changes—the alteration of volume.

Both the appoggiatura and trill are presented in written music as a kind of musical shorthand. Like many forms of ornamentation, they are often open to the interpretation of the player. Explicit instructions for the meanings of bars 8 and 11 are shown below.

INTERPRETING THE APPOGGIATURA

Appoggiatura literally means "leaning." It is shown as a tiny "grace note" linked by a curve to a regular note. In practice it means that the appoggiatura is played on the beat "leaning into" the principal note. Although it is often shown as an eighth note, it doesn't necessarily mean that it "eats" an eighth note out of the main note. The generally accepted practice is that if the principal note is divisible by two, then the appoggiatura is worth half its value; if divisible by three, the appoggiatura is worth two-thirds of the principle note. A literal interpretation of bar 8 is shown below on the right.

PLAYING TRILLS

A trill is an ornamentation by which a note is alternated with adjacent notes at rapid speed. There are a number of different types of trill—the one used on bar 11 is called a LOWER MORDENT. This means that the note marked with the mordent symbol is actually played using notes directly below the principal note. As with all ornamentations, the precise playing of a mordent is largely open to the interpretation of the player and depends on the context of the music. This really means playing it the way you think sounds best.

Below on the left you can see bar 11 with the mordent. Alongside, you can see how Bach suggested that the mordent should be played.

MINUET IN G MAJOR

PERFORMANCE MARKS

A note has three defining elements: its pitch, its time value and its volume. The last of these elements is covered by what are termed PERFORMANCE MARKS—instructions written on the music that are concerned with the way in which the music is played rather than alterations to pitch or time.

The general mood of a passage of music is defined by DYNAMIC MARKS. These, like many musical symbols, are shown as abbreviations from the original Italian terminology. You can see some of the most commonly used dynamic marks in the box below.

Music can also be changed fundamentally by emphasizing certain notes. This can be done by playing louder on specific notes, which are shown in written music with an ACCENT MARK (>) above the note. You can also gradually increase or decrease volume over a passage using CRESCENDO or DIMINUENDO marks.

DYNAMIC INSTRUCTIONS

CRESCENDO and DIMINUENDO marks are shown in music using "hairpin" symbols. The staff below shows a crescendo mark stretched over four bars. This means that during the course of those four bars, the music should gradually be increased until it reaches a new volume at the end of the fourth bar. The reverse would show a diminuendo over the four bars; this would appear on the music starting with the "open hairpin" and reaching its point where the volume is at its quietest.

The problem with these two symbols is that there is no strict instruction as to precisely how loud or soft you should play. For this, DYNAMIC MARKS are used.

Dynamic marks can be used to set the the mood of a piece of music, and are often used in conjunction with foot pedals on a piano. These marks are shown in their abbreviated forms. They can also be used with crescendo and diminuendo marks.

In the staff above, for example, if the beginning of the first bar was marked with *p* before the crescendo mark, and the end of the fourth bar with *ff*, the instruction would be to play from "soft" to "very loud" over the course of four bars.

ITALIAN NAME	DESCRIPTION	ABBREVIATION
FORTE	Loud	*f*
PIANO	Soft	*p*
MEZZO-FORTE	Medium loud	*mf*
MEZZO-PIANO	Medium soft	*mp*
FORTISSIMO	Very loud	*ff*
FORTISSISSIMO	Extremely loud	*fff*
PIANISSIMO	Very soft	*pp*
PIANISSISSIMO	Extremely soft	*ppp*
FORTE PIANO	Loud then immediately soft	*fp*
POCO FORTE	Slightly loud	*pf*
SFORZATO/SFORZANDO	Played with force	*sf*
RINFORZATO/RINFORZANDO	Becoming stronger	*rf*
SMORZANDO	Gradually fading	*smorz*
CALANDO	Slower with decreasing volume	*cal*

PLAYING STACCATO

An additional mark that you will need to understand before you can play the next piece is the STACCATO. The term quite literally means "detached" in Italian, and it is an instruction to reduce the length of a note.

Although there are a number ways the staccato can be shown, the most common is the placement of a dot above or below the head of the note.

As with other stylistic effects, the staccato mark is more likely to indicate a manner of playing rather than imparting a precise measurement. It is NOT, however, an instruction to shorten the note as much as possible.

As a general rule, the staccato can be treated as halving the value of the note and replacing the second half with a rest. In the two bars shown below, you can see that four staccato quarter notes are broadly equivalent in in their effect to four eighth notes, each followed by an eighth-note rest.

Quarter notes with staccato marks   Equivalent note and rest values

ARTICULATION

Just as the way we speak can be broken into self-contained paragraphs and sentences, so too can a piece of music. The musical equivalent of a sentence is referred to as a PHRASE.

Consider this well-known children's rhyme: you could view the line "twinkle twinkle little star" as a musical phrase in its own right. You could also extend that by two bars to create a longer phrase—"twinkle twinkle little star, how I wonder what you are." Many such phrases are passages of music that make some sort of sense when heard in isolation.

There are no strict rules governing what specifically constitutes a musical phrase, but they have a practical value in the way a piece of music can be performed.

A musical phrase can be shown formally using ARTICULATION MARKS, in particular a symbol called a SLUR. This is a curve that can be placed around a phrase of any length.

A defining characteristic of a musical phrase is a natural pause at its end, again, rather like the spoken word. A slur placed around a phrase has the practical effect of shortening the final note within its boundary, thus emphasizing the self-contained nature of the grouping.

The example below is taken from bars 3, 4 and 5 of Bach's *Partita in E Minor*—the next piece of music that you can try out for yourself (*see page 103*). As you can see, there are two slurs on the treble staff.

STACCATO AND PERFORMANCE MARKS IN PRACTICE

In the staff below, you can also see practical examples of the performance marks and staccato notes. The f in the middle of the second bar below (the fourth bar of the piece) indicates that the phrase should be played quite loud at that point.

The staccato notes in the first and third bars below work in the same way as the example at the top of the page—think of each quarter note as an eighth note followed by a rest.

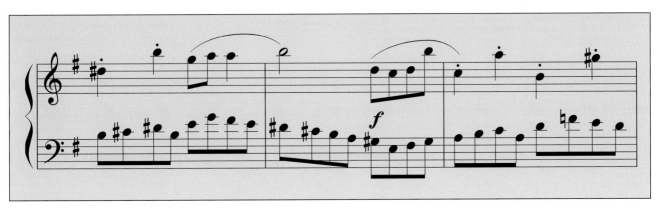

PLAYING WITH PHRASES

Other than informally identifying a musical phrase, implicit within the boundaries of a slur is the need for the notes to be played in a smooth and flowing manner, creating a cohesion that once again emphasizes the "togetherness" of the phrase. Playing in this way is known as "LEGATO." The most important factor when playing legato is that all of the notes within the slur must be played without any breaks—rather as if they were the result of single movement or gesture. In effect, legato is the opposite of staccato.

Now take a look at the staff below. In the first bar, you will see that the group of four beamed eighth notes makes use of two slurs. This effectively breaks the group into two pairs, since there

is an implication of a slight—if barely perceptible—pause between the second and third notes. If a single slur joined all four notes in the group, this pause would not exist; if there were no slurs, all four notes would be played in the same way. Notice, however, that the curve joining the half note to the quarter note across the bar line is NOT a slur but a tie. This is shown merely to demonstrate the two curved lines; since the half note is effectively the start of phrase, a more orthodox notation would begin the slur with the half note, meaning that the notes from the half note to the end of the second bar should be played legato.

In the hands of a good musician the interpretation of the slur is subtle and can't really be defined in any precise way. Indeed, the term "feel" is probably as good as any to describe a process aimed at making the music sound as natural as possible.

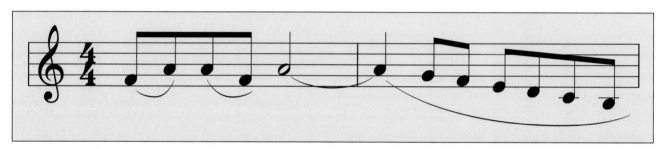

TRIPLET DIVISIONS

With the exception of the blues example that you've already seen on page 85, all of the note values you have used so far have been divisible by two. However, a beat can also be divided into three equal parts. The notes that result are known as TRIPLETS. Every type of note can be subdivided in this way.

There are various ways in which triplets can be notated. Three alternatives are shown below. In each case, a quarter note has been subdivided into three triplet eighth notes. Each of these methods is equally legitimate and their use is largely down to personal taste.

Although this is the most common way in which they are used, a triplet division does not necessarily mean that three notes of equal value will be produced. It is also

possible to create groups of mixed triplets made up from notes and rests of different values.

If a piece of music makes extensive use of triplets throughout the number "3" is sometimes dropped from the score. However, it's reasonable to say that such heavy use of triplets is relatively unusual within a simple time signature—it would be more usual for the piece to be written in the equivalent compound time signature. For example, a piece of music written in four-four time that uses groups of four eighth note triplets in each bar (as they could appear on the staff below) could perhaps more easily be shown in twelve-eight—comprising twelve eighth-note beats in each bar. In this way, the notation would be neater and simpler to understand.

PARTITA IN E MINOR

This piece is reasonably demanding. It brings together some of the ideas to which you've been introduced over the past few pages.

Let's begin by looking at the time signature. At first there doesn't seem to be one. Notice, however, the symbol "₵" that follows the key signature. This tells you the piece is in two-two time, which is also called "ALLA BREVE." The same symbol without the vertical stroke ("𝄵") means the music is written in four-four time. Also pay attention to the dynamic marks. In bar 9 you'll notice the term "cresc." This is an alternative to a "hairpin" crescendo mark.

The key signature tells you that the piece is in E minor. Since E minor is the relative minor of G major, this means that it is the "one sharp" key. Consequently, F is played as F♯ throughout, except in bar 6, where the natural symbol is used.

MUSETTE IN D MAJOR

NOTES ON MUSETTE IN D MAJOR

Bach's *Musette in D Major* has a time signature of two-four, so when you are working out the rhythm, makes sure that you count in multiples of two, always emphasizing the first beat.

Notice the repeat symbols used throughout the piece. Begin by playing bars 1 to 8. The end repeat sign at the end of bar 8 indicates that you should play bars 1 to 8 again. Continue playing through to bar 28. This also has a end repeat sign, meaning that bars 9 to 28 should be played again. Bar 28 ends the piece this time.

The piece has a key signature of D major—the "two sharps" key. This means that the notes C and F are played throughout as C♯ and F♯ respectively. Naturals only occur twice, on bars 13 and 15, this is to return the D♯ created earlier in each bar back to its original state.

Where a tie carries over a staff line, the tie is shown on both notes. This explains the notation between bars 13 and 14. Thus, the first eighth note in the treble staff of bar 14 (D) is not played, but sustained from the last eighth note of bar 13.

Whenever you approach a new piece of music, always look out for patterns of repeating notes. For example, the same notes and rhythms feature in bars 1, 2, 5, 6, 21, 22, 25 and 26, so once you've figured out the first bar, you've almost mastered a quarter of the entire piece.

DIFFERENT VOICES

Take a look at the staff below. Do you see anything odd about it? There are two things to notice: firstly, some of the notes have their stems pointing in the "wrong" direction; secondly, if you total the value of the notes in the first bar you'll see that they come to eight beats (four quarter notes + two half notes = eight beats), which shouldn't be possible in a bar of four-four. However, it IS allowed when two or more notes are played at the same time, but do NOT have identical time values. When this happens, each of the notes is referred to as having a separate VOICE.

In the bar shown below, on the first beat there is the instruction to play a half note and a quarter note. While a second quarter note is played on the second beat, the half note is sustained until the third beat where, once again a quarter note and half note are played together. Whenever multiple voices occur on the same beat, the normal rules of stem direction are ignored: the higher note points upward; the lower note points downward.

You can easily hear how this sequence works in practice if you let the thumb play the two half notes on the first and third beats, and the four fingers play the four quarter notes on every beat.

In the second bar, you might think that the first beat looks a little strange. This doesn't mean that you have to play the same note at the same time with two different fingers, but is there so that you know that a quarter note has to be played on the SECOND beat.

The basic rule here is that each voice on the staff has to conform to the rules governed by the time signature. The lower voice comprises two half notes (two beats + two beats) which is correct in four-four time; the upper voice comprises four quarter notes (four beats) which is also correct in four-four time. If that first quarter note in the second bar did not exist, then that voice could not fulfil the rules of four-four time, since there would be only three beats. One acceptable alternative to the method shown would be to position a quarter note rest on the first beat above the half note.

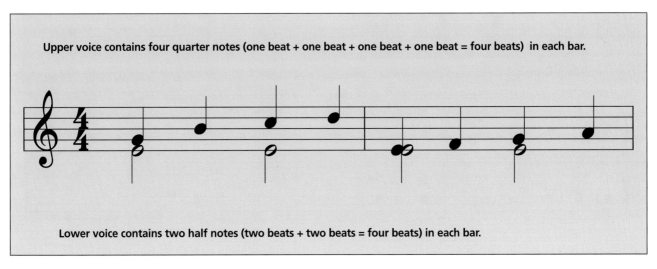

Upper voice contains four quarter notes (one beat + one beat + one beat + one beat = four beats) in each bar.

Lower voice contains two half notes (two beats + two beats = four beats) in each bar.

JESU, JOY OF MAN'S DESIRING (I)

Although this is the most demanding piece in the book, once you are comfortable with the triplet eighth notes that form the basic rhythm, you should find it manageable.

You'll notice that the number "3" is only shown on the beam in the first bar; the word "simile" in the second bar tells you that this is the rule throughout the piece.

To play these triplets, count out the beats in each bar as "ONE-two-three-TWO-two-three-THREE-two-three." Here, the emphasized beats give you the basic three-four rhythm; the other beats provide you with the rhythm of the triplet eighth notes.

One of the trickiest aspects of this triplet rhythm can be found on the bass line. If you look at bar 3, you will see a quarter note and an eighth note "joined" by a number "3." This means that these two notes should be treated as triplet eighth notes, so in this case the quarter note represents not "one" beat but two-thirds of a beat. The count is marked beneath the bar.

JESU, JOY OF MAN'S DESIRING (II)

JESU, JOY OF MAN'S DESIRING (III)

JESU, JOY OF MAN'S DESIRING (IV)

THE GREAT KEYBOARD COMPOSERS

Since the majority of the most popular "classic" composers lived and worked during the 18th and 19th centuries, their works are now deemed to be in the public domain. This means that collections of piano music by the likes of Schumann, Mendelssohn, Schubert, Brahms, Mozart, Beethoven, Chopin and Haydn are widely available in music stores, often for less than the price of a compact disc. Any of these composers will provide most keyboard players with enough of a musical challenge to last a lifetime.

It's also interesting to hear professional recordings or performances of the great piano works, especially since their interpretations can differ so greatly.

CHAPTER 3
CHORD DICTIONARY
IMPROVING YOUR VOCABULARY

An expansive chord vocabulary, and a firm understanding of the way in which chords are constructed, is arguably the most useful capability that a musician can acquire. Not only does it provide players, composers and songwriters with a more sophisticated palette from which to draw, it also teaches valuable lessons in the use of alternative voicings and inversions.

HOW THE CHORD DICTIONARY WORKS

The Chord Dictionary offers a useful reference guide for playing 27 different chord types in all twelve keys. In all, there are 324 different chord positions shown over the next 24 pages. They are primarily intended as a reference. If you want to know how to play the chord—or the notes or "spellings" that define the chord—you can find them in the Chord Dictionary.

You can also treat the Chord Dictionary as a series of playing exercises. By working methodically through all of the chords for each key you may come across certain types of sounds that you might have heard used on familiar recordings, but not previously been able to name or play. You will also hopefully be newly acquainted with some of the more unusual or esoteric types of chord.

Another useful playing exercise is to work out inversions for the chords listed. This is straightforward for those containing just three or four notes (*see Lesson 5, pages 54–65*), but far more demanding for the ninth. eleventh and thirteenth series.

THE KEY TO THE CHORD DICTIONARY

Each set of chords is grouped according to their key, and is positioned across a two-page spread. The name of the key is marked in the pale blue box on the top left-hand corner of of the first page. Alongside the key identity, you'll see a larger pale blue box containing the notes of the major scale shown on the treble clef for that key. Each note is identified by its name and its scale degree. To make things clearer, each also has a unique color shading.

Each chord type is shown in its own box. In the top left-hand corner you will find the name of the chord. Directly beneath, you can see how the chord looks when written down on the staff. The main diagram shows an overhead view of a keyboard. The colored dots on the keyboard represent the

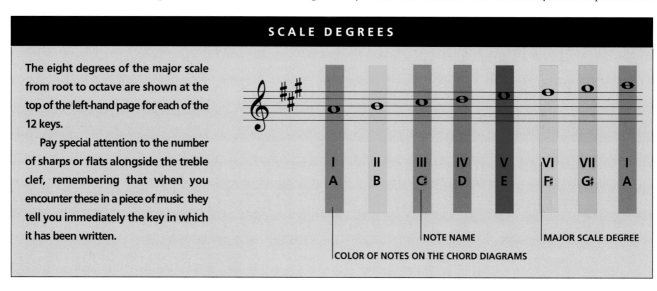

SCALE DEGREES

The eight degrees of the major scale from root to octave are shown at the top of the left-hand page for each of the 12 keys.

Pay special attention to the number of sharps or flats alongside the treble clef, remembering that when you encounter these in a piece of music they tell you immediately the key in which it has been written.

I	II	III	IV	V	VI	VII	I
A	B	C♯	D	E	F♯	G♯	A

NOTE NAME   MAJOR SCALE DEGREE

COLOR OF NOTES ON THE CHORD DIAGRAMS

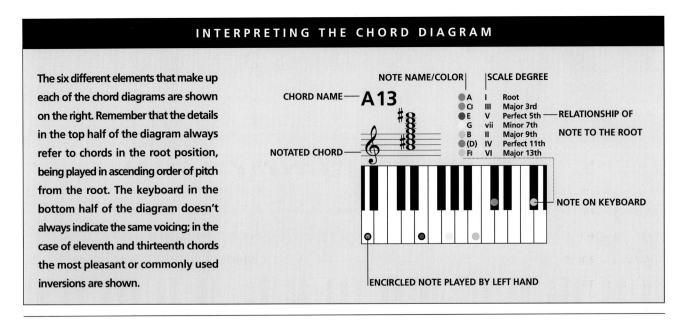

INTERPRETING THE CHORD DIAGRAM

The six different elements that make up each of the chord diagrams are shown on the right. Remember that the details in the top half of the diagram always refer to chords in the root position, being played in ascending order of pitch from the root. The keyboard in the bottom half of the diagram doesn't always indicate the same voicing; in the case of eleventh and thirteenth chords the most pleasant or commonly used inversions are shown.

---

notes that have to be played. The same colors are used for each scale degree throughout the chord dictionary.

Some of the lowest-pitched notes are shown encircled. This occurs when the chord is impractical (or impossible) to play with just one hand. In these cases, the encircled notes are to be played with the left hand, the remainder with the right hand.

There is no instruction as to which finger should be used to play a particular note, since many of the chords can be played by either hand. These positions are easy enough to work out for yourself, since you should play them in whatever way feels most comfortable. In practice, this is likely to mean that when using the right hand, the thumb will play the lowest note, and when playing with the left hand, the thumb will play the highest note.

On the top right-hand area of each box, you will find the names of the notes that make up the chord (alongside the corresponding colored dots). Any note that is shown surrounded by a bracket means that although it is a part of the chord, it is optional in practice. Finally, alongside the note names you will see the description and abbreviated degree of each note's relationship to the root. For example, in the key of C, the note G is the perfect 5th, which can be abbreviated as the Roman numeral "V."

ROOT POSITIONS AND INVERSIONS

You may notice that in some cases, the notes on the fingerboard diagram don't quite match those shown in the information directly above. There is a good reason for this. The notes on the staff, as well as the names and relationships shown alongside, refer to each chord in its "root position." This means that the notes defining that chord appear in ascending pitch from the root. However, in the case of the eleventh and thirteenth series of chords, the simple truth is that like any other chord types

containing six or more different notes, they don't always sound very pleasant when played from the root. Therefore, in these cases, more effective inversions are shown.

Of course, as you've already seen, understanding inversion is of crucial importance in all forms of music. So when you work through each of the chord types it's a good idea to practice inverting them in as many ways as possible. The easiest way to do this is to take the lowest-pitch note and replace it with one an octave above. For example, when playing C seven, begin with C-E-G-B♭ (root position), then move to E-G-B♭-C (first inversion), then onto G-B♭-C-E (second inversion), before finishing with B♭-C-E-G (third inversion).

ENHARMONIC ISSUES

Finally, here is brief word on the subject of the enharmonic notes: these are the ones that share the same pitch but can have two possible names. To keep matters simple, the keys have been identified by the most commonly used key names. For example, we've shown chords in the key of B♭ rather than A♯: similarly, the keys C♯, E♭, F♯ and A♭ are shown rather than D♭, D♯, G♭ and G♯. However, the note names shown for each chord are are ALWAYS enharmonically correct for the given key. For example, the chord D augmented requires the use of the augmented fifth note, which in the key of D is A♯, NOT B♭, even though the two notes have the same pitch.

One area that does deviate from classical practice is in the naming of certain diminished notes. In the key of F, for example, to avoid confusing the complete beginner, the diminished fifth is referred to as B when technically (since the perfect fifth is C) it should be called C♭: although there is no such note on the keyboard, a flattened C is C♭, NOT B, although, of course, they have identical pitches.

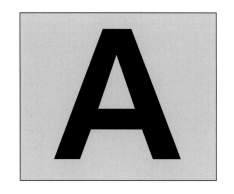

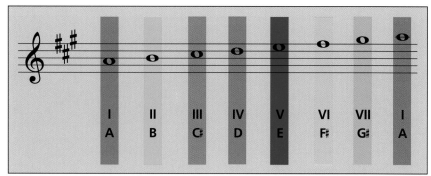

	I	II	III	IV	V	VI	VII	I
	A	B	C♯	D	E	F♯	G♯	A

A maj

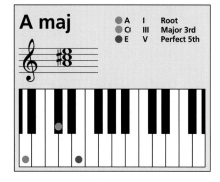

A	I	Root
C♯	III	Major 3rd
E	V	Perfect 5th

A m

A	I	Root
C	iii	Minor 3rd
E	V	Perfect 5th

A 7

A	I	Root
C♯	III	Major 3rd
E	V	Perfect 5th
G	vii	Minor 7th

A min 7

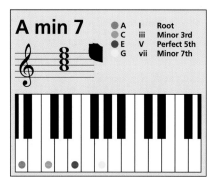

A	I	Root
C	iii	Minor 3rd
E	V	Perfect 5th
G	vii	Minor 7th

A maj 7

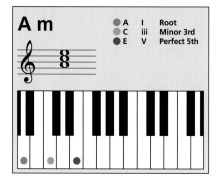

A	I	Root
C♯	III	Major 3rd
E	V	Perfect 5th
G♯	VII	Major 7th

A sus 4

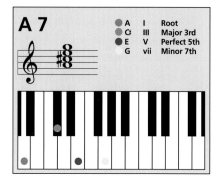

A	I	Root
D	IV	Perfect 4th
E	V	Perfect 5th

A sus 2

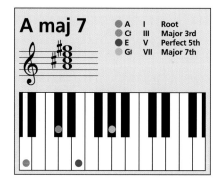

A	I	Root
B	II	Major 2nd
E	V	Perfect 5th

A 6

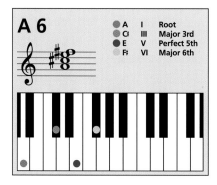

A	I	Root
C♯	III	Major 3rd
E	V	Perfect 5th
F♯	VI	Major 6th

A min 6

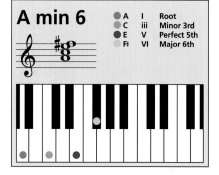

A	I	Root
C	iii	Minor 3rd
E	V	Perfect 5th
F♯	VI	Major 6th

A aug

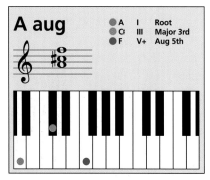

A	I	Root
C♯	III	Major 3rd
F	V+	Aug 5th

A dim 7

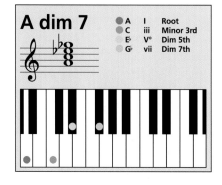

A	I	Root
C	iii	Minor 3rd
E♭	V°	Dim 5th
G♭	vii	Dim 7th

A 7-5

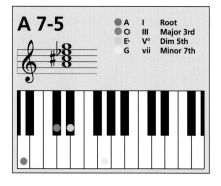

A	I	Root
C♯	III	Major 3rd
E♭	V°	Dim 5th
G	vii	Minor 7th

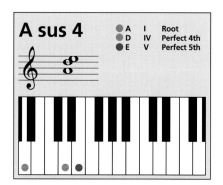

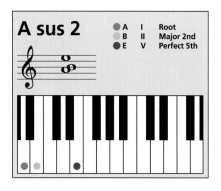

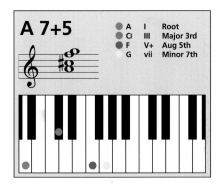

A 7+5

A	I	Root
C♯	III	Major 3rd
F	V+	Aug 5th
G	vii	Minor 7th

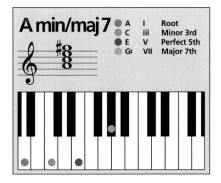

A min/maj7

A	I	Root
C	iii	Minor 3rd
E	V	Perfect 5th
G♯	VII	Major 7th

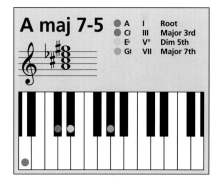

A maj 7-5

A	I	Root
C♯	III	Major 3rd
E♭	V°	Dim 5th
G♯	VII	Major 7th

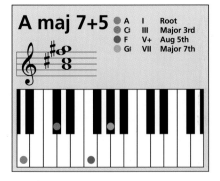

A maj 7+5

A	I	Root
C♯	III	Major 3rd
F	V+	Aug 5th
G♯	VII	Major 7th

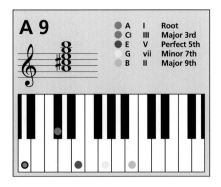

A 9

A	I	Root
C♯	III	Major 3rd
E	V	Perfect 5th
G	vii	Minor 7th
B	II	Major 9th

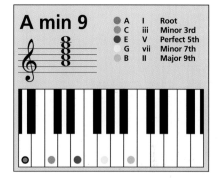

A min 9

A	I	Root
C	iii	Minor 3rd
E	V	Perfect 5th
G	vii	Minor 7th
B	II	Major 9th

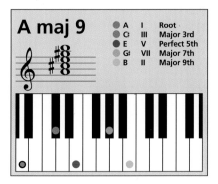

A maj 9

A	I	Root
C♯	III	Major 3rd
E	V	Perfect 5th
G♯	VII	Major 7th
B	II	Major 9th

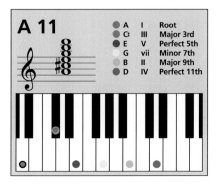

A 11

A	I	Root
C♯	III	Major 3rd
E	V	Perfect 5th
G	vii	Minor 7th
B	II	Major 9th
D	IV	Perfect 11th

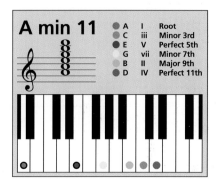

A min 11

A	I	Root
C	iii	Minor 3rd
E	V	Perfect 5th
G	vii	Minor 7th
B	II	Major 9th
D	IV	Perfect 11th

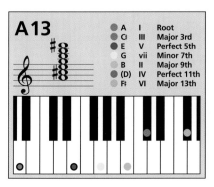

A 13

A	I	Root
C♯	III	Major 3rd
E	V	Perfect 5th
G	vii	Minor 7th
B	II	Major 9th
(D)	IV	Perfect 11th
F♯	VI	Major 13th

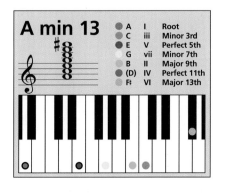

A min 13

A	I	Root
C	iii	Minor 3rd
E	V	Perfect 5th
G	vii	Minor 7th
B	II	Major 9th
(D)	IV	Perfect 11th
F♯	VI	Major 13th

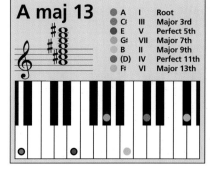

A maj 13

A	I	Root
C♯	III	Major 3rd
E	V	Perfect 5th
G♯	VII	Major 7th
B	II	Major 9th
(D)	IV	Perfect 11th
F♯	VI	Major 13th

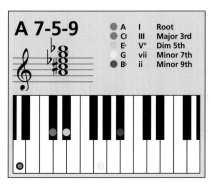

A 7-5-9

A	I	Root
C♯	III	Major 3rd
E♭	V°	Dim 5th
G	vii	Minor 7th
B♭	ii	Minor 9th

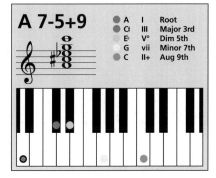

A 7-5+9

A	I	Root
C♯	III	Major 3rd
E♭	V°	Dim 5th
G	vii	Minor 7th
C	II+	Aug 9th

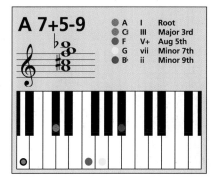

A 7+5-9

A	I	Root
C♯	III	Major 3rd
F	V+	Aug 5th
G	vii	Minor 7th
B♭	ii	Minor 9th

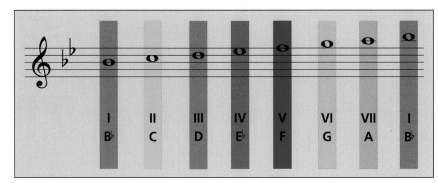

I	II	III	IV	V	VI	VII	I
B♭	C	D	E♭	F	G	A	B♭

B♭ maj

B♭	I	Root
D	III	Major 3rd
F	V	Perfect 5th

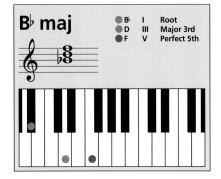

B♭ m

B♭	I	Root
D♭	iii	Minor 3rd
F	V	Perfect 5th

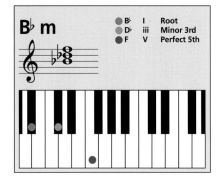

B♭ 7

B♭	I	Root
D	III	Major 3rd
F	V	Perfect 5th
A♭	vii	Minor 7th

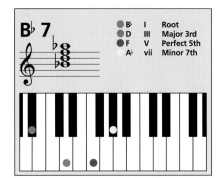

B♭ min 7

B♭	I	Root
D♭	iii	Minor 3rd
F	V	Perfect 5th
A♭	vii	Minor 7th

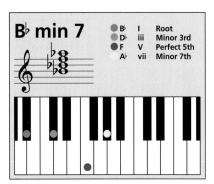

B♭ maj 7

B♭	I	Root
D	III	Major 3rd
F	V	Perfect 5th
A	VII	Major 7th

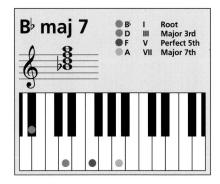

B♭ sus 4

B♭	I	Root
E♭	IV	Perfect 4th
F	V	Perfect 5th

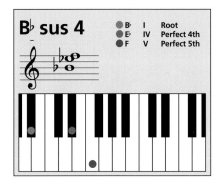

B♭ sus 2

B♭	I	Root
C	II	Major 2nd
F	V	Perfect 5th

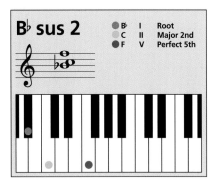

B♭ 6

B♭	I	Root
D	III	Major 3rd
F	V	Perfect 5th
G	VI	Major 6th

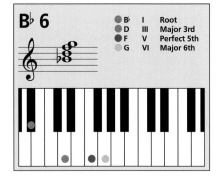

B♭ min 6

B♭	I	Root
D♭	iii	Minor 3rd
F	V	Perfect 5th
G	VI	Major 6th

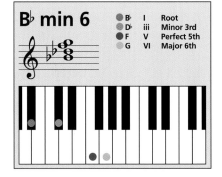

B♭ aug

B♭	I	Root
D	III	Major 3rd
F♯	V+	Aug 5th

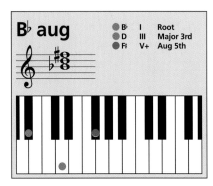

B♭ dim 7

B♭	I	Root
D♭	iii	Minor 3rd
E	V°	Dim 5th
G	vii	Dim 7th

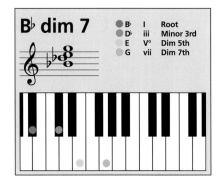

B♭ 7-5

B♭	I	Root
D	III	Major 3rd
E	V°	Dim 5th
A♭	vii	Minor 7th

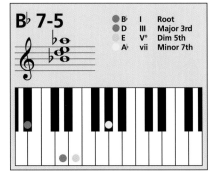

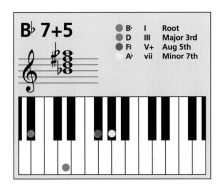

B♭ 7+5

B♭	I	Root
D	III	Major 3rd
F♯	V+	Aug 5th
A♭	vii	Minor 7th

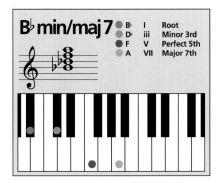

B♭ min/maj7

B♭	I	Root
D♭	iii	Minor 3rd
F	V	Perfect 5th
A	VII	Major 7th

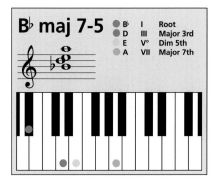

B♭ maj 7-5

B♭	I	Root
D	III	Major 3rd
E	V°	Dim 5th
A	VII	Major 7th

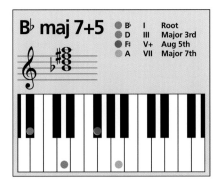

B♭ maj 7+5

B♭	I	Root
D	III	Major 3rd
F♯	V+	Aug 5th
A	VII	Major 7th

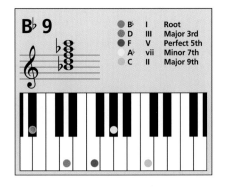

B♭ 9

B♭	I	Root
D	III	Major 3rd
F	V	Perfect 5th
A♭	vii	Minor 7th
C	II	Major 9th

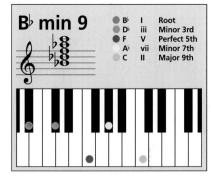

B♭ min 9

B♭	I	Root
D♭	iii	Minor 3rd
F	V	Perfect 5th
A♭	vii	Minor 7th
C	II	Major 9th

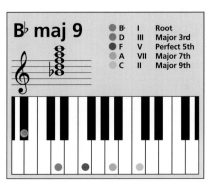

B♭ maj 9

B♭	I	Root
D	III	Major 3rd
F	V	Perfect 5th
A	VII	Major 7th
C	II	Major 9th

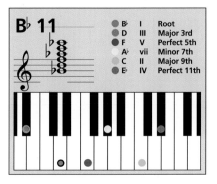

B♭ 11

B♭	I	Root
D	III	Major 3rd
F	V	Perfect 5th
A♭	vii	Minor 7th
C	II	Major 9th
E♭	IV	Perfect 11th

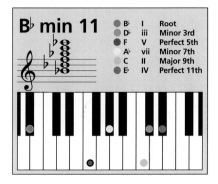

B♭ min 11

B♭	I	Root
D♭	iii	Minor 3rd
F	V	Perfect 5th
A♭	vii	Minor 7th
C	II	Major 9th
E♭	IV	Perfect 11th

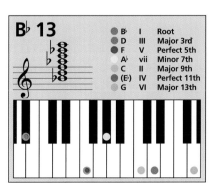

B♭ 13

B♭	I	Root
D	III	Major 3rd
F	V	Perfect 5th
A♭	vii	Minor 7th
C	II	Major 9th
(E♭)	IV	Perfect 11th
G	VI	Major 13th

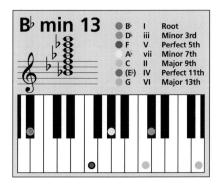

B♭ min 13

B♭	I	Root
D♭	iii	Minor 3rd
F	V	Perfect 5th
A♭	vii	Minor 7th
C	II	Major 9th
(E♭)	IV	Perfect 11th
G	VI	Major 13th

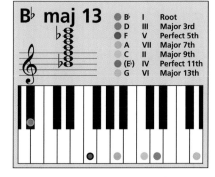

B♭ maj 13

B♭	I	Root
D	III	Major 3rd
F	V	Perfect 5th
A	VII	Major 7th
C	II	Major 9th
(E♭)	IV	Perfect 11th
G	VI	Major 13th

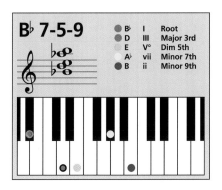

B♭ 7-5-9

B♭	I	Root
D	III	Major 3rd
E	V°	Dim 5th
A♭	vii	Minor 7th
B	ii	Minor 9th

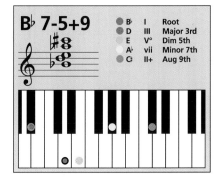

B♭ 7-5+9

B♭	I	Root
D	III	Major 3rd
E	V°	Dim 5th
A♭	vii	Minor 7th
C♯	II+	Aug 9th

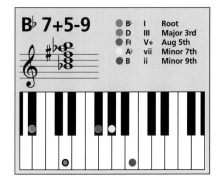

B♭ 7+5-9

B♭	I	Root
D	III	Major 3rd
F♯	V+	Aug 5th
A♭	vii	Minor 7th
B	ii	Minor 9th

B

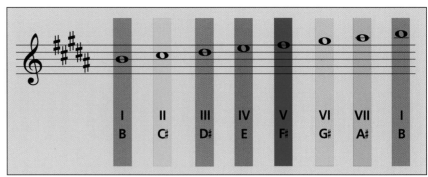

I	II	III	IV	V	VI	VII	I
B	C#	D#	E	F#	G#	A#	B

B maj

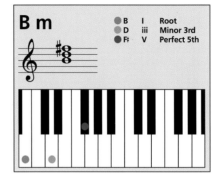

B	I	Root
D#	III	Major 3rd
F#	V	Perfect 5th

B m

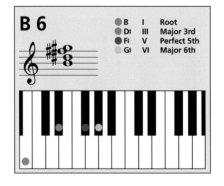

B	I	Root
D	iii	Minor 3rd
F#	V	Perfect 5th

B 7

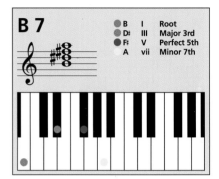

B	I	Root
D#	III	Major 3rd
F#	V	Perfect 5th
A	vii	Minor 7th

B min 7

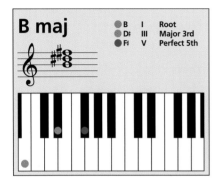

B	I	Root
D	iii	Minor 3rd
F#	V	Perfect 5th
A	vii	Minor 7th

B maj 7

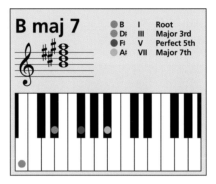

B	I	Root
D#	III	Major 3rd
F#	V	Perfect 5th
A#	VII	Major 7th

B sus 4

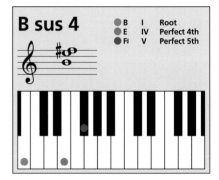

B	I	Root
E	IV	Perfect 4th
F#	V	Perfect 5th

B sus 2

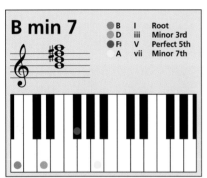

B	I	Root
C#	II	Major 2nd
F#	V	Perfect 5th

B 6

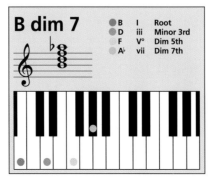

B	I	Root
D#	III	Major 3rd
F#	V	Perfect 5th
G#	VI	Major 6th

B min 6

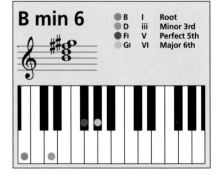

B	I	Root
D	iii	Minor 3rd
F#	V	Perfect 5th
G#	VI	Major 6th

B aug

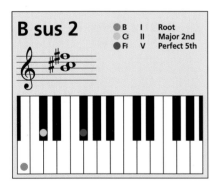

B	I	Root
D#	III	Major 3rd
G	V+	Aug 5th

B dim 7

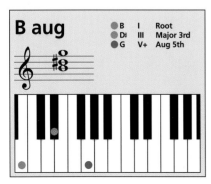

B	I	Root
D	iii	Minor 3rd
F	V°	Dim 5th
A♭	vii	Dim 7th

B 7-5

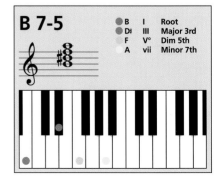

B	I	Root
D#	III	Major 3rd
F	V°	Dim 5th
A	vii	Minor 7th

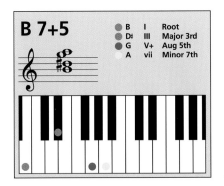

B 7+5

B	I	Root
D♯	III	Major 3rd
G	V+	Aug 5th
A	vii	Minor 7th

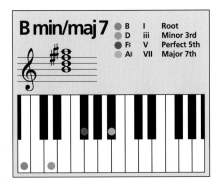

B min/maj 7

B	I	Root
D	iii	Minor 3rd
F♯	V	Perfect 5th
A♯	VII	Major 7th

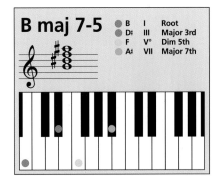

B maj 7-5

B	I	Root
D♯	III	Major 3rd
F	V°	Dim 5th
A♯	VII	Major 7th

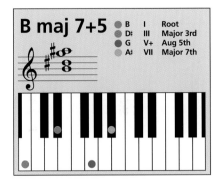

B maj 7+5

B	I	Root
D♯	III	Major 3rd
G	V+	Aug 5th
A♯	VII	Major 7th

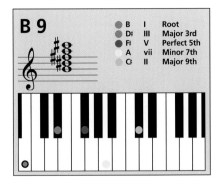

B 9

B	I	Root
D♯	III	Major 3rd
F♯	V	Perfect 5th
A	vii	Minor 7th
C♯	II	Major 9th

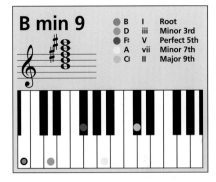

B min 9

B	I	Root
D	iii	Minor 3rd
F♯	V	Perfect 5th
A	vii	Minor 7th
C♯	II	Major 9th

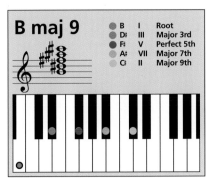

B maj 9

B	I	Root
D♯	III	Major 3rd
F♯	V	Perfect 5th
A♯	VII	Major 7th
C♯	II	Major 9th

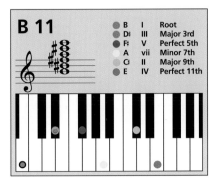

B 11

B	I	Root
D♯	III	Major 3rd
F♯	V	Perfect 5th
A	vii	Minor 7th
C♯	II	Major 9th
E	IV	Perfect 11th

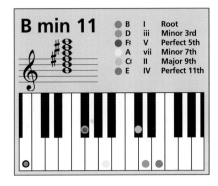

B min 11

B	I	Root
D	iii	Minor 3rd
F♯	V	Perfect 5th
A	vii	Minor 7th
C♯	II	Major 9th
E	IV	Perfect 11th

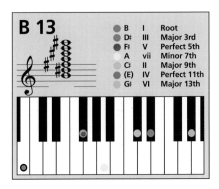

B 13

B	I	Root
D♯	III	Major 3rd
F♯	V	Perfect 5th
A	vii	Minor 7th
C♯	II	Major 9th
(E)	IV	Perfect 11th
G♯	VI	Major 13th

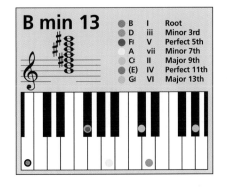

B min 13

B	I	Root
D	iii	Minor 3rd
F♯	V	Perfect 5th
A	vii	Minor 7th
C♯	II	Major 9th
(E)	IV	Perfect 11th
G♯	VI	Major 13th

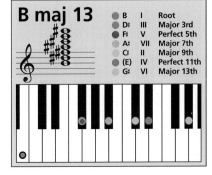

B maj 13

B	I	Root
D♯	III	Major 3rd
F♯	V	Perfect 5th
A♯	VII	Major 7th
C♯	II	Major 9th
(E)	IV	Perfect 11th
G♯	VI	Major 13th

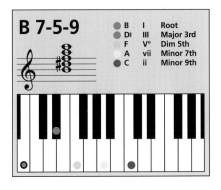

B 7-5-9

B	I	Root
D♯	III	Major 3rd
F	V°	Dim 5th
A	vii	Minor 7th
C	ii	Minor 9th

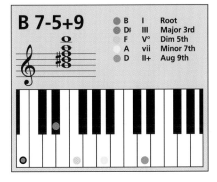

B 7-5+9

B	I	Root
D♯	III	Major 3rd
F	V°	Dim 5th
A	vii	Minor 7th
D	II+	Aug 9th

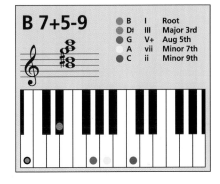

B 7+5-9

B	I	Root
D♯	III	Major 3rd
G	V+	Aug 5th
A	vii	Minor 7th
C	ii	Minor 9th

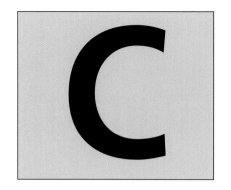

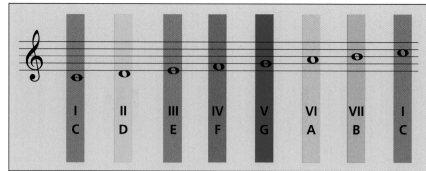

I	II	III	IV	V	VI	VII	I
C	D	E	F	G	A	B	C

C maj

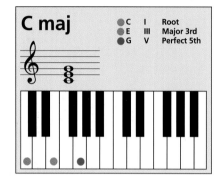

C	I	Root
E	III	Major 3rd
G	V	Perfect 5th

C m

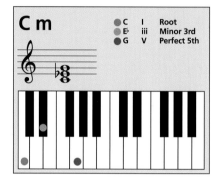

C	I	Root
E♭	iii	Minor 3rd
G	V	Perfect 5th

C 7

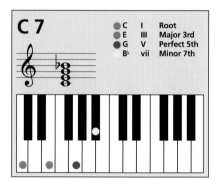

C	I	Root
E	III	Major 3rd
G	V	Perfect 5th
B♭	vii	Minor 7th

C min 7

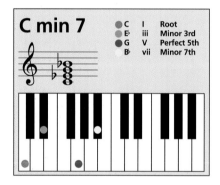

C	I	Root
E♭	iii	Minor 3rd
G	V	Perfect 5th
B♭	vii	Minor 7th

C maj 7

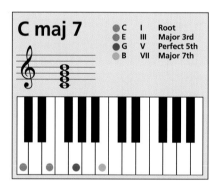

C	I	Root
E	III	Major 3rd
G	V	Perfect 5th
B	VII	Major 7th

C sus 4

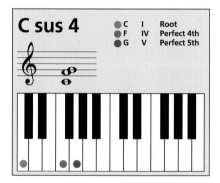

C	I	Root
F	IV	Perfect 4th
G	V	Perfect 5th

C sus 2

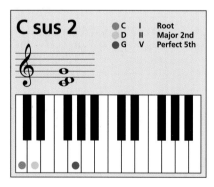

C	I	Root
D	II	Major 2nd
G	V	Perfect 5th

C 6

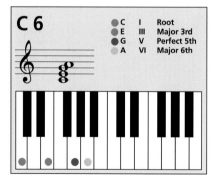

C	I	Root
E	III	Major 3rd
G	V	Perfect 5th
A	VI	Major 6th

C min 6

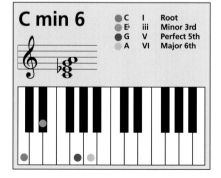

C	I	Root
E♭	iii	Minor 3rd
G	V	Perfect 5th
A	VI	Major 6th

C aug

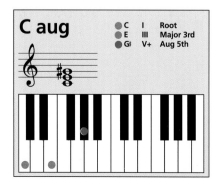

C	I	Root
E	III	Major 3rd
G♯	V+	Aug 5th

C dim 7

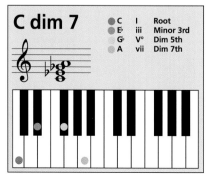

C	I	Root
E♭	iii	Minor 3rd
G♭	V°	Dim 5th
A	vii	Dim 7th

C 7-5

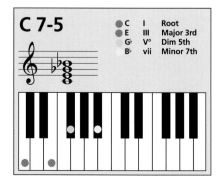

C	I	Root
E	III	Major 3rd
G♭	V°	Dim 5th
B♭	vii	Minor 7th

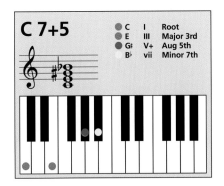

C 7+5

C	I	Root
E	III	Major 3rd
G#	V+	Aug 5th
B♭	vii	Minor 7th

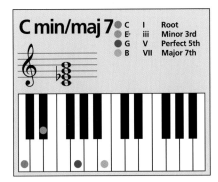

C min/maj 7

C	I	Root
E♭	iii	Minor 3rd
G	V	Perfect 5th
B	VII	Major 7th

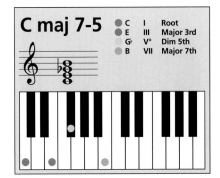

C maj 7-5

C	I	Root
E	III	Major 3rd
G♭	V°	Dim 5th
B	VII	Major 7th

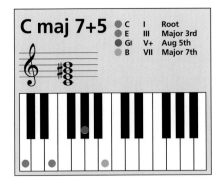

C maj 7+5

C	I	Root
E	III	Major 3rd
G#	V+	Aug 5th
B	VII	Major 7th

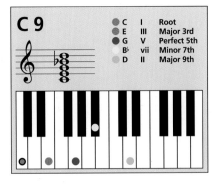

C 9

C	I	Root
E	III	Major 3rd
G	V	Perfect 5th
B♭	vii	Minor 7th
D	II	Major 9th

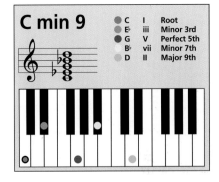

C min 9

C	I	Root
E♭	iii	Minor 3rd
G	V	Perfect 5th
B♭	vii	Minor 7th
D	II	Major 9th

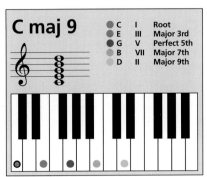

C maj 9

C	I	Root
E	III	Major 3rd
G	V	Perfect 5th
B	VII	Major 7th
D	II	Major 9th

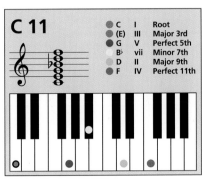

C 11

C	I	Root
(E)	III	Major 3rd
G	V	Perfect 5th
B♭	vii	Minor 7th
D	II	Major 9th
F	IV	Perfect 11th

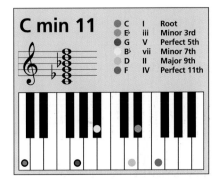

C min 11

C	I	Root
E♭	iii	Minor 3rd
G	V	Perfect 5th
B♭	vii	Minor 7th
D	II	Major 9th
F	IV	Perfect 11th

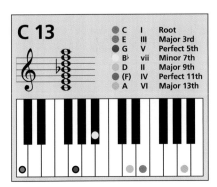

C 13

C	I	Root
E	III	Major 3rd
G	V	Perfect 5th
B♭	vii	Minor 7th
D	II	Major 9th
(F)	IV	Perfect 11th
A	VI	Major 13th

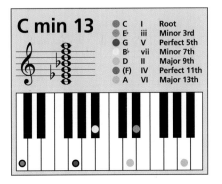

C min 13

C	I	Root
E♭	iii	Minor 3rd
G	V	Perfect 5th
B♭	vii	Minor 7th
D	II	Major 9th
(F)	IV	Perfect 11th
A	VI	Major 13th

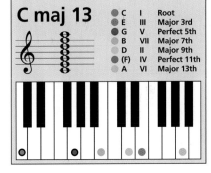

C maj 13

C	I	Root
E	III	Major 3rd
G	V	Perfect 5th
B	VII	Major 7th
D	II	Major 9th
(F)	IV	Perfect 11th
A	VI	Major 13th

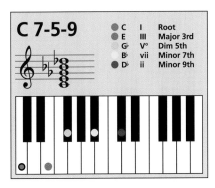

C 7-5-9

C	I	Root
E	III	Major 3rd
G♭	V°	Dim 5th
B♭	vii	Minor 7th
D♭	ii	Minor 9th

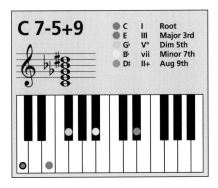

C 7-5+9

C	I	Root
E	III	Major 3rd
G♭	V°	Dim 5th
B♭	vii	Minor 7th
D#	II+	Aug 9th

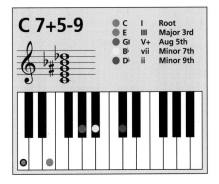

C 7+5-9

C	I	Root
E	III	Major 3rd
G#	V+	Aug 5th
B♭	vii	Minor 7th
D♭	ii	Minor 9th

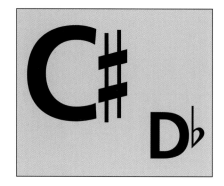

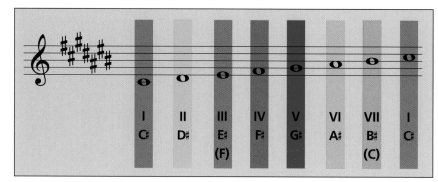

I	II	III	IV	V	VI	VII	I
C#	D#	E#	F#	G#	A#	B#	C#
		(F)				(C)	

C# maj
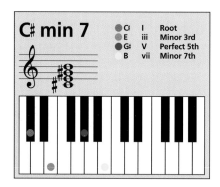

C#	I	Root
F	III	Major 3rd
G#	V	Perfect 5th

C# m
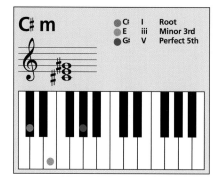

C#	I	Root
E	iii	Minor 3rd
G#	V	Perfect 5th

C# 7

C#	I	Root
F	III	Major 3rd
G#	V	Perfect 5th
B	vii	Minor 7th

C# min 7
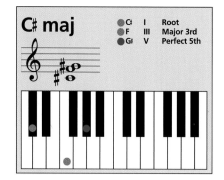

C#	I	Root
E	iii	Minor 3rd
G#	V	Perfect 5th
B	vii	Minor 7th

C# maj 7
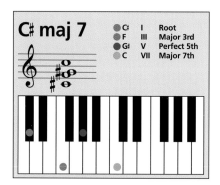

C#	I	Root
F	III	Major 3rd
G#	V	Perfect 5th
C	VII	Major 7th

C# sus 4
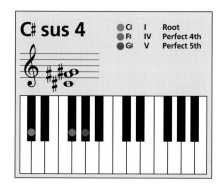

C#	I	Root
F#	IV	Perfect 4th
G#	V	Perfect 5th

C# sus 2
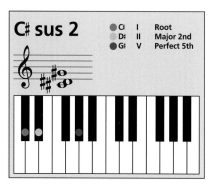

C#	I	Root
D#	II	Major 2nd
G#	V	Perfect 5th

C# 6
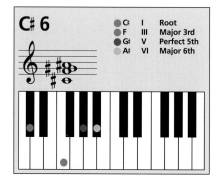

C#	I	Root
F	III	Major 3rd
G#	V	Perfect 5th
A#	VI	Major 6th

C# min 6
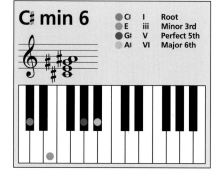

C#	I	Root
E	iii	Minor 3rd
G#	V	Perfect 5th
A#	VI	Major 6th

C# aug
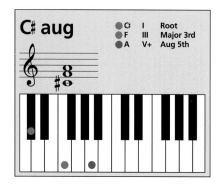

C#	I	Root
F	III	Major 3rd
A	V+	Aug 5th

C# dim 7
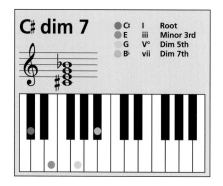

C#	I	Root
E	iii	Minor 3rd
G	V°	Dim 5th
B♭	vii	Dim 7th

C# 7-5
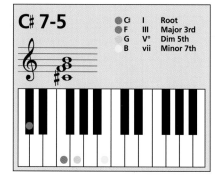

C#	I	Root
F	III	Major 3rd
G	V°	Dim 5th
B	vii	Minor 7th

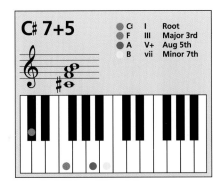

C# 7+5

C#	I	Root
F	III	Major 3rd
A	V+	Aug 5th
B	vii	Minor 7th

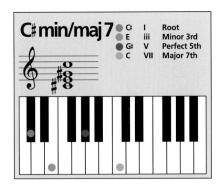

C# min/maj7

C#	I	Root
E	iii	Minor 3rd
G#	V	Perfect 5th
C	VII	Major 7th

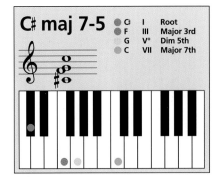

C# maj 7-5

C#	I	Root
F	III	Major 3rd
G	V°	Dim 5th
C	VII	Major 7th

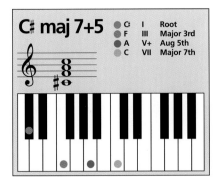

C# maj 7+5

C#	I	Root
F	III	Major 3rd
A	V+	Aug 5th
C	VII	Major 7th

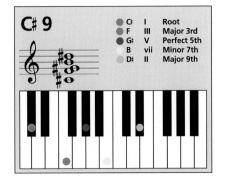

C# 9

C#	I	Root
F	III	Major 3rd
G#	V	Perfect 5th
B	vii	Minor 7th
D#	II	Major 9th

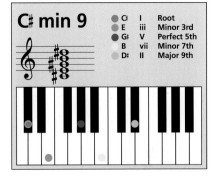

C# min 9

C#	I	Root
E	iii	Minor 3rd
G#	V	Perfect 5th
B	vii	Minor 7th
D#	II	Major 9th

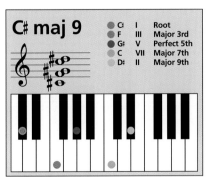

C# maj 9

C#	I	Root
F	III	Major 3rd
G#	V	Perfect 5th
C	VII	Major 7th
D#	II	Major 9th

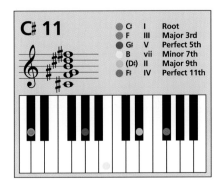

C# 11

C#	I	Root
F	III	Major 3rd
G#	V	Perfect 5th
B	vii	Minor 7th
(D#)	II	Major 9th
F#	IV	Perfect 11th

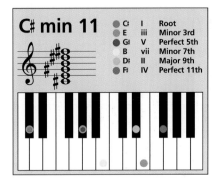

C# min 11

C#	I	Root
E	iii	Minor 3rd
G#	V	Perfect 5th
B	vii	Minor 7th
D#	II	Major 9th
F#	IV	Perfect 11th

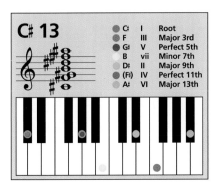

C# 13

C#	I	Root
F	III	Major 3rd
G#	V	Perfect 5th
B	vii	Minor 7th
D#	II	Major 9th
(F#)	IV	Perfect 11th
A#	VI	Major 13th

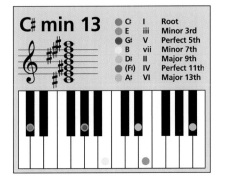

C# min 13

C#	I	Root
E	iii	Minor 3rd
G#	V	Perfect 5th
B	vii	Minor 7th
D#	II	Major 9th
(F#)	IV	Perfect 11th
A#	VI	Major 13th

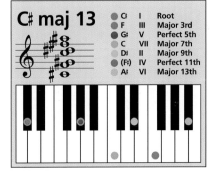

C# maj 13

C#	I	Root
F	III	Major 3rd
G#	V	Perfect 5th
C	VII	Major 7th
D#	II	Major 9th
(F#)	IV	Perfect 11th
A#	VI	Major 13th

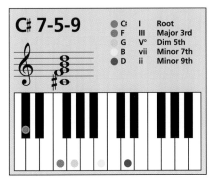

C# 7-5-9

C#	I	Root
F	III	Major 3rd
G	V°	Dim 5th
B	vii	Minor 7th
D	ii	Minor 9th

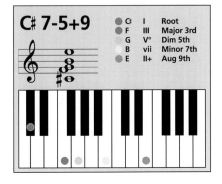

C# 7-5+9

C#	I	Root
F	III	Major 3rd
G	V°	Dim 5th
B	vii	Minor 7th
E	II+	Aug 9th

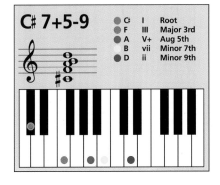

C# 7+5-9

C#	I	Root
F	III	Major 3rd
A	V+	Aug 5th
B	vii	Minor 7th
D	ii	Minor 9th

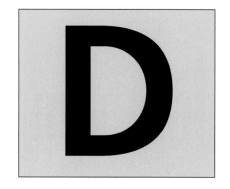

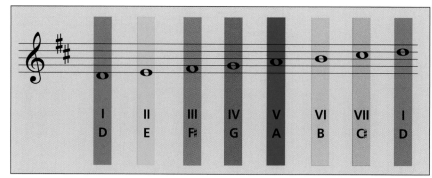

I	II	III	IV	V	VI	VII	I
D	E	F#	G	A	B	C#	D

D maj

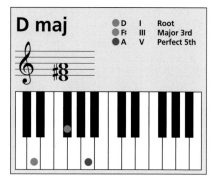

D	I	Root
F#	III	Major 3rd
A	V	Perfect 5th

D m

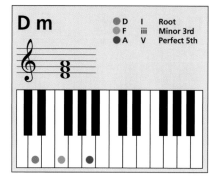

D	I	Root
F	iii	Minor 3rd
A	V	Perfect 5th

D 7

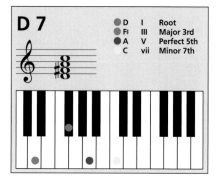

D	I	Root
F#	III	Major 3rd
A	V	Perfect 5th
C	vii	Minor 7th

D min 7

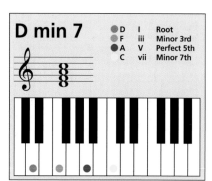

D	I	Root
F	iii	Minor 3rd
A	V	Perfect 5th
C	vii	Minor 7th

D maj 7

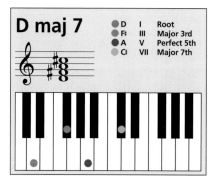

D	I	Root
F#	III	Major 3rd
A	V	Perfect 5th
C#	VII	Major 7th

D sus 4

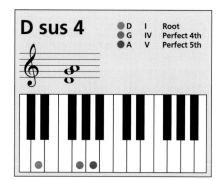

D	I	Root
G	IV	Perfect 4th
A	V	Perfect 5th

D sus 2

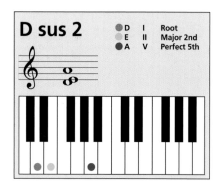

D	I	Root
E	II	Major 2nd
A	V	Perfect 5th

D 6

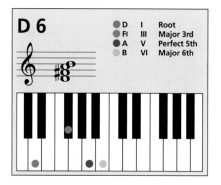

D	I	Root
F#	III	Major 3rd
A	V	Perfect 5th
B	VI	Major 6th

D min 6

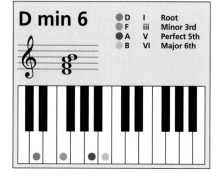

D	I	Root
F	iii	Minor 3rd
A	V	Perfect 5th
B	VI	Major 6th

D aug

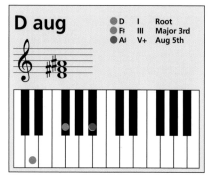

D	I	Root
F#	III	Major 3rd
A#	V+	Aug 5th

D dim 7

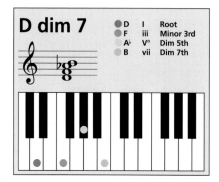

D	I	Root
F	iii	Minor 3rd
A♭	V°	Dim 5th
B	vii	Dim 7th

D 7-5

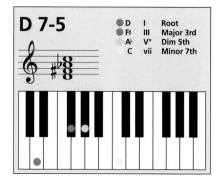

D	I	Root
F#	III	Major 3rd
A♭	V°	Dim 5th
C	vii	Minor 7th

D 7+5

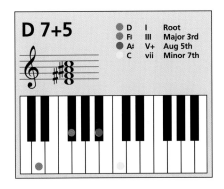

D	I	Root
F♯	III	Major 3rd
A♯	V+	Aug 5th
C	vii	Minor 7th

D min/maj7

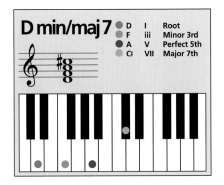

D	I	Root
F	iii	Minor 3rd
A	V	Perfect 5th
C♯	VII	Major 7th

D maj 7-5

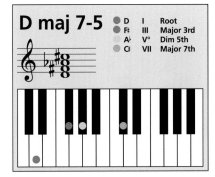

D	I	Root
F♯	III	Major 3rd
A♭	V°	Dim 5th
C♯	VII	Major 7th

D maj 7+5

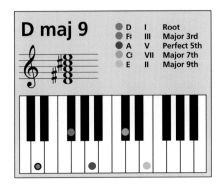

D	I	Root
F♯	III	Major 3rd
A♯	V+	Aug 5th
C♯	VII	Major 7th

D 9

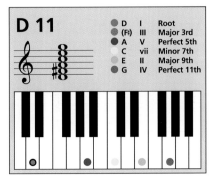

D	I	Root
F♯	III	Major 3rd
A	V	Perfect 5th
C	vii	Minor 7th
E	II	Major 9th

D min 9

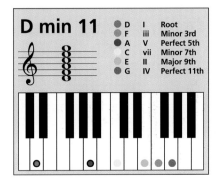

D	I	Root
F	iii	Minor 3rd
A	V	Perfect 5th
C	vii	Minor 7th
E	II	Major 9th

D maj 9

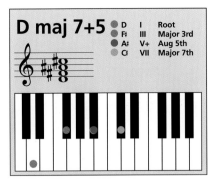

D	I	Root
F♯	III	Major 3rd
A	V	Perfect 5th
C♯	VII	Major 7th
E	II	Major 9th

D 11

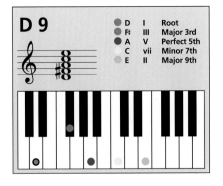

D	I	Root
(F♯)	III	Major 3rd
A	V	Perfect 5th
C	vii	Minor 7th
E	II	Major 9th
G	IV	Perfect 11th

D min 11

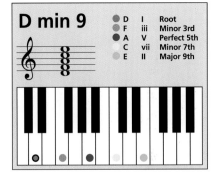

D	I	Root
F	iii	Minor 3rd
A	V	Perfect 5th
C	vii	Minor 7th
E	II	Major 9th
G	IV	Perfect 11th

D 13

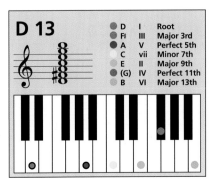

D	I	Root
F♯	III	Major 3rd
A	V	Perfect 5th
C	vii	Minor 7th
E	II	Major 9th
(G)	IV	Perfect 11th
B	VI	Major 13th

D min 13

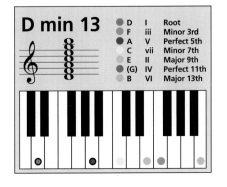

D	I	Root
F	iii	Minor 3rd
A	V	Perfect 5th
C	vii	Minor 7th
E	II	Major 9th
(G)	IV	Perfect 11th
B	VI	Major 13th

D maj 13

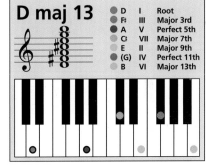

D	I	Root
F♯	III	Major 3rd
A	V	Perfect 5th
C♯	VII	Major 7th
E	II	Major 9th
(G)	IV	Perfect 11th
B	VI	Major 13th

D 7-5-9

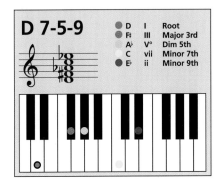

D	I	Root
F♯	III	Major 3rd
A♭	V°	Dim 5th
C	vii	Minor 7th
E♭	ii	Minor 9th

D 7-5+9

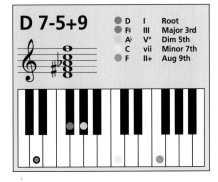

D	I	Root
F♯	III	Major 3rd
A♭	V°	Dim 5th
C	vii	Minor 7th
F	II+	Aug 9th

D 7+5-9

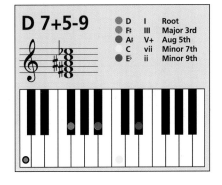

D	I	Root
F♯	III	Major 3rd
A♯	V+	Aug 5th
C	vii	Minor 7th
E♭	ii	Minor 9th

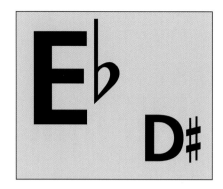

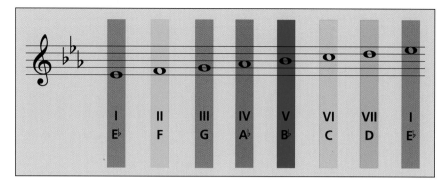

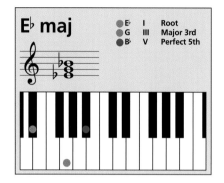

E♭ maj
- E♭ — I — Root
- G — III — Major 3rd
- B♭ — V — Perfect 5th

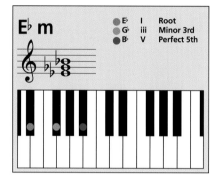

E♭ m
- E♭ — I — Root
- G♭ — iii — Minor 3rd
- B♭ — V — Perfect 5th

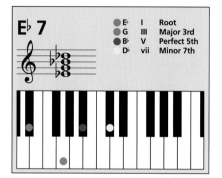

E♭ 7
- E♭ — I — Root
- G — III — Major 3rd
- B♭ — V — Perfect 5th
- D♭ — vii — Minor 7th

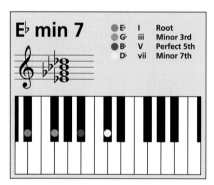

E♭ min 7
- E♭ — I — Root
- G♭ — iii — Minor 3rd
- B♭ — V — Perfect 5th
- D♭ — vii — Minor 7th

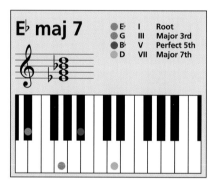

E♭ maj 7
- E♭ — I — Root
- G — III — Major 3rd
- B♭ — V — Perfect 5th
- D — VII — Major 7th

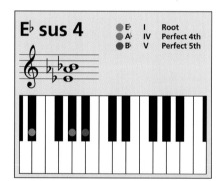

E♭ sus 4
- E♭ — I — Root
- A♭ — IV — Perfect 4th
- B♭ — V — Perfect 5th

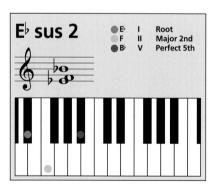

E♭ sus 2
- E♭ — I — Root
- F — II — Major 2nd
- B♭ — V — Perfect 5th

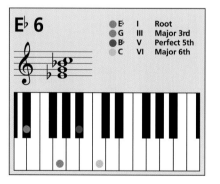

E♭ 6
- E♭ — I — Root
- G — III — Major 3rd
- B♭ — V — Perfect 5th
- C — VI — Major 6th

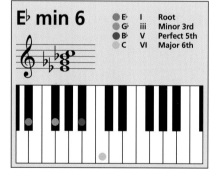

E♭ min 6
- E♭ — I — Root
- G♭ — iii — Minor 3rd
- B♭ — V — Perfect 5th
- C — VI — Major 6th

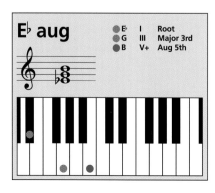

E♭ aug
- E♭ — I — Root
- G — III — Major 3rd
- B — V+ — Aug 5th

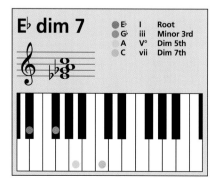

E♭ dim 7
- E♭ — I — Root
- G♭ — iii — Minor 3rd
- A — V° — Dim 5th
- C — vii — Dim 7th

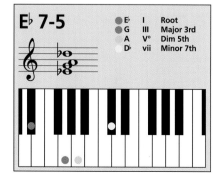

E♭ 7-5
- E♭ — I — Root
- G — III — Major 3rd
- A — V° — Dim 5th
- D♭ — vii — Minor 7th

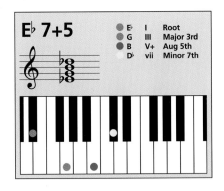

E♭ 7+5

E♭	I	Root
G	III	Major 3rd
B	V+	Aug 5th
D♭	vii	Minor 7th

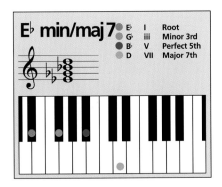

E♭ min/maj7

E♭	I	Root
G♭	iii	Minor 3rd
B♭	V	Perfect 5th
D	VII	Major 7th

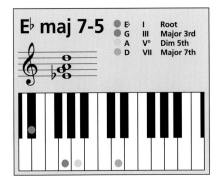

E♭ maj 7-5

E♭	I	Root
G	III	Major 3rd
A	V°	Dim 5th
D	VII	Major 7th

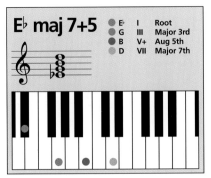

E♭ maj 7+5

E♭	I	Root
G	III	Major 3rd
B	V+	Aug 5th
D	VII	Major 7th

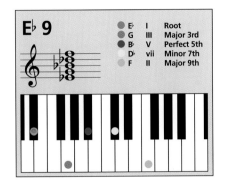

E♭ 9

E♭	I	Root
G	III	Major 3rd
B♭	V	Perfect 5th
D♭	vii	Minor 7th
F	II	Major 9th

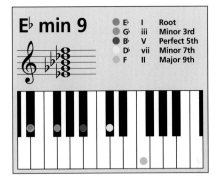

E♭ min 9

E♭	I	Root
G♭	iii	Minor 3rd
B♭	V	Perfect 5th
D♭	vii	Minor 7th
F	II	Major 9th

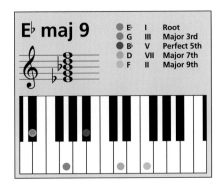

E♭ maj 9

E♭	I	Root
G	III	Major 3rd
B♭	V	Perfect 5th
D	VII	Major 7th
F	II	Major 9th

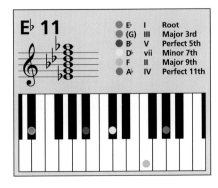

E♭ 11

E♭	I	Root
(G)	III	Major 3rd
B♭	V	Perfect 5th
D♭	vii	Minor 7th
F	II	Major 9th
A♭	IV	Perfect 11th

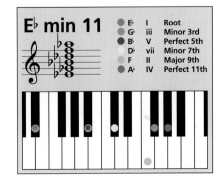

E♭ min 11

E♭	I	Root
G♭	iii	Minor 3rd
B♭	V	Perfect 5th
D♭	vii	Minor 7th
F	II	Major 9th
A♭	IV	Perfect 11th

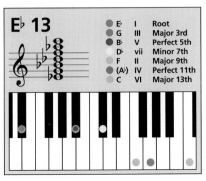

E♭ 13

E♭	I	Root
G	III	Major 3rd
B♭	V	Perfect 5th
D♭	vii	Minor 7th
F	II	Major 9th
(A♭)	IV	Perfect 11th
C	VI	Major 13th

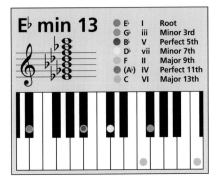

E♭ min 13

E♭	I	Root
G♭	iii	Minor 3rd
B♭	V	Perfect 5th
D♭	vii	Minor 7th
F	II	Major 9th
(A♭)	IV	Perfect 11th
C	VI	Major 13th

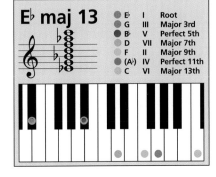

E♭ maj 13

E♭	I	Root
G	III	Major 3rd
B♭	V	Perfect 5th
D	VII	Major 7th
F	II	Major 9th
(A♭)	IV	Perfect 11th
C	VI	Major 13th

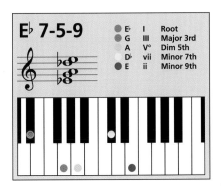

E♭ 7-5-9

E♭	I	Root
G	III	Major 3rd
A	V°	Dim 5th
D♭	vii	Minor 7th
E	ii	Minor 9th

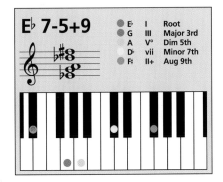

E♭ 7-5+9

E♭	I	Root
G	III	Major 3rd
A	V°	Dim 5th
D♭	vii	Minor 7th
F♯	II+	Aug 9th

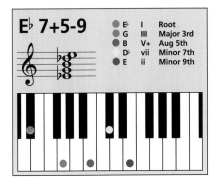

E♭ 7+5-9

E♭	I	Root
G	III	Major 3rd
B	V+	Aug 5th
D♭	vii	Minor 7th
E	ii	Minor 9th

E

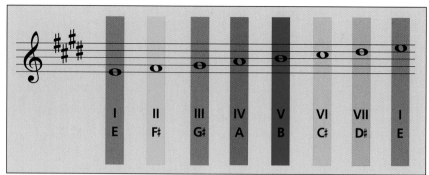

I	II	III	IV	V	VI	VII	I
E	F#	G#	A	B	C#	D#	E

E maj
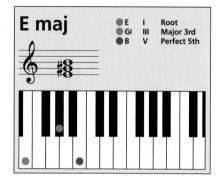

E	I	Root
G#	III	Major 3rd
B	V	Perfect 5th

E m
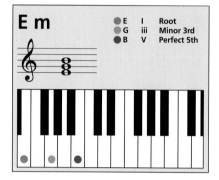

E	I	Root
G	iii	Minor 3rd
B	V	Perfect 5th

E 7
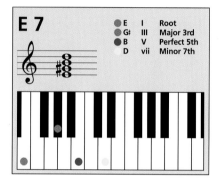

E	I	Root
G#	III	Major 3rd
B	V	Perfect 5th
D	vii	Minor 7th

E min 7
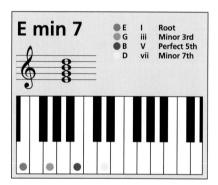

E	I	Root
G	iii	Minor 3rd
B	V	Perfect 5th
D	vii	Minor 7th

E maj 7
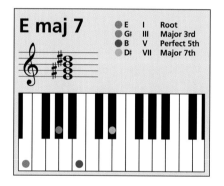

E	I	Root
G#	III	Major 3rd
B	V	Perfect 5th
D#	VII	Major 7th

E sus 4
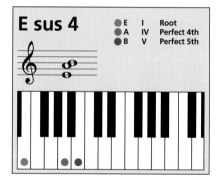

E	I	Root
A	IV	Perfect 4th
B	V	Perfect 5th

E sus 2
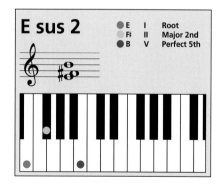

E	I	Root
F#	II	Major 2nd
B	V	Perfect 5th

E 6
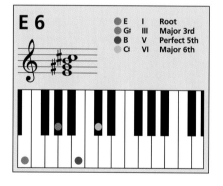

E	I	Root
G#	III	Major 3rd
B	V	Perfect 5th
C#	VI	Major 6th

E min 6
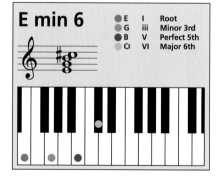

E	I	Root
G	iii	Minor 3rd
B	V	Perfect 5th
C#	VI	Major 6th

E aug
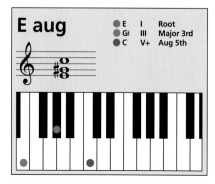

E	I	Root
G#	III	Major 3rd
C	V+	Aug 5th

E dim 7
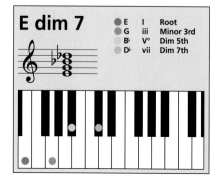

E	I	Root
G	iii	Minor 3rd
B♭	V°	Dim 5th
D♭	vii	Dim 7th

E 7-5
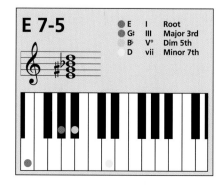

E	I	Root
G#	III	Major 3rd
B♭	V°	Dim 5th
D	vii	Minor 7th

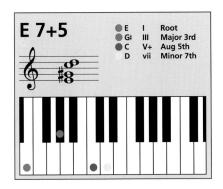

E 7+5

E	I	Root
G♯	III	Major 3rd
C	V+	Aug 5th
D	vii	Minor 7th

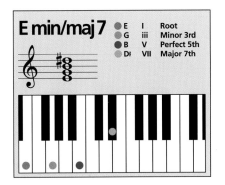

E min/maj7

E	I	Root
G	iii	Minor 3rd
B	V	Perfect 5th
D♯	VII	Major 7th

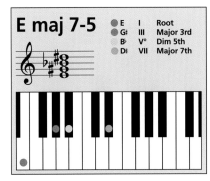

E maj 7-5

E	I	Root
G♯	III	Major 3rd
B♭	V°	Dim 5th
D♯	VII	Major 7th

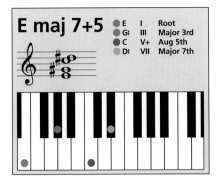

E maj 7+5

E	I	Root
G♯	III	Major 3rd
C	V+	Aug 5th
D♯	VII	Major 7th

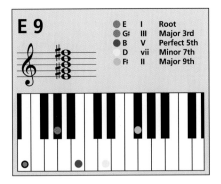

E 9

E	I	Root
G♯	III	Major 3rd
B	V	Perfect 5th
D	vii	Minor 7th
F♯	II	Major 9th

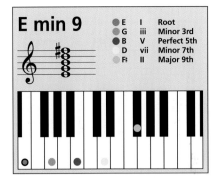

E min 9

E	I	Root
G	iii	Minor 3rd
B	V	Perfect 5th
D	vii	Minor 7th
F♯	II	Major 9th

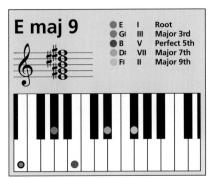

E maj 9

E	I	Root
G♯	III	Major 3rd
B	V	Perfect 5th
D♯	VII	Major 7th
F♯	II	Major 9th

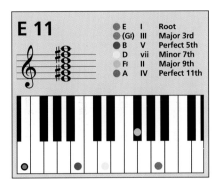

E 11

E	I	Root
(G♯)	III	Major 3rd
B	V	Perfect 5th
D	vii	Minor 7th
F♯	II	Major 9th
A	IV	Perfect 11th

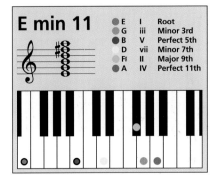

E min 11

E	I	Root
G	iii	Minor 3rd
B	V	Perfect 5th
D	vii	Minor 7th
F♯	II	Major 9th
A	IV	Perfect 11th

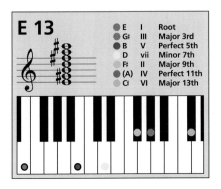

E 13

E	I	Root
G♯	III	Major 3rd
B	V	Perfect 5th
D	vii	Minor 7th
F♯	II	Major 9th
(A)	IV	Perfect 11th
C♯	VI	Major 13th

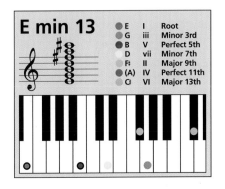

E min 13

E	I	Root
G	iii	Minor 3rd
B	V	Perfect 5th
D	vii	Minor 7th
F♯	II	Major 9th
(A)	IV	Perfect 11th
C♯	VI	Major 13th

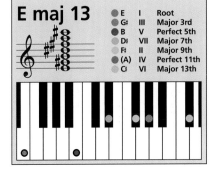

E maj 13

E	I	Root
G♯	III	Major 3rd
B	V	Perfect 5th
D♯	VII	Major 7th
F♯	II	Major 9th
(A)	IV	Perfect 11th
C♯	VI	Major 13th

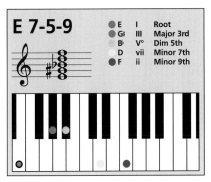

E 7-5-9

E	I	Root
G♯	III	Major 3rd
B♭	V°	Dim 5th
D	vii	Minor 7th
F	ii	Minor 9th

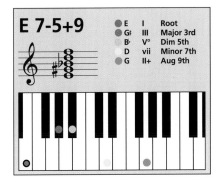

E 7-5+9

E	I	Root
G♯	III	Major 3rd
B♭	V°	Dim 5th
D	vii	Minor 7th
G	II+	Aug 9th

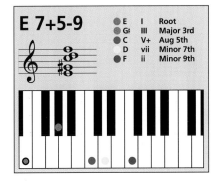

E 7+5-9

E	I	Root
G♯	III	Major 3rd
C	V+	Aug 5th
D	vii	Minor 7th
F	ii	Minor 9th

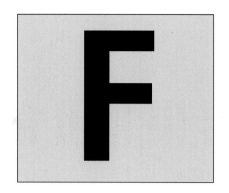

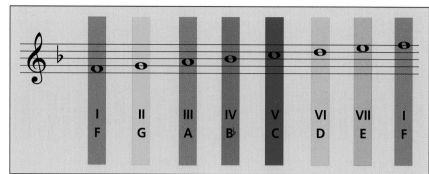

I	II	III	IV	V	VI	VII	I
F	G	A	B♭	C	D	E	F

F maj

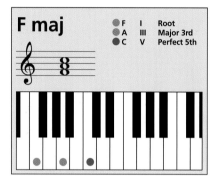

F	I	Root
A	III	Major 3rd
C	V	Perfect 5th

F min

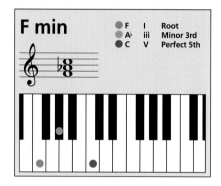

F	I	Root
A♭	iii	Minor 3rd
C	V	Perfect 5th

F 7

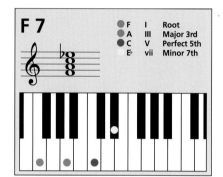

F	I	Root
A	III	Major 3rd
C	V	Perfect 5th
E♭	vii	Minor 7th

F min 7

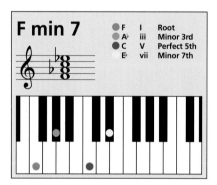

F	I	Root
A♭	iii	Minor 3rd
C	V	Perfect 5th
E♭	vii	Minor 7th

F maj 7

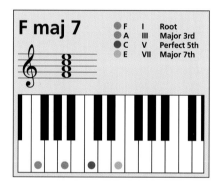

F	I	Root
A	III	Major 3rd
C	V	Perfect 5th
E	VII	Major 7th

F sus 4

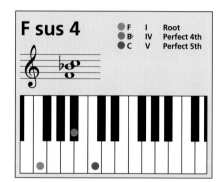

F	I	Root
B♭	IV	Perfect 4th
C	V	Perfect 5th

F sus 2

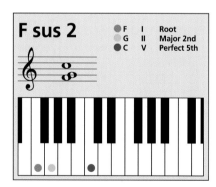

F	I	Root
G	II	Major 2nd
C	V	Perfect 5th

F 6

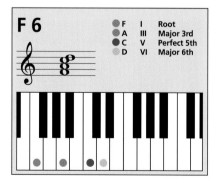

F	I	Root
A	III	Major 3rd
C	V	Perfect 5th
D	VI	Major 6th

F min 6

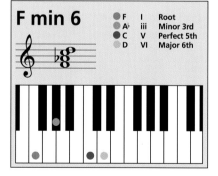

F	I	Root
A♭	iii	Minor 3rd
C	V	Perfect 5th
D	VI	Major 6th

F aug

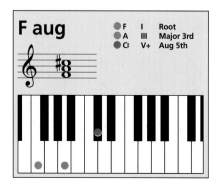

F	I	Root
A	III	Major 3rd
C♯	V+	Aug 5th

F dim 7

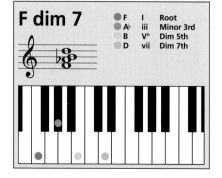

F	I	Root
A♭	iii	Minor 3rd
B	V°	Dim 5th
D	vii	Dim 7th

F 7-5

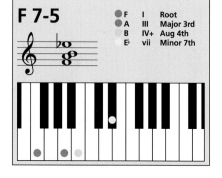

F	I	Root
A	III	Major 3rd
B	IV+	Aug 4th
E♭	vii	Minor 7th

F 7+5
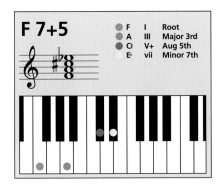

F	I	Root
A	III	Major 3rd
C♯	V+	Aug 5th
E♭	vii	Minor 7th

F min/maj7
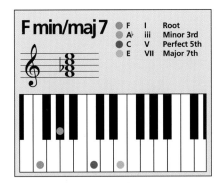

F	I	Root
A♭	iii	Minor 3rd
C	V	Perfect 5th
E	VII	Major 7th

F maj 7-5
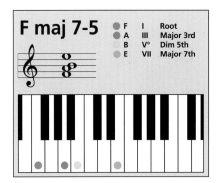

F	I	Root
A	III	Major 3rd
B	V°	Dim 5th
E	VII	Major 7th

F maj 7+5
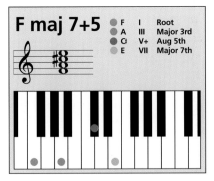

F	I	Root
A	III	Major 3rd
C♯	V+	Aug 5th
E	VII	Major 7th

F 9
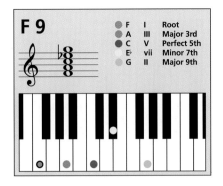

F	I	Root
A	III	Major 3rd
C	V	Perfect 5th
E♭	vii	Minor 7th
G	II	Major 9th

F min 9
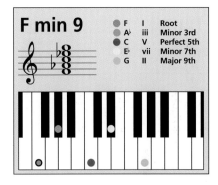

F	I	Root
A♭	iii	Minor 3rd
C	V	Perfect 5th
E♭	vii	Minor 7th
G	II	Major 9th

F maj 9
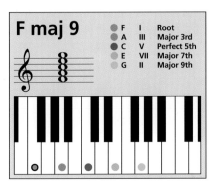

F	I	Root
A	III	Major 3rd
C	V	Perfect 5th
E	VII	Major 7th
G	II	Major 9th

F 11
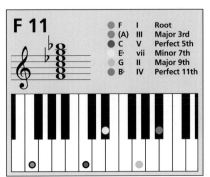

F	I	Root
(A)	III	Major 3rd
C	V	Perfect 5th
E♭	vii	Minor 7th
G	II	Major 9th
B♭	IV	Perfect 11th

F min 11
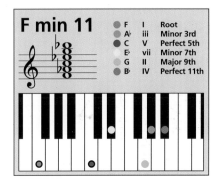

F	I	Root
A♭	iii	Minor 3rd
C	V	Perfect 5th
E♭	vii	Minor 7th
G	II	Major 9th
B♭	IV	Perfect 11th

F 13
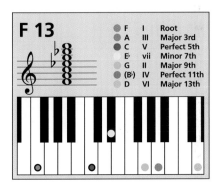

F	I	Root
A	III	Major 3rd
C	V	Perfect 5th
E♭	vii	Minor 7th
G	II	Major 9th
(B♭)	IV	Perfect 11th
D	VI	Major 13th

F min 13
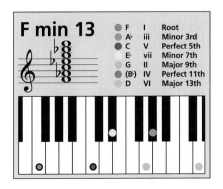

F	I	Root
A♭	iii	Minor 3rd
C	V	Perfect 5th
E♭	vii	Minor 7th
G	II	Major 9th
(B♭)	IV	Perfect 11th
D	VI	Major 13th

F maj 13
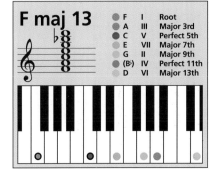

F	I	Root
A	III	Major 3rd
C	V	Perfect 5th
E	VII	Major 7th
G	II	Major 9th
(B♭)	IV	Perfect 11th
D	VI	Major 13th

F 7-5-9
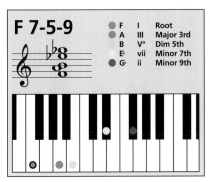

F	I	Root
A	III	Major 3rd
B	V°	Dim 5th
E♭	vii	Minor 7th
G♭	ii	Minor 9th

F 7-5+9
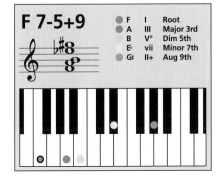

F	I	Root
A	III	Major 3rd
B	V°	Dim 5th
E♭	vii	Minor 7th
G♯	II+	Aug 9th

F 7+5-9
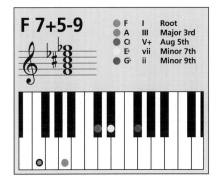

F	I	Root
A	III	Major 3rd
C♯	V+	Aug 5th
E♭	vii	Minor 7th
G♭	ii	Minor 9th

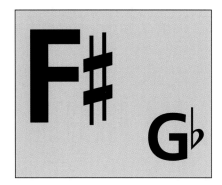

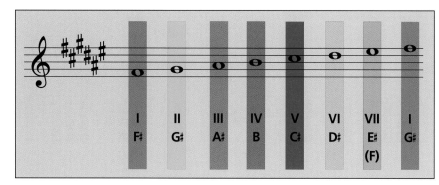

I	II	III	IV	V	VI	VII	I
F#	G#	A#	B	C#	D#	E#	G#
						(F)	

F# maj

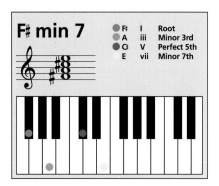

●	F#	I	Root
●	A#	III	Major 3rd
●	C#	V	Perfect 5th

F# m

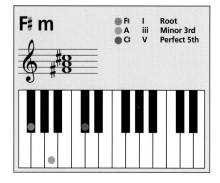

●	F#	I	Root
●	A	iii	Minor 3rd
●	C#	V	Perfect 5th

F# 7

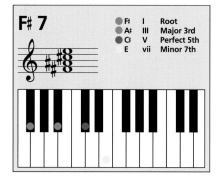

●	F#	I	Root
●	A#	III	Major 3rd
●	C#	V	Perfect 5th
	E	vii	Minor 7th

F# min 7

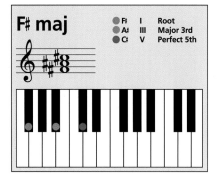

●	F#	I	Root
●	A	iii	Minor 3rd
●	C#	V	Perfect 5th
	E	vii	Minor 7th

F# maj 7

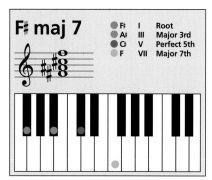

●	F#	I	Root
●	A#	III	Major 3rd
●	C#	V	Perfect 5th
●	F	VII	Major 7th

F# sus 4

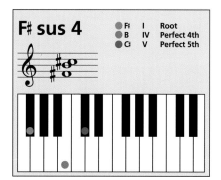

●	F#	I	Root
●	B	IV	Perfect 4th
●	C#	V	Perfect 5th

F# sus 2

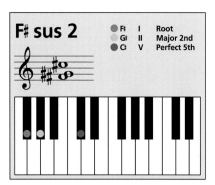

●	F#	I	Root
●	G#	II	Major 2nd
●	C#	V	Perfect 5th

F# 6

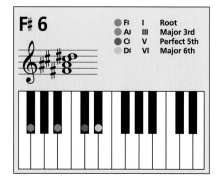

●	F#	I	Root
●	A#	III	Major 3rd
●	C#	V	Perfect 5th
●	D#	VI	Major 6th

F# min 6

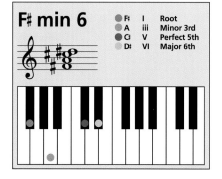

●	F#	I	Root
●	A	iii	Minor 3rd
●	C#	V	Perfect 5th
●	D#	VI	Major 6th

F# aug

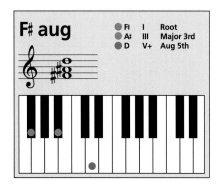

●	F#	I	Root
●	A#	III	Major 3rd
●	D	V+	Aug 5th

F# dim 7

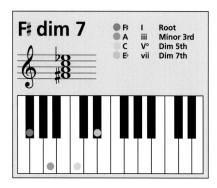

●	F#	I	Root
●	A	iii	Minor 3rd
	C	V°	Dim 5th
	E♭	vii	Dim 7th

F# 7-5

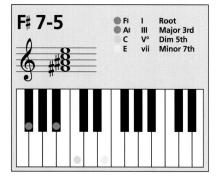

●	F#	I	Root
●	A#	III	Major 3rd
	C	V°	Dim 5th
	E	vii	Minor 7th

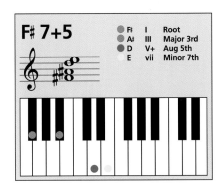

F♯ 7+5

F♯	I	Root
A♯	III	Major 3rd
D	V+	Aug 5th
E	vii	Minor 7th

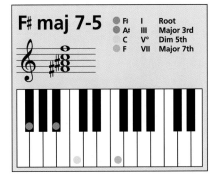

F♯min/maj7

F♯	I	Root
A	iii	Minor 3rd
C♯	V	Perfect 5th
F	VII	Major 7th

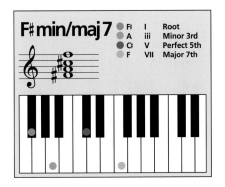

F♯ maj 7-5

F♯	I	Root
A♯	III	Major 3rd
C	V°	Dim 5th
F	VII	Major 7th

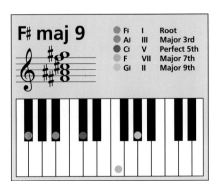

F♯ maj 7+5

F♯	I	Root
A♯	III	Major 3rd
D	V+	Aug 5th
F	VII	Major 7th

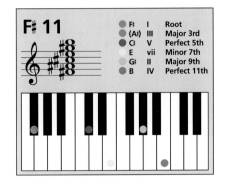

F♯ 9

F♯	I	Root
A♯	III	Major 3rd
C♯	V	Perfect 5th
E	vii	Minor 7th
G♯	II	Major 9th

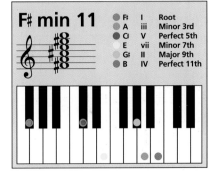

F♯ min 9

F♯	I	Root
A	iii	Minor 3rd
C♯	V	Perfect 5th
E	vii	Minor 7th
G♯	II	Major 9th

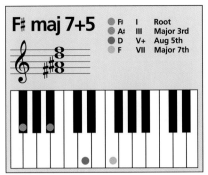

F♯ maj 9

F♯	I	Root
A♯	III	Major 3rd
C♯	V	Perfect 5th
F	VII	Major 7th
G♯	II	Major 9th

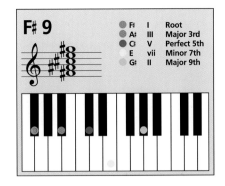

F♯ 11

F♯	I	Root
(A♯)	III	Major 3rd
C♯	V	Perfect 5th
E	vii	Minor 7th
G♯	II	Major 9th
B	IV	Perfect 11th

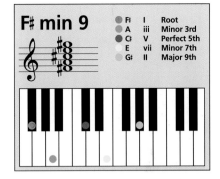

F♯ min 11

F♯	I	Root
A	iii	Minor 3rd
C♯	V	Perfect 5th
E	vii	Minor 7th
G♯	II	Major 9th
B	IV	Perfect 11th

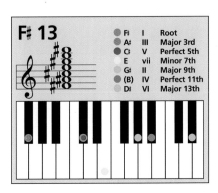

F♯ 13

F♯	I	Root
A♯	III	Major 3rd
C♯	V	Perfect 5th
E	vii	Minor 7th
G♯	II	Major 9th
(B)	IV	Perfect 11th
D♯	VI	Major 13th

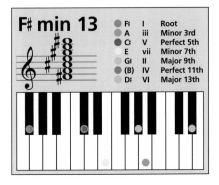

F♯ min 13

F♯	I	Root
A	iii	Minor 3rd
C♯	V	Perfect 5th
E	vii	Minor 7th
G♯	II	Major 9th
(B)	IV	Perfect 11th
D♯	VI	Major 13th

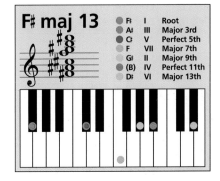

F♯ maj 13

F♯	I	Root
A♯	III	Major 3rd
C♯	V	Perfect 5th
F	VII	Major 7th
G♯	II	Major 9th
(B)	IV	Perfect 11th
D♯	VI	Major 13th

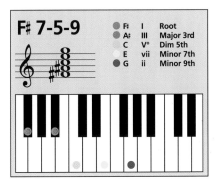

F♯ 7-5-9

F♯	I	Root
A♯	III	Major 3rd
C	V°	Dim 5th
E	vii	Minor 7th
G	ii	Minor 9th

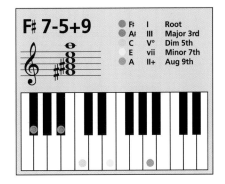

F♯ 7-5+9

F♯	I	Root
A♯	III	Major 3rd
C	V°	Dim 5th
E	vii	Minor 7th
A	II+	Aug 9th

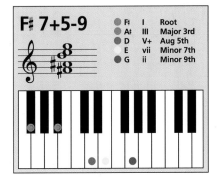

F♯ 7+5-9

F♯	I	Root
A♯	III	Major 3rd
D	V+	Aug 5th
E	vii	Minor 7th
G	ii	Minor 9th

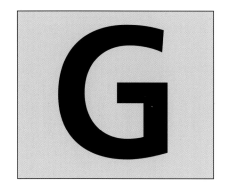

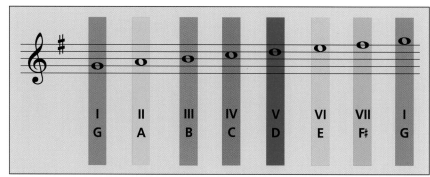

I	II	III	IV	V	VI	VII	I
G	A	B	C	D	E	F#	G

G maj

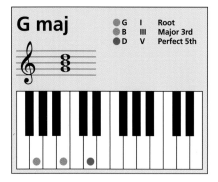

G	I	Root
B	III	Major 3rd
D	V	Perfect 5th

G m

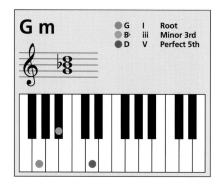

G	I	Root
B♭	iii	Minor 3rd
D	V	Perfect 5th

G 7

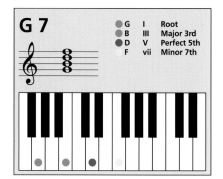

G	I	Root
B	III	Major 3rd
D	V	Perfect 5th
F	vii	Minor 7th

G min 7

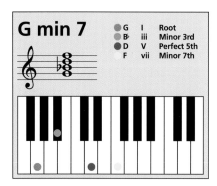

G	I	Root
B♭	iii	Minor 3rd
D	V	Perfect 5th
F	vii	Minor 7th

G maj 7

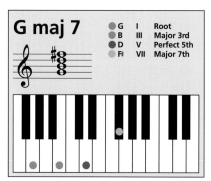

G	I	Root
B	III	Major 3rd
D	V	Perfect 5th
F#	VII	Major 7th

G sus 4

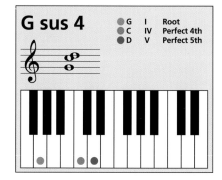

G	I	Root
C	IV	Perfect 4th
D	V	Perfect 5th

G sus 2

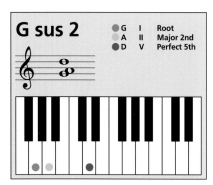

G	I	Root
A	II	Major 2nd
D	V	Perfect 5th

G 6

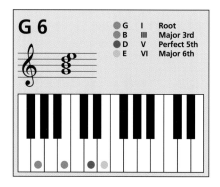

G	I	Root
B	III	Major 3rd
D	V	Perfect 5th
E	VI	Major 6th

G min 6

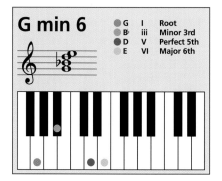

G	I	Root
B♭	iii	Minor 3rd
D	V	Perfect 5th
E	VI	Major 6th

G aug

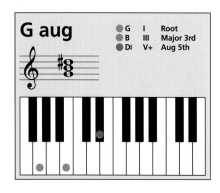

G	I	Root
B	III	Major 3rd
D#	V+	Aug 5th

G dim 7

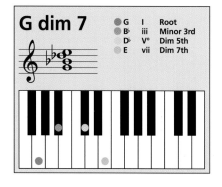

G	I	Root
B♭	iii	Minor 3rd
D♭	V°	Dim 5th
E	vii	Dim 7th

G 7-5

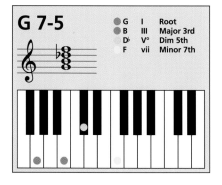

G	I	Root
B	III	Major 3rd
D♭	V°	Dim 5th
F	vii	Minor 7th

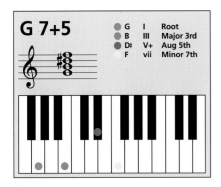

G 7+5

G	I	Root
B	III	Major 3rd
D♯	V+	Aug 5th
F	vii	Minor 7th

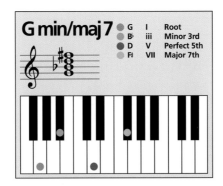

G min/maj7

G	I	Root
B♭	iii	Minor 3rd
D	V	Perfect 5th
F♯	VII	Major 7th

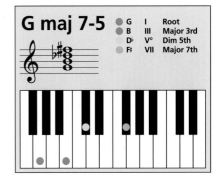

G maj 7-5

G	I	Root
B	III	Major 3rd
D♭	V°	Dim 5th
F♯	VII	Major 7th

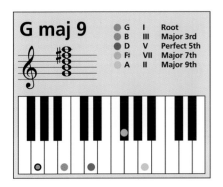

G maj 7+5

G	I	Root
B	III	Major 3rd
D♯	V+	Aug 5th
F♯	VII	Major 7th

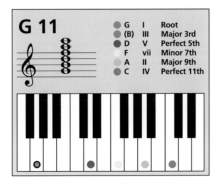

G 9

G	I	Root
B	III	Major 3rd
D	V	Perfect 5th
F	vii	Minor 7th
A	II	Major 9th

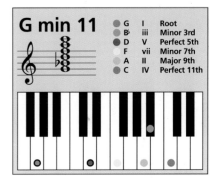

G min 9

G	I	Root
B♭	iii	Minor 3rd
D	V	Perfect 5th
F	vii	Minor 7th
A	II	Major 9th

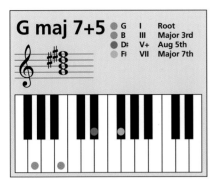

G maj 9

G	I	Root
B	III	Major 3rd
D	V	Perfect 5th
F♯	VII	Major 7th
A	II	Major 9th

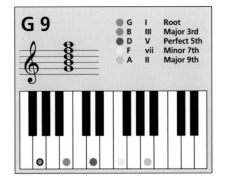

G 11

G	I	Root
(B)	III	Major 3rd
D	V	Perfect 5th
F	vii	Minor 7th
A	II	Major 9th
C	IV	Perfect 11th

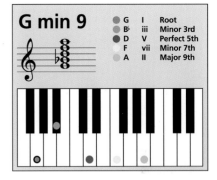

G min 11

G	I	Root
B♭	iii	Minor 3rd
D	V	Perfect 5th
F	vii	Minor 7th
A	II	Major 9th
C	IV	Perfect 11th

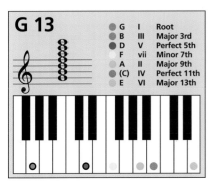

G 13

G	I	Root
B	III	Major 3rd
D	V	Perfect 5th
F	vii	Minor 7th
A	II	Major 9th
(C)	IV	Perfect 11th
E	VI	Major 13th

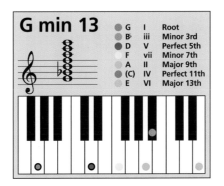

G min 13

G	I	Root
B♭	iii	Minor 3rd
D	V	Perfect 5th
F	vii	Minor 7th
A	II	Major 9th
(C)	IV	Perfect 11th
E	VI	Major 13th

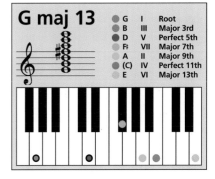

G maj 13

G	I	Root
B	III	Major 3rd
D	V	Perfect 5th
F♯	VII	Major 7th
A	II	Major 9th
(C)	IV	Perfect 11th
E	VI	Major 13th

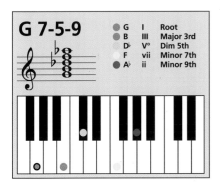

G 7-5-9

G	I	Root
B	III	Major 3rd
D♭	V°	Dim 5th
F	vii	Minor 7th
A♭	ii	Minor 9th

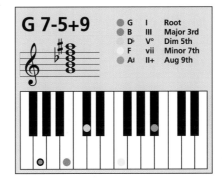

G 7-5+9

G	I	Root
B	III	Major 3rd
D♭	V°	Dim 5th
F	vii	Minor 7th
A♯	II+	Aug 9th

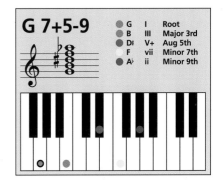

G 7+5-9

G	I	Root
B	III	Major 3rd
D♯	V+	Aug 5th
F	vii	Minor 7th
A♭	ii	Minor 9th

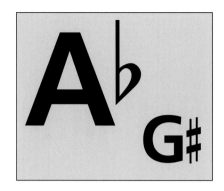

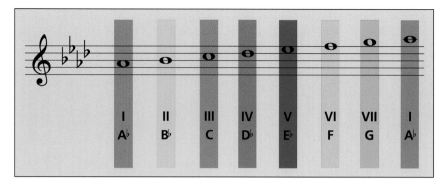

I	II	III	IV	V	VI	VII	I
A♭	B♭	C	D♭	E♭	F	G	A♭

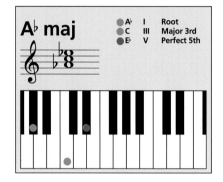

A♭ maj

●	A♭	I	Root
●	C	III	Major 3rd
●	E♭	V	Perfect 5th

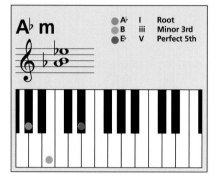

A♭ m

●	A♭	I	Root
●	B	iii	Minor 3rd
●	E♭	V	Perfect 5th

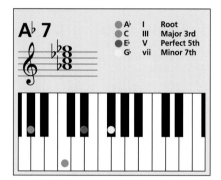

A♭ 7

●	A♭	I	Root
●	C	III	Major 3rd
●	E♭	V	Perfect 5th
○	G♭	vii	Minor 7th

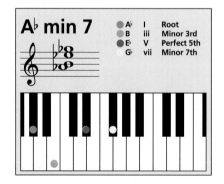

A♭ min 7

●	A♭	I	Root
●	B	iii	Minor 3rd
●	E♭	V	Perfect 5th
○	G♭	vii	Minor 7th

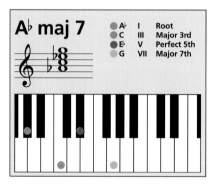

A♭ maj 7

●	A♭	I	Root
●	C	III	Major 3rd
●	E♭	V	Perfect 5th
●	G	VII	Major 7th

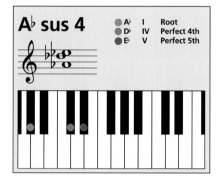

A♭ sus 4

●	A♭	I	Root
●	D♭	IV	Perfect 4th
●	E♭	V	Perfect 5th

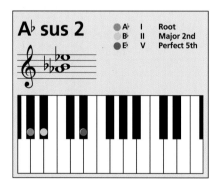

A♭ sus 2

●	A♭	I	Root
●	B♭	II	Major 2nd
●	E♭	V	Perfect 5th

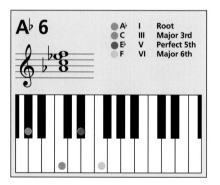

A♭ 6

●	A♭	I	Root
●	C	III	Major 3rd
●	E♭	V	Perfect 5th
●	F	VI	Major 6th

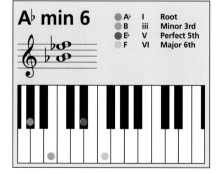

A♭ min 6

●	A♭	I	Root
●	B	iii	Minor 3rd
●	E♭	V	Perfect 5th
●	F	VI	Major 6th

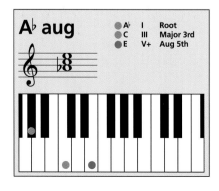

A♭ aug

●	A♭	I	Root
●	C	III	Major 3rd
●	E	V+	Aug 5th

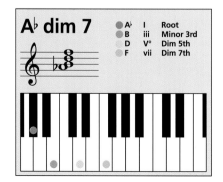

A♭ dim 7

●	A♭	I	Root
●	B	iii	Minor 3rd
●	D	V°	Dim 5th
●	F	vii	Dim 7th

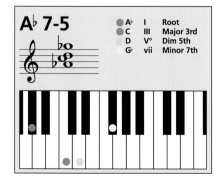

A♭ 7-5

●	A♭	I	Root
●	C	III	Major 3rd
●	D	V°	Dim 5th
○	G♭	vii	Minor 7th

A♭ 7+5

A♭	I	Root
C	III	Major 3rd
E	V+	Aug 5th
G♭	vii	Minor 7th

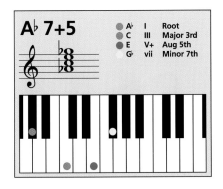

A♭ min/maj7

A♭	I	Root
B	iii	Minor 3rd
E♭	V	Perfect 5th
G	VII	Major 7th

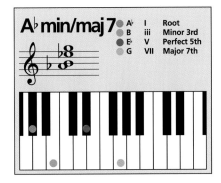

A♭ maj 7-5

A♭	I	Root
C	III	Major 3rd
D	V°	Dim 5th
G	VII	Major 7th

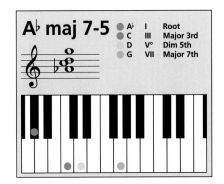

A♭ maj 7+5

A♭	I	Root
C	III	Major 3rd
E	V+	Aug 5th
G	VII	Major 7th

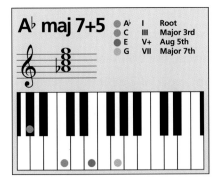

A♭ 9

A♭	I	Root
C	III	Major 3rd
E♭	V	Perfect 5th
G♭	vii	Minor 7th
B♭	II	Major 9th

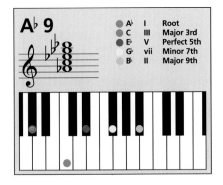

A♭ min 9

A♭	I	Root
B	iii	Minor 3rd
E♭	V	Perfect 5th
G♭	vii	Minor 7th
B♭	II	Major 9th

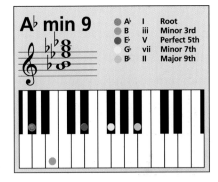

A♭ maj 9

A♭	I	Root
C	III	Major 3rd
E♭	V	Perfect 5th
G	VII	Major 7th
B♭	II	Major 9th

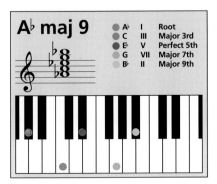

A♭ 11

A♭	I	Root
C	III	Major 3rd
E♭	V	Perfect 5th
G♭	vii	Minor 7th
B♭	II	Major 9th
D♭	IV	Perfect 11th

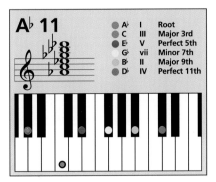

A♭ min 11

A♭	I	Root
B	iii	Minor 3rd
E♭	V	Perfect 5th
G♭	vii	Minor 7th
B♭	II	Major 9th
D♭	IV	Perfect 11th

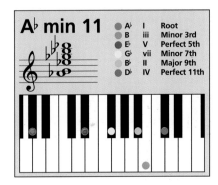

A♭ 13

A♭	I	Root
C	III	Major 3rd
E♭	V	Perfect 5th
G♭	vii	Minor 7th
B♭	II	Major 9th
(D♭)	IV	Perfect 11th
F	VI	Major 13th

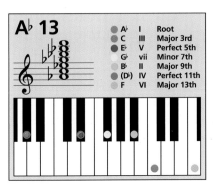

A♭ min 13

A♭	I	Root
B	iii	Minor 3rd
E♭	V	Perfect 5th
G♭	vii	Minor 7th
B♭	II	Major 9th
(D♭)	IV	Perfect 11th
F	VI	Major 13th

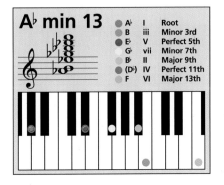

A♭ maj 13

A♭	I	Root
C	III	Major 3rd
E♭	V	Perfect 5th
G	VII	Major 7th
B♭	II	Major 9th
(D♭)	IV	Perfect 11th
F	VI	Major 13th

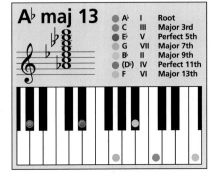

A♭ 7-5-9

A♭	I	Root
C	III	Major 3rd
D	V°	Dim 5th
G♭	vii	Minor 7th
A	ii	Minor 9th

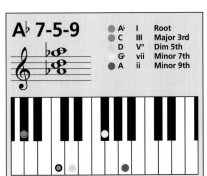

A♭ 7-5+9

A♭	I	Root
C	III	Major 3rd
D	V°	Dim 5th
G♭	vii	Minor 7th
B	II+	Aug 9th

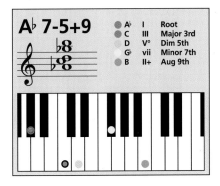

A♭ 7+5-9

A♭	I	Root
C	III	Major 3rd
E	V+	Aug 5th
G♭	vii	Minor 7th
A	ii	Minor 9th

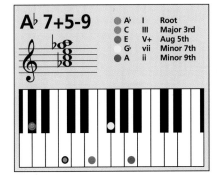

CHAPTER 4
MODERN KEYBOARDS

WHAT'S IT ALL ABOUT?

For most modern keyboard musicians, the ability the play music in the conventional sense is only one aspect of the total picture. It's all very well using preset sounds, but even the humblest modern keyboards offer the scope for creating and storing your own sound "patches." Furthermore, the boundaries between keyboard technology and studio recording are becoming increasingly blurred, especially with the advance of MIDI, digital sampling and computer hard-disk recording. For the newcomer, this can mean having to wade through a maze of technological jargon to understand the possibilities offered by even the simplest pieces of equipment. The aim of this chapter is to bring you up to speed, equipping you with enough basic knowledge to take an informed look into areas of potential interest.

SYNTHESIZER OPTIONS

Synthesizers can be broadly grouped into one of two categories: MONOPHONIC or POLYPHONIC. Each has its own merits and potential uses. The principal difference between the two is that a monophonic synth can only play one note at a time—to play chords you need a polyphonic synth. Most synths consist typically of a keyboard with a series of knobs, faders or other means of controlling sound parameters.

The keyboard and sounds don't necessarily have to be in the same box. An increasingly common approach is to buy a MOTHER KEYBOARD and a series of EXTERNAL SOUND MODULES. The keyboard itself doesn't make a sound, but sends MIDI signals (*see page 146*) that trigger the sounds in the external units. The advantage of this approach is that a wide variety of sounds can be used without the need for a hefty stand full of keyboards. The external modules can also be neatly stored in a rack unit.

MULTITIMBRAL SYNTHESIZERS

Some of the more high-performance (and expensive) keyboards available on the market are called WORKSTATION synthesizers. These are aimed to provide the keyboard player with nothing less than a studio in a box. They have a number of distinct differences to regular polyphonic synths.

Firstly, workstations are MULTITIMBRAL. This means that a number of the different sounds stored internally can be accessed at the same time. You will see why this is useful in a moment. Workstations also have a built-in MIDI sequencer (*see page 146*) capable of recording and playing back a large number of tracks simultaneously. If, for example, the specification of a workstation indicates that it is 16-voice multitimbral, and has a built-in 16-track sequencer, then any 16 sounds stored on the synth can be recorded on the sequencer one track at a time, and then all played back simultaneously. When used for professional recording, if the synthesizer has a sufficient number of audio output sockets, each sound could be connected to a different channel on a mixing desk, and processed individually (*see page 164*).

The only limitation on using a multitimbral synth in this way is its polyphonic capability. If a workstation in question is decribed as being "32-note polyphonic" then this means that over the entire spread of multitimbral sounds, a maximum of 32 notes can be played at once. That might sound a lot, but it isn't. Consider that tracks using piano and organ voices could, theoretically, play up to 20 notes at one time. If you put string and brass arrangements on top of that then you quickly start to run out of notes. Where an arrangement exceeds this capacity, notes start getting "left out" from the play back, which is obviously not desirable.

ANALOG VERSUS DIGITAL

A great deal has been written over the past 15 years about the so-called analog-digital divide. Much of it has tended to echo the same "old-versus-new" arguments that have permeated similar issues, such as vinyl versus CD, or tube versus transistor amplification.

It's a little difficult to be objective about the sounds produced by a synthesizer since it generally comes to down to issues of personal taste and prevailing fashions in sound. When the DX7 came out in 1983, analog synthesis became outdated almost overnight. Keyboards that a few years earlier had been considered the ultimate in music technology now languished in second-hand stores. However, it didn't take long for the differences to make themselves plain. Digital synths may have produced extremely clean noises, but for many users they sounded overly harsh and clinical. Furthermore, bass sounds were accompanied by unavoidable low-end digital "noise." The old analog synths made nothing like as "realistic" imitations of acoustic sounds, but they had a warmth of tone and ease of programmability that many missed. As manufacturers responded to these criticisms, purely digital systems also went out of fashion.

Snobbery continues to play a part in this ongoing process. Fuelled by the speed at which manufacturers bring out new models, keyboard players can easily get dragged into an endless cycle of upgrades, ever off-loading "obsolete" technology at a fraction of its original cost.

Unlike computers, which genuinely do become obsolete after a while, music technology rarely stops working—unless there has been physical abuse, a 20-year-old synth will more than probably still sound fine. With such rapid developments, its easy to lose sight of what should be the only important issue here: making music. When you buy the latest in high-performance keyboard technology it doesn't come with a guarantee that your music will be any better as a result.

HOW A SYNTHESIZER WORKS

When forming any sound, a synthesizer uses electrical currents moving in an circuit to simulate the vibration of air waves. All sounds—especially those produced by musical instruments—are composed of complex soundwaves. Synthesizers have traditionally sought to reconstruct these waveforms using a number of different means.

Traditional analog synthesis—the kind utilized by all synthesizers until the early 1980s—created sounds by taking a basic waveform and filtering out unwanted harmonics until the desired sound was created. This process is referred to as SUBTRACTIVE SYNTHESIS.

The rapid development and gradual falling price of computer technology from the early 1980s opened up other DIGITAL alternatives. This allowed sounds to be created in the opposite way—constructed from the bottom up. This process is known as ADDITIVE SYNTHESIS.

Although the analog system began to fall from favor when digital synthesizers came on the market during the mid-1980s, users soon tired of the sometimes clinical sounds they made. As as result, new approaches were sought that combined the best of analog and digital processing with the newly popular sampling technology. Consequently, most of the developments that have taken place over the past 15 years have brought together synthesizer and sampling technology to produce a hybrid format. Digital samples are used along with traditional basic waveforms which can then be processed using the familiar system of modulators, filters and envelopes.

Recent years have also seen a resurrection in purely analog sounds, especially in dance music. This has resulted in the launch of new analog models. Although they may make extensive use of digital technology, the basic sound principles remain the same. Indeed, the fundamental processes and terminology of the original analog synthesizers have remained the basis of every new development since the first Moog modular system appeared back in 1965.

ANALOG PRINCIPLES

To show how analog synthsis work, it's convenient to break the various functions down into their component parts. Indeed, in the early days of synthesis, these modules *were* physically separate units, and had to be connected with patch leads.

Let's start with the keyboard. Synthesizers traditionally work on the principle of an electronic keyboard sending a control voltage, the specific value of which dependends on which key has been pressed. These voltages are then used to control a variety of parameters within each subsequent module, namely the voltage controlled oscillator (VCO), voltage controlled filter (VCF) and the voltage controlled amplifier (VCA). These three elements respectively govern the pitch, tone and volume of the sound created.

VOLTAGE CONTROLLED OSCILLATOR (VCO)

The voltage from the keyboard is routed into the voltage controlled oscillator. This determines the frequency at which the VCO oscillates, and hence the pitch of the note. A variety of different types of soundwave can be generated, each has its own characteristic and use. Here are the most common forms:

- **Sine wave—pure tone, rather like a flute.**
- **Sawtooth wave—used for brass-like sounds.**
- **Square wave—"hollow" sound, rather like a clarinet.**
- **Triangle—like sine wave with brighter tone.**

Only one oscillator is needed to create a sound, however most modern synths using this type of system have three oscillators. This means that one note on a keyboard can trigger three independent sounds, all of which can be tuned and processed individually. There is also generally some kind of facility on the synth for controlling the respective volumes of each oscillator allowing for the creation of some extremely detailed and complex sounds.

MODULATING THE OSCILLATOR

Oscillators can also be modified by a number of other controls. The majority of electronic keyboards have at least one PERFORMANCE WHEEL positioned alongside the keyboard. The most commonly used control is the pitch wheel, which can be moved back and forth to alter the pitch of the oscillator, creating portamento and glissando effects. Additional performance wheels are used to modulate the sound, creating vibrato and tremolo effects.

Many synths also have what is called a LOW FREQUENCY OSCILLATOR control. This routes a sub-audio frequency into the VCO, disturbing the sound and creating modulation. The type of waveform generated governs the sound produced: a sine wave, for example, can create a smooth vibrato; a square wave can be used to produce a trill effect.

FILTERING THE SOUND

The audio signal that emerges from each of the oscillators is then routed into a filtering system. The voltage controlled filter is essentially a set of tone controls, rather like an extremely sophisticated version of the bass and treble knobs found on most hi-fi systems. VCFs are used to remove specific frequencies across the audio spectrum, thus refining the sound. Although every manufacturer uses a different design, each model will have at least some kind of high-pass filter—which removes frequencies below a specified level—and low-pass filter, which removes frequencies above a specified level. On some models,

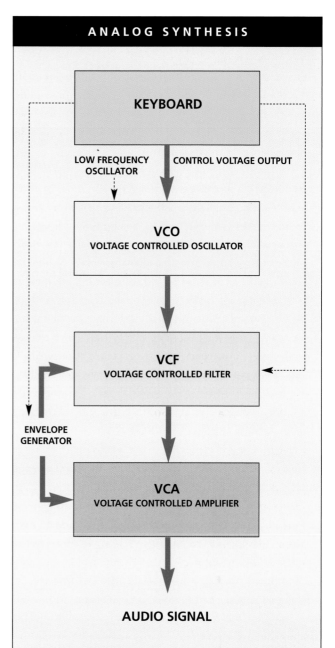

ANALOG SYNTHESIS

KEYBOARD

LOW FREQUENCY OSCILLATOR   CONTROL VOLTAGE OUTPUT

VCO
VOLTAGE CONTROLLED OSCILLATOR

VCF
VOLTAGE CONTROLLED FILTER

ENVELOPE GENERATOR

VCA
VOLTAGE CONTROLLED AMPLIFIER

AUDIO SIGNAL

The three principle building blocks in analog synthesis are the voltage controlled oscillator (VCO), voltage controlled filter (VCF) and the voltage controlled amplifier (VCA). In most synthesizers, the control voltage from the keyboard is routed to the the oscillator, then on to the filter, and finally to the amplifier, which emerges as an audio output signal.

The voltages from the keyboard can also be used to control the filter and the envelope generator, which governs the attack, decay and sustain of the note.

The low frequency oscillator (LFO) is a separate entity in which "sub-audio" frequencies are routed to the voltage contolled oscillator to produce modulation effects, such as vibrato or more extreme sounds.

a band-pass filter can also be used to remove signals from all but the selected frequency.

Most filter systems comprise two separate elements—cut-off and resonance: the cut-off controls the specified levels at which filtering takes place; the resonance alters the amplitude or intensity of the soundwave at the cut-off frequency, which can dramatically alter the sound.

CONTROLLING THE ENVELOPE

The way a sound behaves from the moment the finger presses the key to the moment that key is released is called the ENVELOPE. This can be controlled with a high degree of precision. Although they can work in very different ways, every type of synthesizer has to have at least one envelope shaping function, the most common of which is known as ADSR. The letters stand for "attack," "decay," "sustain," and "release," each of which has its own separate control.

- **ATTACK controls the speed at which the sound moves from minimum to maximum volume. A slow attack will means that when you press the key, the sound slowly fades in.**
- **DECAY controls the rate at which the sound fades away until reaching the SUSTAIN threshold, after which the volume remains constant until the note is released. If the sustain control is set to minimum, then the note will stop playing the moment the finger is removed from the keyboard.**
- **RELEASE controls the rate at which the sound fades out when the finger is taken off the key. The higher the setting the longer the sound takes to die away.**

Enveloped generators can also be used to control the way in which notes are filtered, creating "sweeps" or "wah" effects.

THE VOLTAGE CONTROLLED AMPLIFIER

The signal from the filter is routed into the voltage controlled amplifier and modified by the envelope system. This governs the volume of the final audio signal output to the amplifier and loudspeaker or mixing board.

OTHER FORMS OF SYNTHESIS

Manufacturers have attempted many different approaches to synthesizing sound. Whilst the analog model you've just seen shows the most basic of principles, even those keyboards that do not work in this way tend to use similar terminologies when referring to filtering and envelope shaping. The main difference comes in the way in which original sounds are created.

The Yamaha FM (Frequency Modulation) system that was so popular during the 1980s, used a series of six sine-wave oscillators that could be either configured as an "operator" (sound source) or "modulator" using a variety of complex algorithms. Although great sounds could be created, the programming was too complex for most musicians.

Roland's LA (Linear Arithmetic) system, introduced in 1987, was the first to make use of digital samples. Sounds were created using a conventional modulator-filter-envelope system.

More recently, "acoustic modelling" synthesis has gained ground, using complex algorithms to recreate the expressiveness of acoustic instruments. Once again, the sounds produced are excellent, but programming them can still be a tricky business.

A DOZEN CLASSIC SYNTHESIZERS

EMS VCS III (1969)
   Revolutionary synth with pinboard patchbay.
Moog MiniMoog (1971)
   The first compact synth with internal patching.
Yamaha CS80 (1978)
   The first great analog polysynth—still highly rated.
Sequential Circuits Prophet 5 (1978)
   Classic analog polysynth with programmable presets.
Fairlight CMI (1979)
   The system that started the digital sampling fashion.
Electronic Dream Plant Wasp (1980)
   The first affordable synthesizer. The keyboard was just a plastic strip, but it helped kick-start the synth-pop boom.

E-MU Emulator (1980)
   The first affordable sampling keyboard.
Roland SH101 (1981)
   Budget monosynth now much beloved of dance producers.
Yamaha DX7 (1983)
   Revolutionery FM synth capable of creating realistic sounds. Sold over 250,000 units.
Roland D-50 (1987)
   LA synthesis with Integrated samples.
Waldorf Wave (1993)
   Digital system that created warm, analog-like sounds.
Kurzweil K2600X (2000)
   Mega synthesizer and sampling with weighted keys.

MAKING A NOISE

With the exception of the cheapest of domestic models, most electronic keyboards require additional equipment for them to be heard. This can pose something of a problem for practising and rehearsing since in gig situations, most keyboard players are connected directly through to the PA system, using no prior amplification of their own. On these pages we'll take a look at the issue of amplifying keyboard sounds, as well as some of the options for connecting to other pieces of equipment.

KEYBOARD AMPLIFIERS

Given the amount of energy many electric guitarists seem to expend on amplification issues, it may seem a little strange that a market for dedicated keyboard amplifiers barely exists. But when it comes to amplification, there is one problem uniquely peculiar to keyboards. Unlike guitars and basses, electronic keyboards have an amazingly wide frequency range.

The best reproduction would theoretically come from an amplifier and speaker system with a "flat" frequency response —the kind you would expect to find in a recording studio monitoring system, or a high-quality hi-fi. Certainly no traditional guitar amplifier and loudspeaker "combo" would be capable of dealing satisfactorily with such extremes of high and

low frequency. Not that this has stopped keyboard players throughout the ages experimenting with alternatives—fans of "low-fi" sounds can produce some extremely interesting and organic sounds using overdriven valve amplifiers.

Given that most "live" keyboard players plug their equipment into the PA system, how are they supposed to listen to themselves away from gigs? It clearly isn't an issue for owners of home studio gear—they just plug their keyboards into the mixing board. Other alternatives include connecting to a domestic hi-fi system, (*see page 27*) or using headphones.

If none of these options are possible or desirable, the best course of action is possibly to buy a cheap "solid-state" guitar practice amp—the sound might not be fantastic, but at least you'll be able to hear yourself.

LOOKING AROUND THE BACK

Most of the keyboard's external connections are found on the rear panel. We've already taken a brief look at this subject near the beginning of Chapter 2. Here is a more detailed view of the most important connecting sockets found on the majority of electronic keyboards.

THE AUDIO OUTPUTS

To get a sound from your keyboard, a standard quarter-inch "jack-to-jack" cable must be inserted into the audio output socket; the other end is plugged into the input socket of the amplifier or mixing board. The cable you need for this job can

be bought as ready-made leads in music stores. They are easy enough to make at home if you have a soldering kit, some screened audio cable, and a pair of standard quarter-inch jack plugs.

Some synths have multiple audio outputs. This reflects the fact that many modern synthesizers can produce stereo sounds. Each output has to be connected to a mixing board channel— to hear the stereo effect working in full, the pan controls on the input channel must be set so that each output can only be heard coming from one loudspeaker.

Some workstation may have a large number of audio outputs, however, where amplification or mixing facilities are limited, there is invariably a way of getting all sounds coming from a a single output.

Stereo audio outputs | Headphones output | Foot pedal sockets | Foot switch sockets | MIDI connections

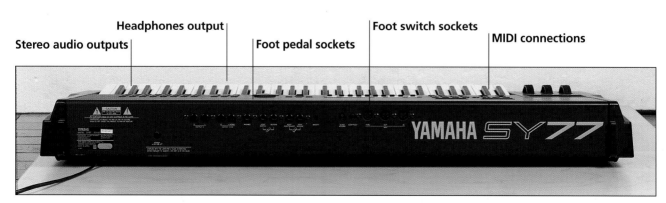

YAMAHA SY77

AMPLIFIERS AND SPEAKERS

Two fundamentally different types of amplifier are used in music: those driven by tube circuitry and those driven by "solid-state" transistor circuitry.

Guitarists have always favored the classic tube amplifier sound, which is characterized by a warmth and smoothness of tone. Tubes also produce a pleasant distortion as the volume increases. Unlike solid-state circuitry, tubes can come loose, or need periodic replacement.

Solid-state "transistor" amplifiers have a sharper, brittle characteristic. They are favored by keyboard players who value a cleaner tone. Transistors are capable of dealing with a wider range of frequencies than tube amplifiers. They also distort less at higher volumes, making them more suited to pure amplification purposes.

Although few dedicated keyboard amplifiers exist, as a rule of thumb, keyboards that are electro-mechanical—such as Hammond organs or electric pianos—are better suited to the warmer tube sound. Since purely electronic instruments, such as any synthesizers, have such a wide frequency range, they are better suited to the cleaner-sounding transistor amplifiers—at least if getting the most accurate sound is the top priority.

Although any loudspeaker can be used with a keyboard (assuming that the impedances are matched with those of the amplifier), some combinations work better than others. When using solid-state amplifiers, a clearer sound can be obtained by using different types of loudspeaker connected by "crossovers." These are electronic circuits that break up the output signals from the amplifier into frequency bands and feed each one into a separate speaker system specifically designed to deal with those frequencies. For example, large "bass bins" can be used for the bass frequencies; "piezo" horns can deal with the highest frequencies.

Unique among loudspeaker systems is the so-called "rotary" cabinet. Designed to bring extra depth to organ sounds, these systems employ a speaker that physically turns at high speed, throwing the sound out in different directions. This means that stationery listeners experience the "Dopler" phase-shifting tremolo effect. Many attempts have been made to produce a synthetic version of this sound—none have succeeded fully.

HEADPHONE OUTPUTS

This socket allows a single stereo signal to be heard over a pair of headphones. All professional audio equipment uses standard quarter-inch jack plugs. If you only have a pair of "personal stereo" headphones you will need a conversion plug, since they are only equipped with "mini-jacks." These cost very little and can be bought from any hi-fi store.

Playing over the headphones is not only useful for keeping noise levels down, but they can also allow you to hear more detail when programming sounds.

FOOT PEDALS AND FOOT SWITCHES

Foot pedals and foot switches are completely different entities. As the name suggests, a foot switch has two positions—on or off. On many electronic keyboards a foot switch can be used to sustain notes. When the switch is pressed, the note "hangs" after the finger has released the keys.

A foot pedal is a variable control. The degree of movement from the foot dictates the extent of its effect. The most common use for such a device is as a volume control, allowing dynamic changes to be made while you are playing.

Some synthesizers have assignable controls so that other elements—such as those normally associated with the performance wheels—can be controlled by the foot.

MIDI CONTROLS

Pretty well every synthesizer made since the mid-1980s has been equipped with MIDI controls. This allows connections to be made with other similarly equipped technology using 5-pin "DIN" leads.

The MIDI OUT socket can be connected to MIDI IN on a different piece of equipment allowing performance information to be transmitted from the keyboard to a sequencer or external sound module.

The MIDI IN connection allows data to be transmitted to the keyboard so that it can be used, for example, as an external sound module for a sequencer or another keyboard.

The MIDI THRU socket can be used for daisychaining several pieces of MIDI equipment. Data received by the MIDI IN socket can be transmitted unchanged from MIDI THRU. For large amounts of MIDI equipment, a patch bay is a more reliable way of making connections.

OTHER POSSIBLE CONNECTIONS

Among the other possible connections are those aimed at communication with computer hardware. Some workstations and samplers, for example, may have SCSI or USB sockets allowing large amounts of data to be quickly transferred to a computer or an external hard disk.

ALTERING SOUNDS

Few modern recordings can be heard using the "dry" sounds of a piano, organ or external MIDI keyboard module. Electronic effects can be used to produce a vastly greater range of sounds. Some of these, like reverberation and delay, are simulations of natural acoustic effects, and are used electronically to give a more natural sound to synthesized electronic voices. Others, like distortion, are used simply to create a wider and more interesting sonic palette from which to draw.

SOUND EFFECTS

If you take the output from any electronic keyboard and connect it to an amplifier or mixing board, the sound you are most likely to hear will be dry and untreated. You can breathe life into almost any keyboard sound by inserting a variety of electronic effects into the signal chain.

The earliest sound processing effects were created in the 1950s and 1960s. They were either mechanical or used crude analog electronics. These days, however, even the simplest and cheapest effects tend to be either digital simulations of natural acoustic phenomena—reverberation and echo—or completely artificial effects based largely on changes in pitch or distorting the original signal.

There are broadly two ways of creating effects. One is to take the output signal from the keyboard and plug into an external effects unit; the output from the effects unit is then passed into the amplifier or mixing board. The second is to use electronic effects that are built into the keyboard. This is an increasingly common approach.

EXTERNAL EFFECTS

The simplest and cheapest way of obtaining an electronic effect is to use a plug-in foot pedal. Most of the commonly heard effects—delay, chorus, phasing, and flanging—can be created using dedicated foot pedals. Although these are primarily used by guitarists, they are equally applicable to any keyboard.

An alternative approach to using foot pedals is to process the sound using rack-mounted professional studio effects. These essentially do the same job as foot pedals, but invariably create a more "hi-fi" sound. At their simplest, electronic effects are extremely easy to use (*see below*). All you need is an additional audio quarter-inch jack cord. The effect is inserted between the keyboard and amplifier: the keyboard is plugged into the "In" socket on the effect using one jack cord; the second jack cord is connected between the "Out" socket on the effect and the amplifier or mixing desk.

MULTIPLE EFFECTS

Electronic effects can be linked together in a "daisychain." This simply means that the output from one unit can be sent directly to the input of another. To all intents and purposes, any number of different sound effects can be joined together in this way.

Single effects units can be a relatively cheap and efficient way of changing a basic sound. However, a major drawback is that complex set-ups can become unwieldy to operate, especially when playing on stage. Additionally, most of these effects have a great number of parameters that can be changed. It is in this area that the use of the more sophisticated rack-mounted effects pays off in that it is generally possible to store individual sound programs, and recall sophisticated effects at the push of a button.

Over the past decade, this has been made even easier by the development of digital multiple effects units. This technology is capable of producing a number of different effects at the same time—at the very least, reverberation, a full range of delays, distortion and compression.

AUDIO OUT	AUDIO IN	AUDIO OUT	AUDIO IN	AUDIO OUT	AUDIO IN
KEYBOARD		**EFFECT A**		**EFFECT B**		**AMPLIFIER/MIXER**

Most professional electronic effects can be mounted in racks for tidy storage and easy portability.

STORING EFFECTS

Many of the digital effects used by modern keyboard players are designed to be fitted into the industry-standard "19-inch" rack, where they are permanently bolted in place. This is a particularly neat and safe way of storing and transporting these units.

This type of studio equipment can physically be described in terms of its height in units, or "U's" (most effects are one or two "U's" high). Racks are available to hold between 4 and 20 units of space. However if you plan on filling up one of the larger racks make sure that you fit castors first, otherwise you will have trouble moving it around.

If you are planning to cart racks of equipment around to live venues, it's a good idea to consider getting a hardy aluminium flight case which is capable of withstanding the occasional knock.

INTERNAL EFFECTS

An increasing number of electronic keyboards and digital samplers come readily equipped with their own internal collection of digital effects. Although in most cases they don't sound as smooth as those created by top professional units, they are certainly good enough for most live uses.

Internal effects are par for the course with the vast majority of "workstation" polysynths. With their vast capability for storing sounds, it becomes possible to build any of these on-board digital effects into a sound patch, which can then be recalled at the push of a button.

Most of the modern workstations also feature multiple output sockets. This means that you can easily mix and match internal effects with those produced externally.

OVERUSING TECHNOLOGY

New and exciting ways of artificially altering sound are continually finding their way into the shops and pages of music technology magazines. But whilst it's always tempting to indulge in the latest state-of-the-art fad, think carefully about its application before you shell out your hard-earned cash. Ask yourself if it REALLY will make an important contribution to your sound.

In fact, the same question applies to all new technology. New products are unleashed with a high degree of market obsolescence, and yet some of the most prized keyboard sounds of the past decade have resulted from ancient technology—old friends such as the MiniMoog synth, Hammond organ, 1980s Roland drum machines and even the Fender Rhodes electric piano.

Here are some considerations to bear in mind when using effects:

- Take great care with effects that are too obviously gimmicky. Any effect that becomes fashionable is certain to date. Even perennial sounds like reverb and delay go through fashions in which certain settings find themselves overused.

- When you first buy an effect unit, spend time working through all the possible sound permutations its parameters will allow. Units can sometimes generate interesting noises that you wouldn't have expected, or that they were not even intended to create.

- Before you use a new effect live or on a recording, try to get its novelty value out of your system. It's always tempting to smother your recordings and playing with the latest sounds and effects, but only once they've become familiar can you make balanced decisions about their potential uses.

- One final word of warning. Effects are not best viewed as an end in themselves. A bad idea or iffy piece of playing rarely (if ever) magically transforms itself simply by masking it with a sound effect.

REVERBERATION

Reverberation is a natural acoustic effect caused by a sound bouncing off the surrounding environment, such as walls, ceilings and objects, before fading away. It is heard as a part of the original sound. Think of the effect of walking through a tunnel; each footstep you take can be heard swirling around as the sound hits the walls.

The diagram at the foot of the page shows precisely how reverb works: the thick black arrow shows the sound reaching the listener directly from the source; the dotted arrows show the early reflections—the first "bounces" off the wall; the gray arrows show the effect of later multiple reflections. In this way, a complex new sound is created, the effect of which lingers on after the direct sound has passed.

ELECTRONIC SIMULATION

Reverberation is now invariably produced electronically. When added to a keyboard signal, "reverb" creates the warm, ambient effect of the sound spreading out.

Simulated reverb effects were originally created in the 1950s using a small spring that was vibrated by the audio signal. Over the next two decades, electronics manufacturers attempted a variety of analog recreations of the sound, but these failed to find too much favor with musicians and producers. It was during the early 1980s that digital reverb first appeared. Initially costing thousands of pounds, these first units were a revelation, allowing the user the luxury of programming parameters based on the attributes of natural reverberation, such as the size, shape, and sound-damping features of an imaginary room.

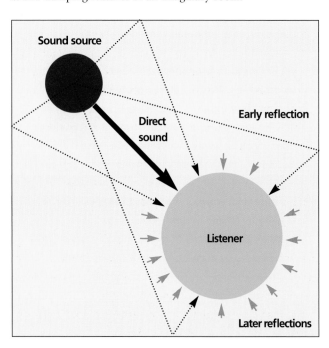

In a studio situation, high-quality reverb is easily the most essential effect. It is reverb that breathes life into "dead" sounds. Keyboards, guitars, lead vocals and drums are rarely mixed down without some reverberation.

DELAY EFFECTS

Most of the other popular electronic effects are created by manipulating a repeating signal. Like reverberation, DELAY is a natural effect produced by a sound being reflected from a distant surface.

Delay effects were originally produced by mechanical means, using what amounted to a cut-down version of a reel-to-reel tape recorder fitted with a continuous loop of quarter-inch tape. The signal was captured by a record head, and then replayed by a series of playback heads. The best-known early model was the famous Watkins Copycat, first produced in 1954. Although these units suffered from poor quality sound and limited frequency response, they created a unique effect that still remains popular today. Indeed, you can see a contemporary equivalent to this effect on page 166, in the form of a computer "plug-in."

Delay effects are now almost entirely produced digitally. Different types of sound can be created by varying the length of the delay.

PHASING

The effect of phasing occurs when the same signal is played back from two different sources at the same time. Every sound comprises a soundwave that passes from peaks to troughs. When two identical signals are slightly out of alignment and the peaks on one signal tie up with the troughs on another, the effect is known as "phase cancellation"—it produces a "sweeping" sound. A delay of between 7 and 12 milliseconds is necessary to create phasing effects.

Phasing is commonly associated with the psychedelic rock sounds of the late-1960s—the first successful song to make use of the effect was the Small Faces' 1967 hit "Itchycoo Park." The effect was produced by playing the same recording simultaneously from two tape recorders—inconsistencies in the speed of the motors took the two signals out of alignment. After falling from fashion during the 1980s, phase effects have since been widely used on numerous dance hits.

FLANGING

Flanging is an extension of phasing. If the delay is greater—between 12 and 20 milliseconds—the sweep becomes more dramatic and "metallic."

COMPRESSORS, LIMITERS AND NOISE GATES

The term "dynamic range" refers to differences between the maximum and minimum volume levels for any audio signal. Some instruments possess a very wide dynamic range, meaning that at various times the overall signal will be naturally too loud and at other times it will be too quiet. A compressor is used to prevent this happening.

In brief, a "threshold" control dictates the volume above which the compression takes effect. When the overall signal is below that level it is left untouched. A manual "ratio" control sets the degree to which the signal is to be compressed once the threshold figure has been passed. Most reasonable-quality compressors also include "attack" and "release" controls to create smoother changes in volume.

Some compressors double up as limiters. This is a much cruder effect than the compressor in that signals passing a preset threshold simply have their gain cut.

Working rather in the reverse way to a limiter, a noise gate is used to shut out unwanted signals. In this case, a threshold setting on the unit dictates the level at which the signal can be heard. Until the audio signal reaches that level nothing at all can be heard.

The noise gate is arguably at its most valuable in the recording chain. By connecting to an audio recorder of any sort via a noise gate you can avoid the kinds of extraneous noises—electrical buzzing, pops and hisses—that can easily find their way onto a recording. Although these are difficult to hear in the context of a mix, they can play a part in "muddying" the sound.

CHORUS AND ADT

Like phasing and flanging, all delay effects were originally created by recording a signal on two tape machines, and then playing them back at the same time. Electronic simulations of these effects were created by adding pitch modulation and speed controls to alter the delayed signal.

ADT ("automatic double tracking") and "chorus" are two such effects. Adding variations in pitch to a delayed signal can create the effect of doubling up the performance. Chorus extends this effect by modulating a number of repeats. As the delay is still very fast, the sound produced gives a rich sustain. ADT and chorus effects require a delay of between 20 and 35 milliseconds.

ADT and chorus effects can be most effective when the original signal is panned to the opposite extreme on the stereo spectrum. This "opens out" the sound, creating the effect of multiple performances.

ECHO

When a signal is sufficiently delayed that the repeated signal can be heard as a distinct sound, this is an echo. A single fast repeat played back at the same volume as the original signal is known as "slap-back" echo.

Echo effects have been used since the early days of rock and roll, most notably on vocals and guitars. Later experiments saw musicians playing with longer delay times.

PITCH SHIFTING/HARMONIZATION

One of the more advanced digital delay effects to achieve widespread popularity over the past two decadse is the pitch shifter or harmonizer unit. These effects generate a preset harmony line from any input signal. The principle on which it operates is that the original signal is delayed by the shortest possible time it takes to turn the audio signal into a digital sample that can be replayed at a different speed.

Most pitch shifter units have a range of a single octave above and below the incoming signal, with half-step "click-stops" in between. For example, if the pitch control is increased to play a perfect 5th, every signal that goes into the unit will come out a perfect 5th higher. If the original signal is mixed in with the output from the effect then automatic harmonies are created. Since the repeated signal is heavily processed, the sound quality can sometimes deteriorate badly.

Some of the more sophisticated units are capable of generating high-quality four-and five-part harmonies. These are often used in live situations to provide backing vocals.

DISTORTION

Although fuzz and distortion effects are most widely used by guitarists, recent times have seen an increase in its popularity among keyboard players.

The principle is relatively simple: a signal is fed into a low-powered amplifier (or pre-amplifier) where the volume is increased to the point of distortion. The treated signal is then itself boosted by a "clean" power amplifier.

Although many electronic simulations exist, the best distortion sounds are created using a tube amplifier.

INTRODUCING MIDI

When MIDI (Musical Instrument Digital Interface) first appeared in 1983, few could have foreseen the impact it would have on the world of electronic music. MIDI represented a new global standard by which electronic instruments could communicate with one another, meaning that suitably equipped keyboards could be connected to other keyboards, drum machines, sequencers and computers. Without MIDI the evolution of electronic dance music simply wouldn't have happened. MIDI has made the keyboard the central instrument in most contemporary music.

WHAT IS MIDI?

Before the inception of MIDI, systems for linking different pieces of equipment did exist and were widely used, however they were largely unique to each manufacturer. Thus, for example, a synthesizer produced by Yamaha could not be controlled by a sequencer made by Roland or Korg.

The drive to create an alternative system came in the early 1980s. The most important figure in this development was Dave Smith of the American Sequential Circuits company. His proposal for a universal system interface met with interest from other manufacturers, and a forum was created that would soon see the birth of MIDI, and a revolution in the way music was made.

PROTOCOL AGREEMENT

A number of different approaches were considered before the MIDI protocol was unanimously adopted. Under considerable influence from Japanese manufacturers, the eventual solution was a system by which data would be transmitted between suitably equipped machines at a rate of 31.25 KBaud (31,250 bits per second, divided into eight-bit "words"). The different types of MIDI function would be identified with digital "markers." Since transmission was serial, only one "event" would be sent at a time, but it was thought that the high speed of data transfer would prevent problems with the timing of information.

The first synthesizers to be equipped with a MIDI operating system were the Sequential Circuits Prophet 600 and the staggeringly popular Yamaha DX7, both of which were launched at the end of 1983. No serious music technology has since appeared without MIDI fitted.

MIDI CONNECTIONS

To communicate with any other piece of MIDI equipment, a keyboard needs at the very least a MIDI IN and MIDI OUT socket. Instruments are connected using cables terminated by regular 5-pin DIN plugs. By connecting the MIDI OUT socket on one machine to the MIDI IN on another a variety of different kinds of data can be transmitted and received.

MIDI FUNCTIONS

MIDI has three distinct but related functions: "recording" keyboard performances; "triggering" other MIDI sound modules; and the storage and transmission of information about sound.

By far the most common MIDI function is in what was once generally referred to as SEQUENCING. By connecting a keyboard to a MIDI sequencer (now more usually simply called a MIDI recorder), it is possible for complete multitrack performances of songs to be captured without storing the sounds themselves on tape or hard disk.

MIDI RECORDING

The principles of MIDI recording are relatively simple. The sequencer records an incoming MIDI signal. The information about that performance is then stored—this will typically include the pitch of the note, its duration and its volume. THE SOUND ITSELF IS NOT RECORDED; it is simply a set of MIDI commands.

To play back the recording, a MIDI OUT signal is sent back to the keyboard where it triggers the internal sounds. Since no audio signal is ever recorded, it's possible to select a completely different sound for playback on the keyboard. You might have recorded the original part using a piano sound on your synthesizer, but you can play back that same performance on a violin, trumpet or any other sound you have programmed in the same keyboard. In fact, any piece of music recorded via MIDI can be played back using the sounds of ANY MIDI-equipped module.

A MIDI recorder works in much the same way as a regular multitrack recorder. To differentiate between the different tracks, each separate performance can be allocated

MIDI DEVICES

MIDI KEYBOARDS

Any electronic keyboard fitted with MIDI IN, MIDI OUT and MIDI THRU sockets. Keyboard performances—note pitches, durations and volumes—can be transmitted to MIDI sequencers or other keyboards. Can also receive transmissions from other MIDI instruments.

MIDI SEQUENCER/RECORDER

Hardware or software that captures MIDI data transmitted from a keyboard. Works on the same principle as a multitrack tape recorder, although MIDI data can be easily edited. Sound parameters from some types of synthesizer can also be stored.

MIDI DRUM MACHINE

Electronic device that enables a musician to program drum rhythms. Usually contains built-in samples from "real" drums that can be triggered according to the programming. Each different drum voice is assigned a note value, so if a keyboard is connected to the drum machine's MIDI IN, its drum sounds can be played back from the keyboard.

MIDI DIGITAL SAMPLER

Unit that stores digital recordings that can be played back via a MIDI keyboard, sequencer or drum machine. A sample is assigned a range of notes—the speed of playback (the pitch of the sound) is determined by the note value of the incoming MIDI signal.

MIDI EXTERNAL SOUND MODULE

A synthesizer or other sound generation module that has no keyboard of its own, but requires a MIDI input signal from another source to trigger a noise.

MOTHER KEYBOARD

MIDI keyboard that is incapable of producing any sounds of its own, but is designed only to trigger external sound modules. Often takes the form of a "weighted" piano-style keyboard.

---

one of 16 MIDI channels. This means that 16 different MIDI sounds or modules can be played back at the same time—assuming you have that many external MIDI devices at your disposal. A major advantage of this approach is that the outputs from each sound module can be connected directly to a mixing board without ever having been consigned to a multitrack tape. This is known as "first-generation sound," which guarantees a completely clean audio signal.

EDITING FEATURES

Another area in which MIDI beats other forms of recording is that since a performance is stored as numerical data any element can be altered after the event. This means that "bum" notes and poor timing can be corrected, and entire songs (or sections of a song) can be transposed to play back in a different key.

All in all, MIDI offers keyboard players an amazing degree of flexibility—you'll see that when we work through a complete MIDI recording on page 158.

COMPUTER OPTIONS

One of the main problems with using a dedicated MIDI sequencer was that the editing process was often quite messy, especially when the information had to be viewed within an LCD screen a few inches in size. Things have changed radically in this area over the past decade.

The vast majority of MIDI recording is now performed using sophisticated computer software such as Cubase, Logic Audio and Performer. Using these programs, it becomes possible to move and edit notes by manipulating a mouse whilst viewing a large monitor screen. Tracks of data can be seen as horizontal bars running across the screen, meaning that whole sections of a song can be copied and pasted to a new position, or deleted altogether.

ADDING AUDIO

The most recent global development in MIDI's evolution has been the integration of digital audio. The rapid increase in processing speeds among each successive generation of new computer system has made made high-quality digital audio recording—once only affordable to professionals—a reality for most musicians. As a result, the designers and manufacturers of MIDI software have sought to integrate audio as seamlessly as possible with their existing MIDI functions. Tracks of audio data now sit alongside tracks of MIDI data; each can be copied, pasted, cut and edited using broadly similar principles.

GETTING CONNECTED

A MIDI system can be as simple or as complicated as a person's musical requirements. A fairly basic set-up would consist of a multi-timbral MIDI keyboard (one that can generate a number of different sounds at the same time) and some kind of MIDI event recorder.

WHAT DO YOU NEED?

Deciding on the kind of MIDI system you want to create will depend on what you want to be able to do with it and how much you want to spend. Let's start with MIDI recording. Although some musicians still prefer to use dedicated MIDI sequencers—specially built "boxes" that do nothing apart from recording MIDI events—it is now more common to use a personal computer equipped with MIDI software.

THE WORKSTATION OPTION

However, there is a third option that is seriously worth contemplating, especially if you are less interested in getting involved with the nitty-gritty of technology. This is the use of a MIDI "workstation"—a keyboard with a built-in MIDI sequencer. This has the major benefit of having everything—keyboard, sounds and sequencer—in a single unit. Since the components are all designed together, you don't have to go through the connection nightmares than can afflict computer systems. Using a workstation keyboard it's possible to make high-quality, professional MIDI recordings. The downside is that

although this is the most straightforward option, such keyboards can be very expensive and exhibit limited sequencing capabilities.

SOFTWARE SEQUENCING

If you have a home computer and are reasonably adept at basic functions such as installing programs and tweaking the various control parameters, then you'll have little problem with the software option. However, there are a number of other pieces of equipment that you need to obtain before you can get your system up and running. Here is a basic list of the things you need:

- **Computer (PC or Apple Macintosh)**
- **MIDI recording software**
- **MIDI-equipped keyboard**
- **MIDI-computer interface unit**
- **MIDI leads; one for each link in each direction**
- **MIDI patch bay (optional)**
- **Additional MIDI sound modules (optional)**

The diagram below shows a very basic MIDI studio set-up. Since few computers are readily equipped with MIDI IN and

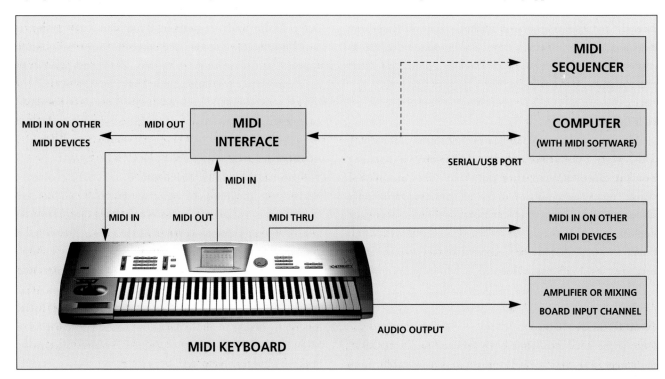

SEQUENCER PROS AND CONS

Each type of MIDI recorder has its own set of benefits and drawbacks. Although it's clear that as far as music technology is concerned, computer-based everything is widely seen as the way forward, it's up to you to decide the way you want to work.

SOFTWARE SEQUENCERS

- Limited only by the quality of computer.
- Unrivalled in flexibility.
- Visually easy to edit.
- Potential for integration of audio recording.
- Heavily supported by technology industries.
- Software constantly under improvement.
- Easy to synchronize to other equipment.
- Requires "technical" attitude.
- Requires you to own a computer.
- Computer technology can be frustrating.
- Software dates quickly.
- Getting connections to work can be a nightmare.
- Computer and hard disk crashes can be a disaster.

DEDICATED SEQUENCERS

- Cheap.
- Simple to operate.
- More reliable than software option.
- Visually difficult to edit.
- Not as intuitive as software.
- Requires external sound devices to be of any use.
- An old-fashioned (if effective) approach to the job.
- Limited data storage.

MIDI WORKSTATION

- Self-contained unit.
- Includes keyboard, sequencer and sounds.
- All connections are internal.
- Portable "studio in a box."
- More reliable than software option.
- Works well as quick and easy musical notebook.
- Easier to handle for "non-technical" users.
- Limited facilities by software standards.
- Limited data storage.

MIDI OUT sockets, the trickiest part of getting connected is in figuring out how to link a keyboard to the computer. This requires a MIDI interface—a tiny box containing a number of MIDI IN and OUT sockets for connecting to musical equipment and another socket for transmitting and receiving data to and from the computer. This connects either to a serial or USB port, depending on your computer.

To make a recording, the MIDI OUT socket on your keyboard must be connected to MIDI IN on the interface. Similarly, to play back a recording, MIDI OUT on the interface must be connected to MIDI IN on the keyboard.

Many MIDI interfaces feature at least four MIDI outputs. This means that at least a further three MIDI devices can easily be added to the configuration. It is also possible to "daisychain" MIDI devices connecting MIDI THRU from one unit to MIDI IN on another. This approach can result in a slight but perceptible delaying in some MIDI signals. If you have a large number of MIDI devices, the most effective way of linking them is to purchase a MIDI patchbay.

CHOOSING A COMPUTER

If you already own a computer, some of the options you have at your disposal will be dictated by your machine, its operating system and the speed at which it can process data. Buying a computer from scratch gives you more scope, although before making a decision, you need to assess the kinds of musical activities you want to perform. If it really is just basic MIDI sequencing, then pretty well any computer produced over the past decade would be powerful enough to do the job. The choice becomes more difficult if you want to integrate audio with your MIDI recordings—most of the best sequencers now have this capability, but it does require certain levels of processing power.

There are two types of home computer in general use. The PC accounts for the vast majority of the world's home computers. Although many different manufacturers produce PCs, the vast majority of them are run with a Microsoft operating system (usually a version of Windows). The other serious option is the Apple Macintosh.

Comparisons between PCs and Macs are rather pointless, and often stir up inexplicably heated passions among users. But whilst both machines can do the job if equipped, there's no question that the majority of serious professional users favour the Apple Macintosh, which is more user-friendly, has a superior operating system and a better reputation for reliability. PCs, on the other hand, offer better value for money since both hardware and software is invariably cheaper than that designed for the Mac.

We'll discuss some of the possibilities of integrating audio with MIDI in a little more detail on page 164.

INSIDE MIDI

For all of its versatility and significance in modern music, MIDI is a pretty straightforward system for anyone to operate. Over the next two pages we'll delve a little more deeply into the way MIDI works, looking at how you can harness its power to the benefit of your keyboard playing and programming.

MIDI CHANNELS

The key to understanding the way MIDI works is to remember that there are two distinct processes at work: data transmission and data reception. Just because two machines are correctly linked via MIDI, there is still no guarantee that they will be able to "speak" to one another. Think, for example, of the way in which a television picks up its signals: the transmission will be "available," but it isn't until the TV set is programmed to receive that particular signal that a picture appears.

A single MIDI connection can contain information for up to sixteen different instruments. These can either be external MIDI sound modules, soft synths running alongside a computer sequencer or multi-timbral modules capable of playing back more than one of their pre-programmed voices at the same time. The way in which these MIDI messages (referred to as EVENTS) are distinguished from one another is by having a unique number prefix from 1 to 16. This is the MIDI CHANNEL. For a pair of MIDI connections to work properly, both the transmitter and receiver must be set to the same MIDI channel.

Here is an example of how multiple channels work in practice. The list on the right represents tracks on a sequencer which has its MIDI OUT connected to the MIDI IN on eight different sound sources.

- **1   Digital Piano Module**
- **2   Digital Sampler (violin)**
- **3   Digital Sampler (cello)**
- **4   Digital Sampler (viola)**
- **5   Digital Sampler (choir)**
- **6   Digital Sampler (trumpet)**
- **7   Digital Sampler (brass ensemble)**
- **8   Digital Sampler (percussion)**
- **9   Drum Machine A (bass/snare drum)**
- **10   Drum Machine B (cymbals)**
- **11   External Synth module A (alternative bass)**
- **12   External Synth module A (bass notes)**
- **13   External Synth module B (organ)**
- **14   External Synth module B (filter sweep)**
- **15   Soft Synth A (internal MIDI connection)**
- **16   Soft Synth B (internal MIDI connection)**

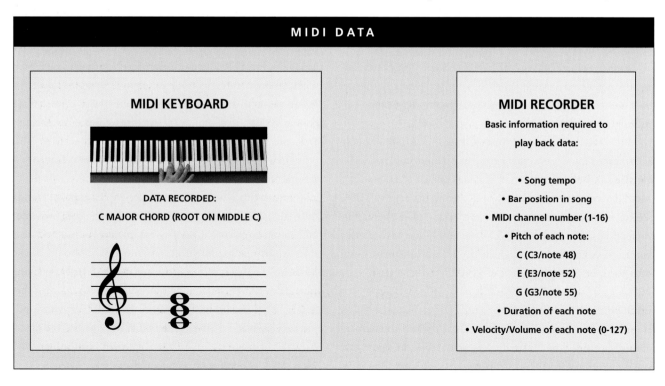

MIDI DATA

MIDI KEYBOARD

DATA RECORDED:

C MAJOR CHORD (ROOT ON MIDDLE C)

MIDI RECORDER

Basic information required to
play back data:

- Song tempo
- Bar position in song
- MIDI channel number (1-16)
  - Pitch of each note:
    C (C3/note 48)
    E (E3/note 52)
    G (G3/note 55)
  - Duration of each note
- Velocity/Volume of each note (0-127)

All of these independent pieces of equipment are connected in one way or another: the piano, sampler, drum machines and external synth modules could be connected through a patchbay or "daisychained" using their MIDI THRU sockets (*see page 148*); the two soft synths are assigned internally.

Now comes the trickiest part. Each MIDI module must have its correct channel number set. Different machines use different methods to achieve this, so you may need to consult operating manuals to find these instructions. This is a crucial process, though. If the digital piano module is assigned to receive signals from MIDI channel 2, then when the sequencer is played back, the data intended to be heard with a violin sound on the digital sampler will also trigger the piano module.

CONFUSED?

If you are completely new to MIDI, some of this can seem a little arcane, but it really is all quite logical. The one distinction you need to get clear in your mind is that whatever form it takes, MIDI is ONLY about similarly equipped machines passing strings of numbers back and forth, it has NOTHING AT ALL to do with audio signals.

MIDI EVENTS

The most important data MIDI communicates is related to the notes themselves. Each different pitch has its own unique MIDI identity. The diagram across the page shows a C major chord being played. Middle C is known to MIDI as "C3" and has a numerical value of 48. Similarly, the notes E and G (E3 and G3) have values of 52 and 55 respectively.

On some pieces of equipment, such as a rhythm machine or drum voice module, each individual sound is allocated to a particular key. For example, many traditional MIDI drum machines have default pitch values of a 36 (C2) for the bass drum and 38 (D2) for the snare drum.

PROGRAM DATA

MIDI can control other aspects of a keyboard performance, such as selecting sounds from a bank of presets. This is done using PROGRAM CHANGE messages, which takes the form of a code between 0 and 127. This can be used for two purposes. For a start, with every MIDI module capable of making so many different sounds, it makes life a lot easier when you don't have to worry about finding the patches you originally used. Secondly, you can use this MIDI message to change patches in the middle of a song. For example, if you only have one sound module, but want different sounds to be played during verse and choruses, the program change message can do this.

MIDI can also allow for other performance data to be sent. For example, information can be sent from the pitch and modulation wheels, or many other synthesizer controls, such as filters, which can be programmed to "sweep"—an effect used widely on modern dance music.

This kind of data can be either be recorded onto a sequencer during the performance or after the event. In the latter case, the notes would be played first and then a second track is recorded for the same MIDI channel in which the various controls are tweaked.

GENERAL MIDI

Storing patch information is all very well for set-ups that always use the same equipment. However, sound patch numbers on different machines may not create the same types of sound. During the 1990s, manufacturers sought to make life a little easier by trying to standardize sounds with program numbers. In doing so, they created GENERAL MIDI. This means that any equipment bearing the "General MIDI" logo has the same types of sound allocated to the same program numbers.

THE PROBLEM WITH MIDI...

MIDI transfers information at a rapid rate. However, this data is transmitted serially, which means that one event is passed after another. If a chord is played, what you hear is the individual notes being sounded very quickly. In most cases, the timing differences—or LATENCY—is not really perceptible. However, this can become a problem when a lot of data is being transferred simultaneously. For example, if every MIDI channel played ten or more notes on the same beat, then not all of that data would be transferred in time.

One way of overcoming this problem has been with the introduction of multiple sets of MIDI channels on some pieces of equipment. For example, on software sequencers, it's possible to set up two independent MIDI systems, each transmitted by a different port on the computer, and each with its own MIDI interface.

In the example across the page, unplugging the digital sampler's MIDI leads and reconnecting them to a second MIDI interface would drastically reduce latency. The only reprogramming needed is the reconfiguration of channels 2–8 on the sequencer so that this data could be transmitted from the second MIDI output.

DIGITAL SAMPLING

One of the most exciting technological developments to hit the music world over the past two decades has been digital sampling. Keyboards and external devices with sampling capabilities can be used to create life-like approximations of "real" instruments by recording an audio signal and playing it back at different pitches. Sampling can also be used to create and play back rhythm loops containing drums and percussion or segments of a complete piece of music.

SAMPLING HISTORY

From the birth of the synthesizer in the 1960s, rather than create a whole new sonic palette from which musicians could draw, designers and programmers had always sought to recreate the sounds of existing instruments. So it should have come as no surprise to find that when a type of keyboard emerged that could play back the sounds of real instruments it would be popular.

The true precursor to the digital sampler was a British-designed keyboard called the Mellotron, which emerged at the same time as Robert Moog's first synthesizers. Like the modern-day sampler, this instrument could play back the sounds of real instruments, albeit in the form of loops of pre-recorded tape.

Although others had experimented with the idea, the Fairlight CMI, launched in 1979, was the first genuine digital sampling keyboard. It was soon followed onto the market by the cheaper American E-mu Emulator. By the late 1980s low-cost digital samplers had been launched by most of the Japanese music technology manufacturers and were featuring on most of the chart hits of the day. Furthermore, most of the string, brass and other orchestral sounds heard on advertisements and film soundtracks were generated by digital sampling keyboards.

PLAYING WITH THE GROOVE

But sampling isn't only about being able to copy real musical instruments. One of its most widely used aspects is the capability for recording and manipulating whole segments of existing tracks for looping and reprocessing. This is especially popular in the production of drum loops for dance music. Sampling gradually moved into the realm of computer recording, which was ideal since the soundwaves that made up the sample could be viewed and manipulated on screen.

The image below is a drum loop taken from a piece of editing software. It is very simple to see what is happening from the pulses on the soundwave, which can be directly translated into beats of a bar. Segments of the soundwave can be copied, cut and pasted as if they were pieces of text in a word processor.

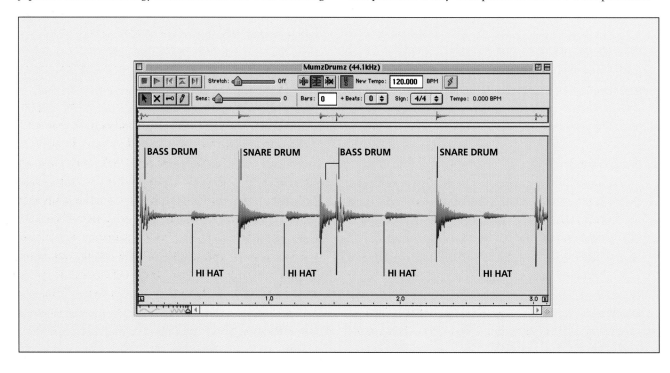

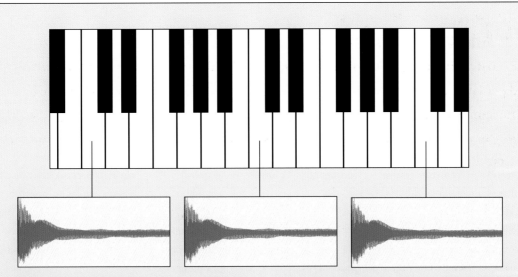

A single sample is triggered over an entire keyboard. The soundwave was recorded at its correct pitch on MIDDLE C (centre). Each time Middle C is pressed, the sample will be replayed at the correct pitch.

When C below Middle C is pressed (left) the sample is replayed at half its original speed, making it twice as long, but half the frequency, and hence one octave lower in pitch.

Similarly, when the highest C is pressed (right), the sample is replayed at twice its original speed. This halves its length but doubles its frequency, and raises its pitch by an octave.

SAMPLING ON THE KEYBOARD

There are two distinct ways in which samples can be played back from a MIDI keyboard. A sample can be allocated to a single key or a range of keys.

It's typical for percussive samples or short melodic "hits" to be allocated a single key. For example, this basic drum kit could be set up on a sampler using a note range of a single octave:

C	Bass Drum
C♯	Snare Drum
D	Rim Shot
D♯	Low Tom
E	Medium Tom
F	High Tom
F♯	Closed Hi-Hat
G	Open Hi-Hat
G♯	Ride Cymbal
A	Crash Cymbal
A♯	Tambourine
B	Shaker
C	Triangle

The alternative is shown at the top of the page, where one sample has been allocated a note range of two whole octaves.

This means that depending on which key is pressed, the same sample is replayed at a different pitch. The fundamental principle on which digital samplers operate is the speed at which a sound is played back. As you already know, the act of doubling the frequency of a soundwave increases its pitch by one octave. This means that a sample triggered by pressing Middle C will be played back at twice the speed as the same sample triggered by pressing the note one octave above Middle C—which also makes the pitch of the sample one octave higher.

SAMPLING MEMORY

The only realistic limit on the number of samples that can be accessed at any given time is the internal memory capacity of the sampler. This is measured in megabytes (Mb) of RAM (Random Access Memory). Using the industry standard sample rate of 44.1 kHz (this is the number of times the signal is sampled per second), stereo CD-quality audio takes up somewhere in the region of 10Mb per minute. The latest generation of samplers usually come equipped with 4Mb of RAM, so that means only 24 seconds of stereo sampling. Additional RAM can be installed by plugging in extra SIMMs (Single In-line Memory Modules) to a maximum of 128Mb. That considerably boosts the potential power of the unit.

DIGITAL SAMPLING ON-BOARD FUNCTIONS

Digital samplers can do a good deal more than simply record and play back sounds. There are also many useful ways in which sounds can be edited.

Samplers typically contain many of the filtering functions associated with other types of synthesizer. For example, filtering, envelope generators and low-frequency oscillators (*see page 138*) can be applied to individual samples or entire banks of samples. On some of the more up-market models, EQ and an array of digital effects can also be programmed in.

SAMPLE EDITORS

One of the problems users of sampling keyboards face is that whilst editing functions are usually very powerful, even the best LCD screens are too small to use effectively. One solution is to use a sample editor on a computer.

To make this work, the sample has to be transferred from the sampling keyboard to the computer—this can be done via MIDI, although a much faster option is to link the sampler to the computer via SCSI (pronounced "scuzzy") connections.

SAMPLE FORMATS

It is at this point that the issue of sample file formats arises. The most significant producers—Akai, E-Mu and Yamaha—each have their own exclusive file formats. Furthermore, digital recordings on PCs use the "WAV" file, whereas Macintosh users are more familiar with the "AIFF" format. You don't need to know too much about each format, other than that they are not interchangeable.

This means that when transferring files between a sampler and a computer, it's crucial that you are clear that the software you use can read your sampler's files, and that it can also write them back once the processing has been completed. Some of the better sample editors can deal with multiple file formats and can thus be used to handle pretty well any possible format. The images you can see at the foot of the page are all taken from a well-known sample editor called TIME BANDIT.

STRETCHING TIME

Samplers alter the pitch of a sound by speeding up and slowing down sounds. This is fine if the sample is, for example, the sound of an instrument sustaining a single note. If, however, the sample contains rhythmic sounds, speeding up

1. Select the sample that you want to process from the contents menu.

2. Choose TIME CORRECTION from the processing options.

Data relating to the original soundfile.

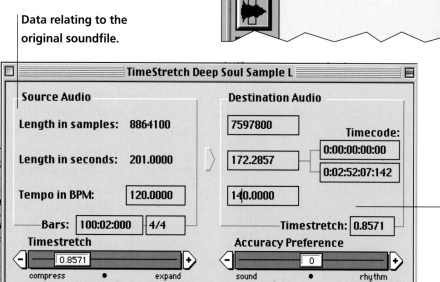

3. Enter the tempo to which you want your sample to be stretched and then click on the PROCESS button.

Data relating to the new soundfile.

4. The time-stretched sample is given a new file name (so that you can easily revert to the old version if required) and appears in its own window where it can be viewed and played using the transport controls.

the sample will also speed up the rhythm recorded on the sample.

Let's look at this from another angle. If you have a drum loop that plays at 120 BPM (beats per minute) but you want it to play at 140 BPM, you have the option of speeding up the sample. However, this will also speed up the frequencies that create the drum sounds, creating an unnatural "Mickey Mouse" effect. To alter the tempo of the rhythm but retain the original characteristics of the sample requires a process known as TIME STRETCHING.

To increase the tempo of the sample's rhythm without altering the pitch, the processing removes tiny amounts of data at equal spaces along the sample and then smooths out the result. To do the reverse, the processing has to add small amounts of data.

The Time Bandit software is capable of stretching according to a number of different criteria. You can specify a new sample length either in seconds or bytes. Other software gives the option of altering the sample length, pitch and tempo by a fixed percentage.

If you know the existing tempo, it's also possible to specify a new tempo in beats per minute, This is especially handy if you are using loops from a sample CD, where the tempo is invariably noted.

Although this process is undoubtedly very clever, it can't work miracles. The greater the processing, the less natural the results. As a rule of thumb, you are unlikely to notice any processing under around 5 per cent in either direction; for more than 20 per cent the difference will be clearly audible, although it can be used as an interesting effect in its own right.

SAMPLE CDS

One of the reasons that sampling is so popular is because of its fundamental simplicity. Unlike even the simplest of analog or digital synthesis systems, absolutely anyone can understand the basic principles of digital sampling.

Another reason is that it allows for the creation of quality-sounding music without the need for vast amounts of equipment and years of musical training.

One of the most popular ways of creating new music is through the use of pre-recorded sample CDs. These are put together by studio producers and musicians specifically to be loaded in to a sampler. They can contain anything from basic drum kits to full orchestras and choirs. They are also usually copyright-free.

HARDWARE SAMPLING VERSUS SOFTWARE SAMPLING

The first digital samplers were dedicated keyboards. Although leading manufacturers such as Kurzweil have continued this trend, the majority of samplers are now bought as rack-mounted MIDI sound modules for connection to a separate MIDI keyboard.

However, recent times have seen a number of technology designers launching their own software-based samplers. These are fully functional samplers that use the processing power of a computer to perform its actions. Since there is no special hardware needed—apart from a soundcard on PC systems (*see page 164*) — they retail at around 20 per cent of the price of a rack-mounted unit. All of this begs the question as to

why anyone would buy the "real thing" if the cheaper alternative could do the job just as well.

The main reason is that computer-based sampling requires a lot of processing power to work. That means a state-of-the-art computer is needed. Another problem is that many of the people to whom the idea appeals are already running audio/MIDI sequencers on their computers, making it difficult to integrate the two functions without a degree of technical heartache.

Computer-based sampling is still in its infancy, but is certain to become widely accepted in future. However, there will always be those for whom a dedicated piece of hardware is a more attractive prospect.

CREATING A NEW TRACK

Now that you've got your basic MIDI system connected, here's how to make a simple recording. This example uses a software sequencer called CUBASE, which is one of the popular music programs for computers. It doesn't really matter which sequencer you use, though: the alternatives may look slightly different, but they all work on broadly the same principles.

CREATING A NEW SONG

The first thing you need to do after loading up the software is to create a new song. Like other sequencers, Cubase automatically loads up a blank song. Before you do anything else, it's a good idea to give your song a working title, and then save it under this name.

Each individual MIDI part you record is known as a "track," which is assigned a MIDI channel number. Before you start to make a recording you must create a new track in which your MIDI information can be stored. In Cubase, you use the "CREATE TRACK" command (found in the "STRUCTURE" menu), which sets up an entry called "Track 1." To prepare the track for recording, click on the track's name in the track list. The entry is highlighted.

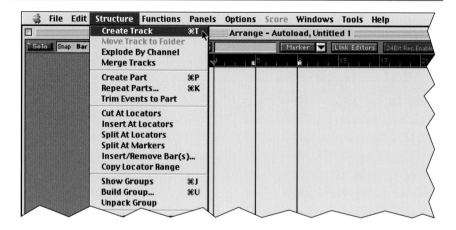

To make the sequencer work, use the features in the Transport window (see below). If you don't have a drum or other rhythm part recorded you can play to a mechanical beat by lighting up the "CLICK" button on the Transport window. Finally, before you start recording, enter the speed of the song (in beats per minute) in the tempo box.

TRACK LIST | CURSOR

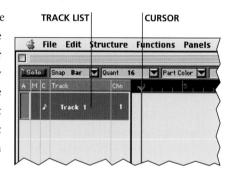

TRANSPORT CONTROLS

The Transport Window contains the functions that control the running of

the sequencer. As you see below, they work in much the same way as the controls of a regular tape recorder. If you click on the "RECORD" button, the software will

start running and the cursor in the main window will move. Any parts you play from a connected MIDI keyboard will be recorded by the software.

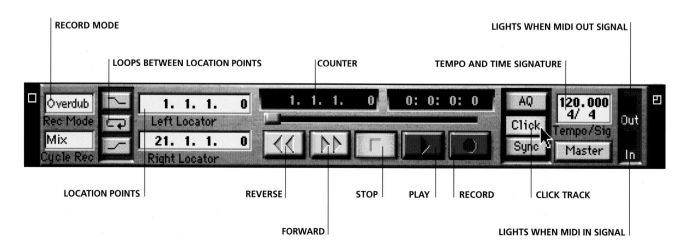

PLAYING BACK A TRACK

When you have finished recording, click on the "STOP" button in the Transport Window. You will see that a horizontal block appears alongside the track within the window. You can see how many bars of music you have recorded by looking at the bar measures at the top of the window. The vertical marks within the block indicate the exact position where the notes have been played. To play back the track, double-click on the "STOP" button (even though the song has already stopped, this will take the cursor back to the start of bar one), and then click on the "PLAY" button. If everything is connected properly you should hear the part you just recorded being played back.

EDITING NOTES

One of the great things about MIDI recording is that if you make a mistake, you don't have to re-record the whole thing from scratch—you can alter the offending notes. To make these changes to Track 1, double-click anywhere on the track's horizontal bar in the song's main window. This opens the Key Window. As the examples on the right illustrate, the Key Window breaks down the contents of the main window (at the top of the page) into a further series of horizontal bars, each one representing a note being played. To alter the pitch of the note, you perform a simple drag-and-drop exercise, clicking on the offending bar, dragging it to the correct position and releasing it. If you want to delete a bar, click to highlight and then press the Delete key on your computer keyboard.

This is a VERY basic overview of MIDI recording. You'll see some of the more complex possibilities shown over the next few pages.

CURSOR **BAR MEASURES**

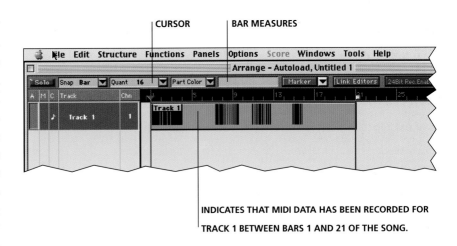

INDICATES THAT MIDI DATA HAS BEEN RECORDED FOR TRACK 1 BETWEEN BARS 1 AND 21 OF THE SONG.

NOTE PITCH **NOTE START POINT** **NOTE END POINT**

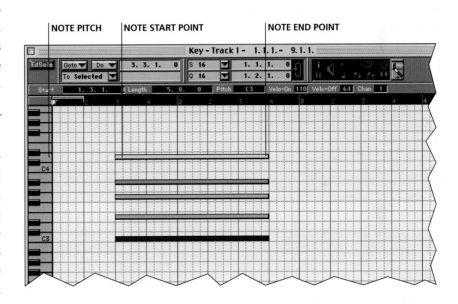

CLICK ON THE NOTE AND DRAG TO A DIFFERENT POSITION TO SELECT A NEW NOTE.

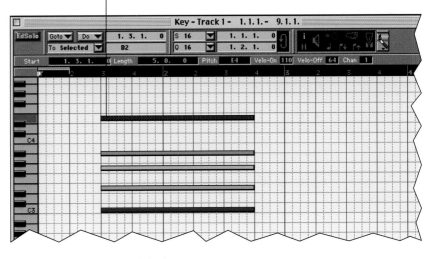

MAKING A MIDI RECORDING

You've just seen an overview of how a MIDI track can be created from scratch. Over the next few pages we'll take a more detailed look at MIDI programming, constructing a song one track at a time. In doing so we'll touch on areas such as drum sounds, bass lines and using score-reading facilities. All of the examples shown are using a CUBASE VST software sequencer running on an Apple Macintosh computer. Although they may look a little different, the other main software sequencers all work in much the same way.

DRUM MACHINES

All software sequencers feature a special window in which rhythms can be programmed. Before you start, if you want to program a drum part you need access to a set of MIDI drum sounds. These may come from drum machines, drum sounds stored in an electronic keyboard or external MIDI device, or from a digital sampler. Each of these sounds will already have been assigned a MIDI note name that must be reflected within the sequencer.

If you look at the drum window shown below, you can see that it appears as a grid, rather like the sequencer's main window. The different drum voices appear in the left-hand column whereas the bars and their sub-divided beats are shown horizontally along the top.

Rhythms are created by setting up trigger points on the grid. This can be done using a mouse; clicking anywhere along one of the horizontal bars will create a trigger point, which is shown by a diamond symbol. Clicking on the same symbol removes the beat. A step-by-step guide to recreating the rhythm below is shown across the page.

You can also program beats from a MIDI keyboard, where each key controls one particular sound. You can draw from any number of drum sounds—you are limited only by the external voices you have at your disposal.

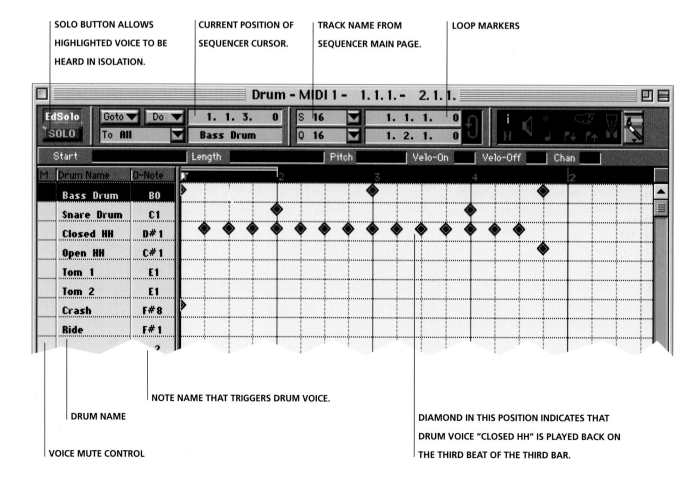

SOLO BUTTON ALLOWS HIGHLIGHTED VOICE TO BE HEARD IN ISOLATION.

CURRENT POSITION OF SEQUENCER CURSOR.

TRACK NAME FROM SEQUENCER MAIN PAGE.

LOOP MARKERS

NOTE NAME THAT TRIGGERS DRUM VOICE.

DRUM NAME

VOICE MUTE CONTROL

DIAMOND IN THIS POSITION INDICATES THAT DRUM VOICE "CLOSED HH" IS PLAYED BACK ON THE THIRD BEAT OF THE THIRD BAR.

PROGRAMMING REALISTIC DRUMS

Anyone can program simple rhythms using a drum machine or appropriate software—as the example you've just seen illustrates, it's a matter of simple maths. However, programming interesting and realistic rhythms is an altogether more advanced skill.

The difference is usually down to timing and dynamics, but it also takes in a fundamental understanding of the way a "real drummer" plays a full kit.

One of the downsides of programming as shown below, is that each of the drum sounds has the same MIDI velocity—this means that each sound will have an identical volume when a beat is generated. A real drummer would not (or could not) ever play so consistently. Furthermore, when the beats are shown as a grid, they are locked (or "quantized") which creates a unnatural mechanical effect. The "feel" or "groove" of a real drummer is provided by the way in which they push or pull the beat. In short, a real drummer never plays in perfect time.

It's possible to edit the contents of the drum window, manually shifting beats forward or backward. It's also possible to edit the velocity of any beat (MIDI has a value range of 1–127, which can provide subtle dynamic variation). However, this can be a labor-intensive, time-consuming operation.

For more realistic drums, it's more effective to program sounds in the same way as recording a MIDI keyboard part. If you switch on the MIDI recorder and tap out the rhythm on a MIDI keyboard, you can capture "real-time" playing and add your own dynamics depending on how hard you strike the keys.

Most keyboard players working in this way are almost certain to make mistakes. However, these can be edited and corrected after the event.

An even better alternative is to use MIDI drum pads, which can be struck with conventional drum sticks.

Non-drummers who program rhythms often lack an understanding of the different components of a drum kit and of what each part does. Although there would seem to be limitless rhythmic possibilities given that a basic kit is made up from around a dozen different sounds, their various functions are used in much the same way irrespective of the kind of music played.

Listen to your favourite music, but focus all of your attention on what the drummer is doing with each part of the kit. This will provide you with a valuable lesson.

STEP-BY-STEP DRUM TRACK

1. Make sure that MIDI IN on the equipment with the drum sounds is connected to MIDI OUT on the sequencer, and that their MIDI channels have been matched so that they can communicate with one another. Also make sure that the audio outputs from the drum sounds are connected to an amplifier, otherwise you won't be able to hear them.

2. Make sure that the note names allocated to the bass drum, snare drum, hi-hat and crash cymbals on the sound module match up with those on the sequencer.

3. Set a four-bar loop on the sequencer's main window, and set up the metronome option on the same page. This provides a consistent click beat for you to work over.

4. Open the drum edit window (as shown on the left). Put the drum machine in "write" mode and start the recorder using the transport window.

5. At this point you will hear a metronome click playing four beats to the bar and see the sequencers cursor looping between bars one to four. You can also see that each bar is sub-divided into four beats.

6. Looking at the "Bass Drum" track, point your mouse at the first beat of the first bar and click right there. A diamond symbol should appear on the line and from then on you should be able to hear a bass drum sound played each time the cursor passes that beat.

7. Add further bass drum notes to the first beat of the third bar, and the third beat of the fourth bar. If you make an error, clicking on any of the diamond symbols will delete that beat.

8. Add the other drum voices as shown across the page: snare drum beats appear at the start of the second and fourth bars; closed hi-hats appear on every beat except the first and last, which feature a crash cymbal and open hi-hat respectively.

ADDING A BASS PART

With the drum part now completed, we can add a bass line using an external MIDI synth module, programmed with a suitable sound. Here is a step-by-step checklist of the actions you need to take:

1. Connect MIDI IN on the synth module to MIDI OUT on the computer's MIDI interface.

2. Create an empty track on the sequencer, which is set up to transmit on MIDI channel 2.

3.Make sure that the MIDI channel on the synth module is also set to "2."

4. Ensure that the synth's output signal is audible.

5. Click on RECORD on the Transport Window.

6. Start playing the bass line.

7. When the performance is ended, click on the STOP button on the Transport Window.

You can see that the recording has been successful because the MIDI events that have been recorded are shown as a series of lines on the track's horizontal bar. From the main window, they simply illustrate that there is some form of MIDI activity at that point in time. To see what that activity is, you will need to a look at the MIDI editing window.

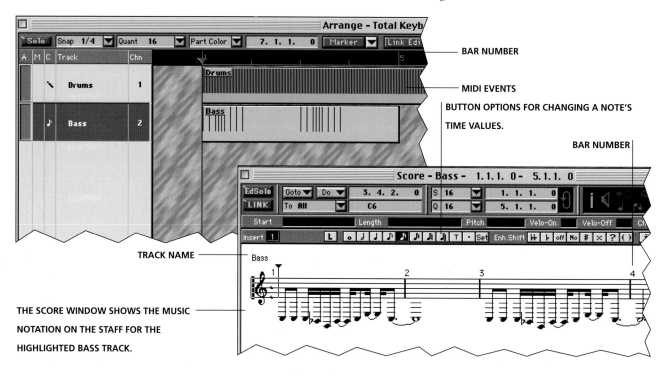

BAR NUMBER

MIDI EVENTS

BUTTON OPTIONS FOR CHANGING A NOTE'S

TIME VALUES.

BAR NUMBER

TRACK NAME

THE SCORE WINDOW SHOWS THE MUSIC
NOTATION ON THE STAFF FOR THE
HIGHLIGHTED BASS TRACK.

WHAT'S THE SCORE?

Most of the better MIDI software recorders also have a facility to allow MIDI data to be viewed and edited as part of a musical score. In the example above, the BASS track is highlighted and the SCORE option selected (in Cubase VST it appears as part of the EDIT drop-down menu).

The Score Window has its own set of menus and button options. For example, any pitch can be altered by highlighting the note on the staff using the mouse, and dragging it up or down to a new position. Similarly, you can change a time value by highlighting the note and choosing a new duration from the buttons on the screen.

Score facilities are excellent for those keyboard players or programmers whose formal notation skills are less than perfect. This can mean, for example, that music could be arranged for a string quartet simply by making a series of MIDI recordings. Each individual track could then be printed out and played by real musicians.

This idea can also be extremely useful for improving sight-reading skills. In this way, any notes that are played on a MIDI keyboard can be viewed in "real-time" in the Score Window.

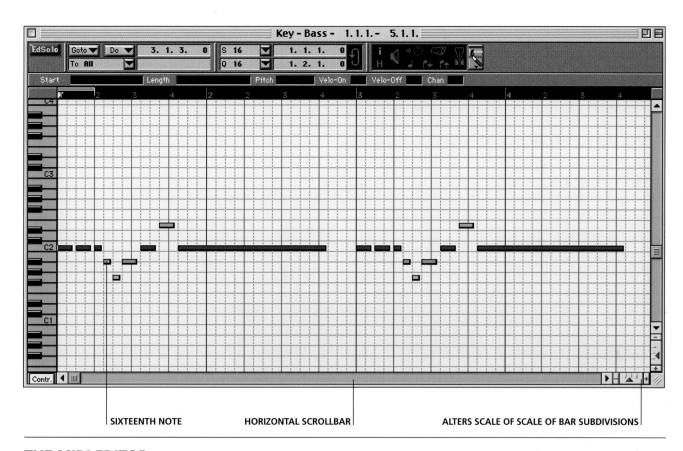

| SIXTEENTH NOTE | HORIZONTAL SCROLLBAR | ALTERS SCALE OF SCALE OF BAR SUBDIVISIONS |

THE MIDI EDITOR

Clicking on any of the horizontal track bars on the sequencer's main window opens up the MIDI editing window (called the Key Window in Cubase VST). This gives you a detailed view of the notes that are being played.

The two axes of this grid are TIME (horizontal) and PITCH (vertical). You can see the pitch clearly from the keyboard on the left-hand side. The horizontal bars represent individual notes.

To make the window easier to read, each pitch can be given a different color.

Time is marked along the top in subdivisions of bars. In this example, each bar is divided into four beats. Each of those beats is further divided into four. This means that a note lasting the smallest of those divisions shown will be a sixteenth note.

The scale of the subdivisions and the thickness of the horizontal bars can be altered by clicking on the arrows on the bottom right-hand corner of the window.

TIMING TIPS

One of the reasons that MIDI has become so popular is that it allows "non-musicians" to make music. The appeal for many is that notes don't have to be played in "real time." Complicated sequences can be "tapped" in one note at a time; fast passages can be recorded at a slow tempo and then replayed faster.

MIDI's ultimate corrective feature is the way in which it can be used to repair timing errors. This is known as QUANTIZATION. If you analyse a MIDI recording using the tiniest of sub-divisions you will see that even the best keyboard players don't play with clinical accuracy. Notes won't necessarily start PRECISELY on a beat, and yet the performance sounds natural.

For the inexperienced players, timing can be a difficult issue. If errors are clearly audible they can be corrected manually using the edit window (*see above*), although this can be a time-consuming operation. The alternative is to quantize a range of notes (or indeed a whole song) to various fractions of a beat. As you can see in the window above, the notes all begin precisely on one of the sixteenth-note subdivisions. The original performance had timing imperfections, which were then quantized to a quarter of a beat.

Take care, though: overuse of quantization can lead to a mechanical sound, which—outside of electronic dance music—is not generally desirable.

COPYING, CUTTING AND PASTING

The horizontal bars on the main window can be treated rather like the text in a word processor. You can move them around by "dragging" the mouse, copy them and paste them to a different position, chop them into smaller bars or delete them altogether.

COPYING SEGMENTS OF A SONG

If you take a look at our main window, you can see that four further MIDI tracks have been added. However, in each case, only four bars have been recorded. We can copy the contents of bars 1, 2, 3 and 4 so that they also play in bars 5, 6, 7 and 8.

1. Highlight the horizontal blocks that you want to copy (in this case, tracks 2 to 5 from bars 1 to 4).

2. Choose the COPY command (usually found in the EDIT drop-down menu).

3. Position the cursor on the start of bar 5.

4. Choose the PASTE command.

5. The contents of bars 1, 2, 3 and 4 are now pasted into bars 5, 6, 7 and 8.

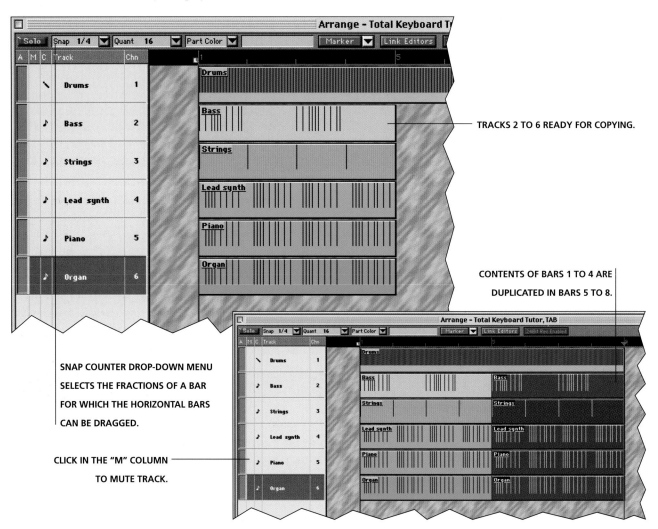

TRACKS 2 TO 6 READY FOR COPYING.

CONTENTS OF BARS 1 TO 4 ARE
DUPLICATED IN BARS 5 TO 8.

SNAP COUNTER DROP-DOWN MENU
SELECTS THE FRACTIONS OF A BAR
FOR WHICH THE HORIZONTAL BARS
CAN BE DRAGGED.

CLICK IN THE "M" COLUMN
TO MUTE TRACK.

SNAPPING INTO POSITION

When processing the horizontal bars, you should pay special attention to the SNAP counter at the top left-hand corner of the screen. This defines the fractions of a bar to which anything you move, copy and paste is positioned. This means that you move blocks of data around the screen with great precision, locking them into place on any specific subdivision of the beat that you wish. If the counter is set to "1/4" (as it is in the example above), then you can only reposition blocks directly on the beat. If you want greater precision, you can choose "1/8," "1/16," "1/32," or "1/64" from the Snap counter menu. You can also turn the snap feature off altogether, giving you total freedom to position blocks of data wherever you wish.

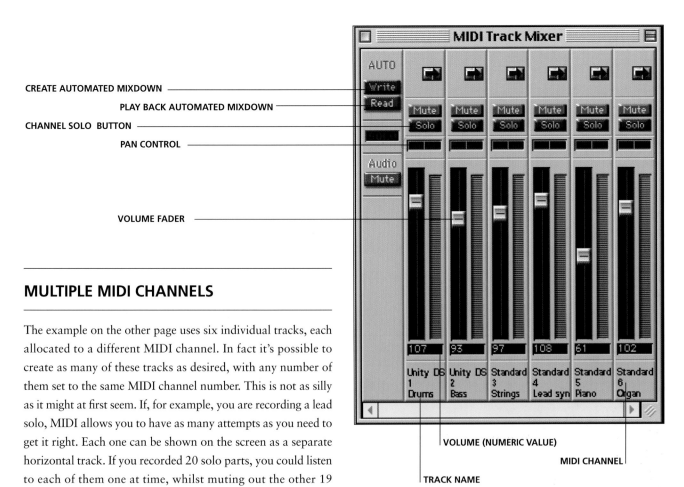

CREATE AUTOMATED MIXDOWN

PLAY BACK AUTOMATED MIXDOWN

CHANNEL SOLO BUTTON

PAN CONTROL

VOLUME FADER

VOLUME (NUMERIC VALUE)

MIDI CHANNEL

TRACK NAME

MULTIPLE MIDI CHANNELS

The example on the other page uses six individual tracks, each allocated to a different MIDI channel. In fact it's possible to create as many of these tracks as desired, with any number of them set to the same MIDI channel number. This is not as silly as it might at first seem. If, for example, you are recording a lead solo, MIDI allows you to have as many attempts as you need to get it right. Each one can be shown on the screen as a separate horizontal track. If you recorded 20 solo parts, you could listen to each of them one at time, whilst muting out the other 19 versions. You could even cut out sections that you like from each one and paste them together to make one composite solo track. You can use the same approach when trying out alternative arrangements of a composition.

One other possibility is to set up different tracks for different segments of the song—for example, one for the verse and another for the chorus. This can make editing a good deal easier.

MIDI MIXER

The MIDI MIXER (*above*) is a simplified on-screen version of a mixing board. It allows you to alter various MIDI parameters, such as volume and panning (the stereo positioning between a pair of loudspeakers). You can even do automated mixdowns.

CONSTRUCTING A MIX

Software sequencers are exceptionally good for modern creative mixing because the main window can be laid out to provide the producer with an at-a-glance overview of the structure of the music.

This approach is especially useful in dance remixes, which are often based around "loops" of different MIDI sounds that are brought in and out of the mix at various times. Whilst this could be done using an automated mix (*see above*) to mute tracks periodically, it is often easier to start off with the screen showing ALL of the tracks making a continuous sound. Various elements are then dropped out of the mix simply by highlighting and deleting the desired range of bars from the screen.

Here is a simple example using the six tracks shown across the page. Each event described below takes place over a cycle of four bars:
- **Bring in piano**
- **Bring in organ**
- **Bring in bass drum**
- **Bring in other drums**
- **Bring in bass**
- **Bring in strings and synth; drop piano and organ**
- **Drop drums**
- **Drop strings and synth; bring in bass drum**
- **Bring in drums, strings and synth**
- **Bring in piano and organ**

INTEGRATING AUDIO WITH MIDI

Over the past decade the processing capabilities of even the most modest computers has increased at a phenomenal rate. One of the implications of such an evolution is that high-performance tasks, such as recording and editing audio signals—once only possible using the most powerful computers—are now open to the average musician. Consequently, designers of music technology now routinely incorporate facilities for audio recording and manipulation into standard MIDI software sequencers.

AUDIO ISSUES

The evolution of MIDI technology has had a profound impact on the way we compose, record and mix music. However, without some method for integrating "real" audio, the only sounds that can be created are those generated by the MIDI equipment connected to the sequencer. Although digital sampling allows a certain degree of manipulation of audio, for most music, the MIDI elements need to be run alongside other audio signals.

TIMECODE

The traditional solution has been to use an audio tape recorder with a TIMECODE STRIPE that could be used to control the MIDI equipment. The timecode (usually in SMPTE format) is recorded onto one of the audio tracks and is then connected to the MIDI sequencer. From this point, the tape recorder has control over the sequencer's clock—the internal mechanism that governs the tempo. This means that any kind of audio signal can be recorded on the free tracks of the tape recorder and played back in perfect time with the sequencer.

THE MIXING BOARD

With all those individual sounds going on, a MIXING BOARD is needed so they can all be heard at the same time. This is effectively a giant patchbay in which a large number of audio signals can be plugged into separate CHANNELS where their individual levels and sounds can be altered.

Mixing boards come in many different forms. At their most basic, each channel may comprise just a volume fader and a PAN control governing where the signal sits in the stereo image. More flexible models provide facilities for altering tone controls and adding external sound effects.

SOUNDCARDS

A soundcard is an integrated circuit board that is slotted into a computer's internal PCI slots. For users of PC computers, the soundcard is a basic necessity: without one, the computer cannot record or play back any kind of sound.

In addition to providing audio connections, some feature basic synthesizer sounds for use in PC games, or others that can be triggered from a MIDI sequencer.

Audio connections to the cheaper soundcard use stereo "mini-jack" plugs, meaning that two-channel signals can be recorded and played back. Soundcards aimed at professional users have multiple audio outputs so that different sounds can be sent to different channels of a mixing desk.

Macintosh users don't need a soundcard to integrate audio: their machines already have reasonable quality audio and video capabilities, although professional PCI soundcards are needed for multiple outputs.

Fitting a soundcard to a PC is not a specialist skill. With care, any PC owner should be able to manage it successfully. The only tool you need is a screwdriver. Here are seven simple steps to fitting any soundcard:

1. Remove the casing from your PC.
2. Before taking the soundcard out of its packaging, touch the chassis of the computer to earth yourself.
3. Holding the edges of the card, insert it carefully into the PCI slot. Make sure that you never touch the gold contact points along the side of the card or you may damage the connection.
4. Screw the soundcard firmly in place to the chassis of the computer.
5. If you have a CD-ROM player you can connect this directly to the soundcard so that you can listen to audio CDs. The cable is generally supplied.
6. Screw the casing back on your PC.

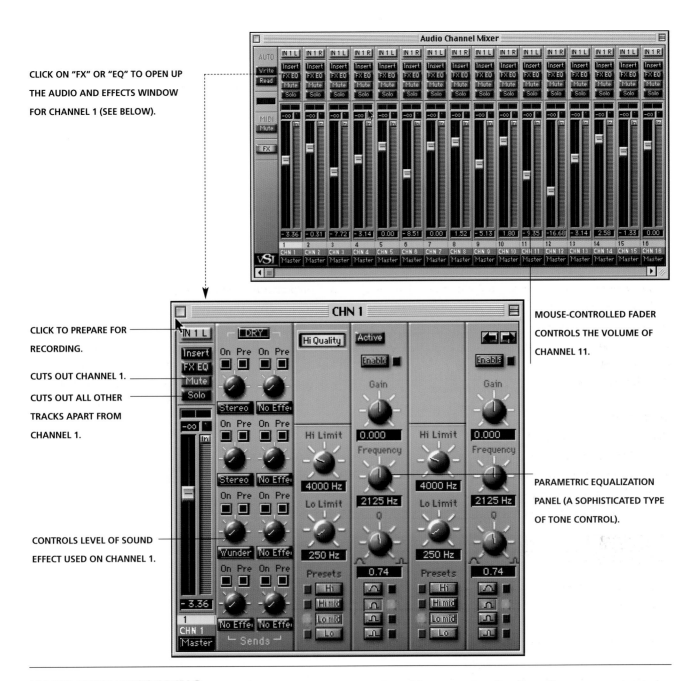

CLICK ON "FX" OR "EQ" TO OPEN UP THE AUDIO AND EFFECTS WINDOW FOR CHANNEL 1 (SEE BELOW).

CLICK TO PREPARE FOR RECORDING.

CUTS OUT CHANNEL 1.

CUTS OUT ALL OTHER TRACKS APART FROM CHANNEL 1.

CONTROLS LEVEL OF SOUND EFFECT USED ON CHANNEL 1.

MOUSE-CONTROLLED FADER CONTROLS THE VOLUME OF CHANNEL 11.

PARAMETRIC EQUALIZATION PANEL (A SOPHISTICATED TYPE OF TONE CONTROL).

HARD-DISK RECORDING

Recording audio on a computer is fundamentally the same as recording on a tape recorder. In essence, you plug your signal into the AUDIO IN socket on the soundcard, click on your sequencer's RECORD button and start making a noise.

Some pieces of software allow a vast number of individual channels to be recorded, although this, as in digital sampling, depends on your computer's internal memory capabilities. A machine with a high specification can cope with as many as 64 audio tracks; when you think that not much more than a decade ago many home musicians felt themselves lucky to have four tracks at their disposal, you can see that technology has moved on somewhat.

One of the greatest benefits of recording on a computer is that the mixing board facilities are all on-screen, and so require no complex connections. The window at the top of the page shows a 16-channel audio mixer screen from Cubase VST. In this case, each of the channels controls a different sound; the balance of the mix can be changed by using the mouse to move the volume faders up or down. This global view of the individual tracks also contains other standard mixing board features, such as MUTE, which cuts out the sound from that track when selected, and SOLO, which cuts out all of the other tracks from the mix so that you can listen to one track in isolation.

Clicking on the FX or EQ button for any individual track calls up a new window in which you can alter the tone controls or set up digital effects that only work on that channel.

PLUG-IN EFFECTS

In computer hard-disk recording systems, the degree to which sounds can be altered depends precisely on the effects that can be accessed. The software itself doesn't produce any digital effects as such, but draws on what are known as PLUG-INS to do the job. Plug-ins take on the traditional roles of digital hardware, produce reverberation, delay distortion and many other effects.

A plug-in is a tiny program that can be called up and run from within the recording software. In most cases, the plug-in is not necessarily produced by the same manufacturer that designs the recording software.

Plug-ins are stored in a special folder so that the software can recognize that they exist. They can then be specified and opened using the channel window (*as shown on the previous page*). When a plug-in is run, it opens its own window on the screen.

On the top right you can see a typical reverb plug-in. Just like a dedicated hardware unit, the various parameters can be altered, stored and recalled at any time. Beneath that you can see a tape-delay-style plug-in. This allows four distinct repeats, the timing of which can be synchronized to the tempo of the track.

FORMATS

Unfortunately, plug-ins are not universal, but work only with the systems for which they were designed. Most PC software can make use of DirectX plug-ins; Steinberg's Cubase sequencers require VST plug-ins; Digidesign's ProTools system use TDM plug-ins (which have much the greatest range of high-quality effects); and MOTU's Digital Performer only uses MAS plug-ins.

AUTOMATION

A good computer-based recording system really does represent remarkable value for money when compared to the hardware equivalent. This is no more evident than when you consider that all of the most popular recording software allows for the luxury of automated mixing. This means that if your mix involves moving faders and EQ, or changing effects parameters, these movements can all be stored.

This system works in the same kind of way as if you were recording an audio track. You press the "record mix" button and from then on any changes you make are recorded. If you play back the recorded "live" mix, you will see the faders moving of their own accord. This feature allows for extremely precise mixes to be made, at a fraction of the cost of an automated hardware mixer.

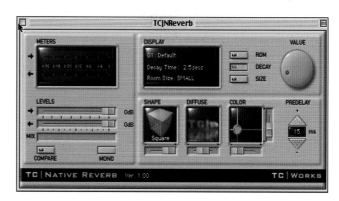

DIGITAL REVERB PLUG-IN

TAPE-STYLE PROGRAMMABLE DELAY PLUG-IN

SOFT VERSUS HARDWARE EFFECTS

Since, in theory, it's possible to use dozens of plug-ins at any one time during a mixing session, these effects represent outstanding value for money when compared to their hardware counterparts. However, in practice, considerable processing power from a state-of-the-art computer is crucial to use that many plug-ins in one go.

One further advantage is that since the effects are in-line—they are "hard-wired" within the computer—there isn't the same loss of signal caused by multiple conversions between digital and analog sound. In short, plug-ins work wholly in the digital domain.

The quality of current plug-ins is variable. Although most do the job well enough, nobody has yet produced a digital reverb that can achieve the same quality as the best external devices.

However, as the popularity of "lo-fi" sounds goes to prove, digital clarity is not to everyone's taste, with "retro" valve processors among the most popular devices on the market.

USING MICROPHONES

Most modern electronic instruments can be recorded simply by plugging them into an audio input socket and playing. However, if you want to add vocals or other acoustic instruments, you need a microphone. Different types of microphone are used for different purposes.

Some home studio owners give little thought or budget to microphones. However, anyone hoping to achieve decent results should seriously consider getting at the very least one reasonable-quality condenser microphone and one dynamic microphone.

DYNAMIC MICROPHONES

Dynamic or "moving coil" microphones are often used in the studio for recording instruments. They are also ideally suited for use in live situations since they can handle high volumes without their coils becoming damaged.

A dynamic microphone comprises a coil joined to a diaphragm that is set around a magnetic cap. When a sound —the movement of air waves—hits the diaphragm the coil moves producing an electrical impulse.

CONDENSER MICROPHONES

Widely used for vocals, condenser microphones feature a diaphragm coated with a thin layer of metal with an separate backing plate. A high "polarizing" voltage is contained between the two pieces of metal, which fluctuates according to pressure changed by movement in the diaphragm.

All condenser microphones have a built-in pre-amp boosting the level of the output. The pre-amp is powered either by batteries or by the "phantom" power supply built into most mixing boards.

PRESSURE ZONE MICROPHONES (PZMS)

PZMs are generically referred to as "ambient" microphones. Each unit consists of a transducer attached to a metal plate that can be fixed to a wall or other alternative upright surfaces. PZMs work best when they are used in pairs, where they can be panned at extremes to produce stereo ambience—the characteristics of space surrounding the area of the recording.

AUDIO RECORDING ISSUES

Making an audio recording on a hard-disk recording system is a straightforward enough business. The basic principle is that every recording you make creates a dedicated computer file. This is then "read" on playback. Here are the basic steps:

1. Plug the audio source (direct connection from electronic equipment or microphone) into the desired input channel on your soundcard.

2. Select the track on which you want to record. This will create an "empty" computer file that will be "written to" as you make your recording.

3. Before recording, check the sound levels by playing your instrument or singing. You should not let the record meter even slightly "go into the red"—unlike in analog recording, digital distortion is very unpleasant.

4. Click on the RECORD button and play.

5. Click on the STOP button when you reach the end of your performance.

RECORDING METHODS

There are various approaches to hard-disk recording. Some treat it like any other type of recording, in which every track contains a single file running the full length of the song. This can only work if the computer system has a large hard disk: a five-minute song requires around 25 megabytes for each track, so a 24-track song would take up a hefty six gigabytes of disk space.

A more economical method is to record shorter segments and repeat them. In this way, a single song could reference fifty or more sound files.

EDITING

All hard-disk systems feature facilities for editing sounds after they've been recorded. These fall into two categories, which are termed DESTRUCTIVE and NON-DESTRUCTIVE.

Audio tracks that appear as horizontal blocks on the main sequencer window can be dragged, cut, copied and pasted in the same way as MIDI data. However, when you do this, the original sound file is unharmed. You can think of it rather like an instruction to play back a short segment of an existing soundfile between two location points. This is non-destructive editing.

Sometimes, however, sound files need permanently altering—for example to remove accidental clicks or pops. This calls upon destructive editing features within the software.

HOME STUDIO ALTERNATIVES

Whatever form it takes, home recording is playing an increasingly significant role in the music world. Knowledge of studio techniques has resulted in a new generation of techno-literate musicians capable of using the recording studio not only as a means to record their music, but as a creative tool every bit as important to the compositional process as instruments themselves. However, although computer-based audio and MIDI recording is an attractive proposition, there are plenty of other alternatives.

RECORDING FORMATS

When Teac introduced the first "Portastudio" in 1979 it revolutionized the home recording market. A four-track cassette recorder with built-in mixer, musicians quickly discovered what a useful medium it was for composition and working out arrangements, even if the sound quality may not have been terribly good. Since then, the all-in-one idea has evolved somewhat to include high-quality 16-track digital recording—ideal for the musician who doesn't want to get involved with computers.

Although analog recording systems are still available, nowadays nearly all new recording systems sold are digital. Apart from computer-based digital recording, which we've already discussed, the most popular multitrack format is the Alesis ADAT, which stores its sound on SuperVHS video tape. ADATs are reasonably priced and can be easily synchronized with other ADATs, MIDI equipment or software sequencers.

THE MIXING BOARD

The heart of any recording studio is its mixing board. Many of the basic principles are shared with the on-screen digital version we have already seen (*see page 165*). The board is used for two distinct but crucial functions: recording and mixing.

RECORDING FORMATS PROS AND CONS

Besides expense, the format you choose may well be linked to the kind of music you play, or the way in which you're most comfortable working. If you only want your machine to capture audio performances, then real-time systems—analog or digital—will work best for you. If your music integrates MIDI and sampling—or you like the idea of tweaking sounds—you will need some kind of computer-based system.

Current technology is so flexible, though, that it's quite feasible to mix and match the different options according to your needs.

ANALOG PORTASTUDIO
- Cheap to buy.
- Built-in mixing facilities.
- Portable.
- Cassette tape is cheap.
- Poor sound quality.
- Limited on-board facilities.
- Multitrack tapes are impossible to edit.
- Out-moded system.

REAL-TIME DIGITAL SYSTEMS
- Excellent sound quality.
- Easy to synchronize with other machines.
- Tapes are relatively inexpensive.
- Reliable technology.
- Impossible to edit tapes without hard-disk facilities.
- Formats are not all compatible.
- Some models feature built-in mixing and effects.

COMPUTER SYSTEMS
- Superb sound quality.
- Matchless editing capabilities.
- Seamless integration with MIDI.
- All-in-one package.
- Different sound-file formats can easily be converted.
- Storage is expensive.
- Can be mentally taxing to work.
- Can be time-consuming.
- Reduces spontaneity.
- Computer systems can be volatile.
- Software and hardware dates at an absurd rate.

RECORDING

Microphones or musical instruments are connected into the mixing board where the sounds can be altered by using the features that are built into the board, such as volume or EQ, or by patching in external effects, such as compression, reverb or delay. The signals are then routed into the channels of a multitrack recorder.

MIXING

After the recording has been finished, each channel from the multitrack is connected to a channel of the board. Here the signal can be altered as before or positioned differently within the stereo spectrum. The sounds from the different channels are played together and balanced to produce a stereo mix.

COMPONENTS OF THE BOARD

Each of the input channels on the mixing board has an identical set of features.

Connections are made to the mixing desk using quarter-inch jack plugs or XLR plugs. The output of any electrical signal is governed by its impedance. Although every piece of equipment has a different impedance, there are two distinct categories: microphone- and line-level. Microphones are connected to the low-impedance inputs; all other electrical equipment can be plugged into the higher-impedance line inputs.

EQUALIZATION

The term "EQ" simply refers to the alteration of the tone of the signal, much like altering the bass and treble controls on a hi-fi system. On most boards the potential for altering the EQ is more dramatic. The sound spectrum (the range of audible signal) is split into separate bandwidths. Frequencies within each category can be cut or boosted according to taste. EQ systems where the specific

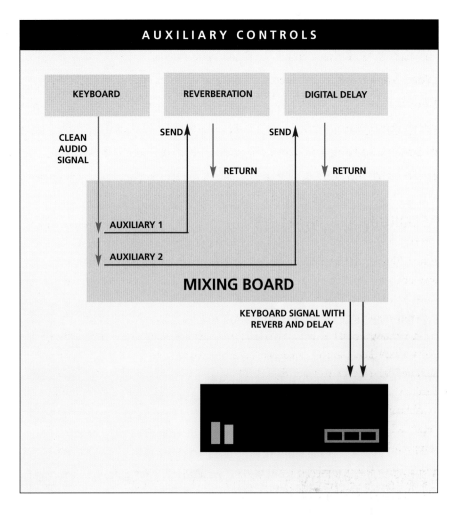

frequency can be fine-tuned before cutting or boosting are called PARAMETRIC. Those where the frequency is fixed are SHELVED.

AUXILIARIES

External effects such as reverb and echo are added using the auxiliary controls. Each board is equipped with a set of auxiliary "sends" and "returns." Each pair can be patched up to an effect (the send and return are connected to the in and out sockets respectively). By rotating the auxiliary control clockwise, increasing amounts of the signal are channelled to the effects unit. The output of the unit is returned to the board where the original clean signal and the new "effected" signal are brought together. The diagram above shows a system where there are two auxiliaries: one connected to a digital delay; the other to a reverberation unit.

PAN

The "Pan" control determines where the signal will be positioned in the stereo spectrum: if the control is panned to the far left, ALL of the signal will come from out of the left-hand speaker, and vice versa.

VOLUME FADER

This a sliding potentiometer that governs the overall volume of the track. The higher it is pushed, the higher the volume.

CHANNEL GROUPING

Mixing boards can also group together different input channels. For example, a complete drum track might be made up from six individual signals. Once they have been EQ'd and their relative levels set, all six channels can be patched through to a group. Thereafter the overall volume of the drums can be controlled as a whole.

BRINGING IT ALL TOGETHER

Mixing boards are described in terms of their input and output characteristics. For example a "24 into 2" desk is one that has 24 input channels and two output channels. If you have a large number of sound modules then you'll need as large a mixing board as you can afford.

The layout on the right shows a system that comprises an eight-track multitrack record linked to a synchronization unit that "clocks" a MIDI sequencer. Five MIDI devices are being controlled by the sequencer: a sampler, two synthesizers, a drum module and a digital piano module. Since these devices have multiple outputs, they each require a channel on the mixing board.

HOME STUDIO ENVIRONMENT

To make the best possible recordings you have to prevent noise from outside from being picked up by your microphone. However, you also need to prevent noise getting out and causing a nuisance to others.

However, the biggest single factor that will affect the quality of your recordings is the acoustic characteristic of your room. Every aspect—from its shape to its contents—will in some way affect the sounds you record or hear.

HORSES FOR COURSES

If your project studio is intended principally as a musical notebook and no more, a small "portastudio" system might well be sufficient for your needs. You don't need too much space to work in and when you've finished work you can unplug everything and put it away in a cupboard. However, for anything more demanding be prepared for a considerable investment of time and energy before you can even lay down a single note.

Professional studios have multi-layered wall structures that are treated with fibreboard and other absorbent materials to soak up different types of sound. Whilst this is unnecessary for most home users, even the simplest acoustic treatment will require time, money, and ingenuity.

REFLECTING SURFACES

The major problem is in dealing with the reflective surfaces from which sounds can bounce back and forth, such as the floor, ceiling and walls. The main aim should be to get the room sounding as "dead" or "dry" as possible. The first option is to cover the main reflective surfaces with an absorbent material such as thick carpet. Another cheap and

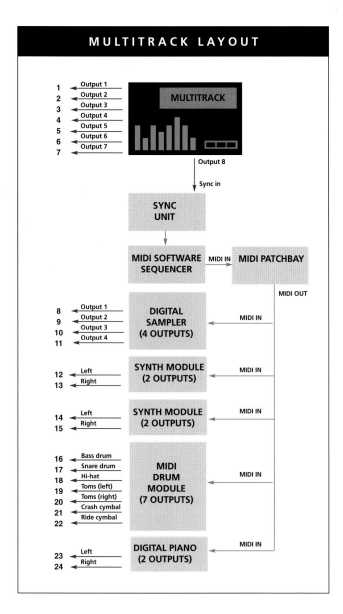

MULTITRACK LAYOUT

traditional acoustic trick is to glue cardboard egg-cartons to the surrounding walls. This type of material is very effective for absorbing sound. If your recording room still has to double for regular domestic use, making permanent fixtures to a room may not be desirable. Less effective temporary alternatives include hanging a sound-absorbent cloth, such as canvas.

ISOLATION

The issue of dealing with external noise is much tougher to face, though. If you live in an small apartment with neighbors in surrounding rooms, there really is NO WAY to avoid noise without literally building a new room within your existing room.

Unless you have very understanding neighbors there are only two realistic options: keep the noise down or find a new place to live.

MONITORING YOUR SOUND

The "soundfield" is a term given to the listening area between the two loudspeakers. For listening to a stereo mixdown, you need to position yourself in the centre of that field. The speakers should ideally be at ear-level height, although if they are positioned higher the correct effect can still be achieved by angling the speakers downward. Monitoring during recording is less critical—as long as you can hear satisfactorily, you can stand or sit where you like.

The quality of monitor speakers is also critical. Basic hi-fi speakers may be adequate for monitoring recordings but they are less appropriate for mixing. This is because hi-fi speakers are designed to make pre-recorded music sound as good as possible; monitors aim to provide a "flat" response that is level across the audible sound spectrum, so that it sounds clear on any system.

Even in a professional studio, a great deal of monitoring work is done using small "near-field" monitors placed only a few feet away from the mixing board.

Headphones can also be used as an occasional mix monitor as they provide a clear view of the stereo positioning. But if you only use headphones or cheap hi-fi speakers you leave a lot to chance. For example, a mix made on bass-deficient monitors can result in over-compensating to correct the sound, which will sound poor when played over an average hi-fi system.

PREVENTATIVE MEDICINE

Home recording technology represents a hefty investment for many people. Taking steps to keep it in good condition not only protects that investment if you later decide to resell, but can help to forestall future problems and extend its working life.

Apart from being physically abused, dropped or knocked around, technology's greatest arch-enemy is dust. Apart from looking unpleasant, dust can stick to the surface of electrical contacts, faders and potentiometers, causing crackling or, in extreme cases, complete failure.

Cigarettes are another menace—and it's not only humans that are affected. Smoke can leave residues on tape recorder heads, switches and faders. No studio equipment benefits from having ash dropped on it.

One simple preventative step you can take is to cover all of your electrical equipment with a dust sheet whenever it isn't being used. You should regularly clean your equipment. A feather duster will do the job in most cases—for faders and other small spaces, artist's paint brushes can be used. It's always a good idea to have a tin of electrical switch cleaning spray to hand, especially if you have an external mixing board. However, you should avoid those that contain lubricants, since they can "gunge" up contacts, making matters worse.

LIVE KEYBOARDS

For many musicians, performing in front of a live audience is by far the most meaningful way of communicating their art. However, many novices are understandably daunted by the prospect: after all, being a great musician doesn't necessarily have anything to do with performing skills. Whenever you walk out on stage, you face the same issues that have affected actors, comedians and other musicians throughout the ages, such as confidence, projection of image and, of course, simple stage nerves.

GETTING THE GEAR

We'll look at the issue of equipment from two different angles. The bits and pieces that you as a keyboard player need to play live, as well as the surrounding performance technology, namely the PA ("public address") system.

THE KEYBOARD PLAYER'S NEEDS

There's no simple answer to the question of what equipment a keyboard player typically needs to play live, since it's governed by many factors, not least of which is the type of music he or she plays. A semi-professional set-up might include two keyboards with a small rack of external sound modules. Your main concern will be how you can get them connected to the PA system and still maintain control over the sounds you want to use.

Unlike guitarists, most keyboard players don't use dedicated amplifiers on stage. It's more regular for the keyboards to be connected directly to the PA system. It is here that relative volumes can be balanced, equalization altered, and sound effects added. However, smaller live venues may not have a sufficient number of inputs on the mixing board—it doesn't take too excessive a keyboard rig to use up 16 input channels, especially where samplers and stereo sounds are used. In these situations, some keyboard players like to provide their own simple mixing facilities, controlling the sounds on their own and sending only a stereo output signal to the PA system.

PROGRAMMABILITY

Of course, there will always be keyboard players whose requirements are relatively simple, and for whom a basic piano or organ sound is all that's needed. However, for most modern players, the main issue is that of programmability: how to recall favourite sounds quickly and efficiently. This can be a tricky problem to solve, especially as even the most modest of keyboard players is likely to have quite a bit of equipment at his or her disposal. But recapturing the sounds

Multiple keyboards were necessary before the advent of MIDI and programmable synthesizers.

used on, say, a studio recording can be impractical or even impossible since it may well require a small studio's worth of keyboard gear to be readily accessible on stage at any given moment. As you can tell from the photograph of 1970s keyboard star Rick Wakeman (*see above*), this can pose a potential nightmare. Luckily, technology has moved on somewhat to the point where even fairly modest low-cost MIDI keyboards are capable of producing excellent imitations of pianos, organs and other instruments—especially those using digital samples—so the most practical approach is to program "preset" voices on one or two instruments that can be called up between or during songs.

LIVE MIDI

The issue of MIDI sequencing also poses a few potential problems when brought into the live arena. Whilst this is more often than not performed using computer software,

PROFESSIONAL PA SYSTEMS

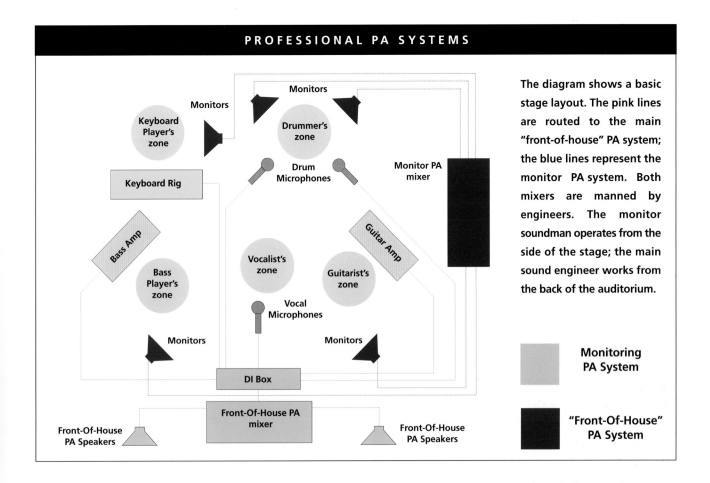

The diagram shows a basic stage layout. The pink lines are routed to the main "front-of-house" PA system; the blue lines represent the monitor PA system. Both mixers are manned by engineers. The monitor soundman operates from the side of the stage; the main sound engineer works from the back of the auditorium.

think twice before using computers on stage—they are notoriously delicate and easily damaged in transit. Again, some musicians choose to convert to more reliable dedicated hardware sequencers for this function.

Of course, when used as a part of a conventional band, sequencing can create a whole new set of problems, especially when the drummer and other musicians have to keep "in sync" with the MIDI recording.

MIDI can play an extremely important function in live music, though, especially since it's possible to program sound "patches" or digital effects to change automatically, leaving the keyboard player to concentrate on the serious business of playing

PA SYSTEMS

In more general terms, the type of equipment you need if you are to perform in public depends both on the nature of your music and the size of the venue. For all but the smallest of club or bar settings, the central requirement is for a PA ("public address") system. At its most basic, a PA may consist of little more than an amplifier and speaker with a single microphone

for vocals. At the opposite end of the scale, a professional artist is likely to require a PA system that bares a closer resemblance to a digital recording studio.

SMALL CLUB SET-UP

When performing in a very small club or bar, it's not uncommon for each of the musicians to provide their own amplification that they control from the stage. This poses a slight problem for keyboard players in that combination amplifiers and speakers used by guitarists and bassists generally have restrictive frequency ranges which fail to do justice to keyboard sounds. That said, there has been a move toward tube-driven keyboard sounds, especially among "lo-fi" aficionados.

Drums and brass instruments in very small venues will be more than loud enough without needing to be miked up. If your music requires a singer an additional amplifier and microphone will most likely be needed. It may be possible to get away with simply plugging a microphone into a spare channel on the guitarist's amplifier, although it probably won't sound too hot.

To be honest, with no mixing board and no external engineer in control of the overall sound, the balance between the instruments is certain to be rather unpredictable. Another frightening issue for inexperienced live performers is the problem of MONITORING—the ability to hear what you're doing while you are playing. Using this kind of set-up, it can be really tempting to keep turning up your own volume. Avoid this: you can be guaranteed that everyone else will do the same, and the whole tenuous sound will deteriorate further.

PRACTICAL APPROACHES TO GETTING STARTED

There's no question that on a level of raw simplicity, the approach described above has considerable appeal. But it really is worth trying to produce something a little more controllable—it will make your sound so much better. To do this properly will involve a couple of new acquisitions: a mixing board and a person prepared to operate it. Both of these may be easier to organize than you might first think.

It's possible to put together a reasonable-quality PA system for very little money. All it takes is a simple eight- or 16-channel mixing board, a reasonably powerful stereo amplifier (500 watts per channel should be ideal for small venues), bass speakers, horns and crossovers, and a few microphones. Many of these components are really easy to pick-up second-hand.

As well as making you self-sufficient when playing gigs, your own PA system will also come in really useful when rehearsing. One thing's certain—there's no bigger motivator than hearing yourself sounding good while you practice.

Having a PA is a fine thing, but finding your own personal sound engineer who knows and understands your music can give you such a boost. Start off by looking close to home. Many a new young band finds itself with hangers on who turn up to rehearsals and gigs just waiting to be asked to get involved in some way.

When you're playing live, learn to trust your soundman. Give him or her as much control as possible so that the musicians can get on with the serious job of performing. A good, sympathetic sound engineer who knows your material is a valuable member of the band.

GOING UP IN THE WORLD

In most professional venues, a professional PA system is likely to be either hired-in for the occasion, or a permanent fixture. Such systems use a lot of standard recording studio technology, such as multiple speaker and amplification systems and rack-mounted digital effects. All of the instruments, as well as the drums, will have their own dedicated inputs or microphones. The individual sound levels of each instrument are controlled by an engineer at a large mixing desk who is positioned behind the audience, at the back of the hall. This type of PA set-up is referred to as a FRONT-OF-HOUSE system.

HEALTH CHECK

Live music is usually a relatively safe pursuit. However, there are some health risks that you should at least be aware of. The first one is the potential damage that may result from too much noise.

A great deal of medical research has now been done on the subject, so much so that there really can be no doubt that prolonged exposure to extremely loud music—at the typical volumes you would experience in a gig or club—is almost certain to cause at least some damage to your hearing.

There is no easy solution to this problem other than, obviously, not performing live, although you should try to take sensible steps like avoiding your ears being too close to loudspeakers, or using earplugs—the kind that swimmers fit to prevent water getting into their ears.

However, if you suffer with persistent hearing problems, such as the infamous "ringing" noise for days after you have performed, you should treat this as a serious warning sign and consult a doctor.

A second problem that faces many semi-professional keyboard players is the physical harm caused by lifting heavy objects. It's surprisingly easy to damage your back in this way. Always get help with the heaviest objects, and when you bend down to pick up something particularly heavy, always bend your knees and then lift upwards, keeping your back as straight as possible; bending from the base of the spine can so easily cause you harm.

Another area to treat with the utmost seriousness is electricity. Numerous musicians have been harmed—some fatally—after receiving electric shocks while performing or recording. Such tragedies are usually a result of faulty earthing on electrical equipment. Frustratingly, in almost all of these occurrences, problems can invariably be avoided by regular servicing of equipment, and checking leads, plugs, and fuses.

As should ALWAYS be the case with all electrical matters, if you have any doubts seek qualified help.

THE LUXURY OF MONITORING

Along with bigger and better systems, playing in larger venues creates a new set of challenges for musicians and engineers alike. Naturally, the larger the venue, the more power and volume is needed to fill the space. It is at this point that the problems of allowing the musicians to hear themselves clearly become more critical.

A professional PA system always incorporates monitoring facilities that allow the musicians to hear a special mix of the overall sound via a wedge-shaped speaker cabinet positioned on the floor in front of them on the stage. At its most basic, the mixing board uses one of the auxiliary controls so that varying amounts from each input channel on the board can be sent out to a monitor amplifier. The problem with this approach is that although the musicians get to hear a monitor mix, they all hear the same thing: in an ideal world, most performers would want to hear an overall mix with their own sound well to the fore.

This desire only becomes a reality at the top end of the professional spectrum, where the largest venues will make use of a completely independent PA system that is used ONLY for monitoring. This invariably means having a mixing board and monitor engineer positioned at the side of the stage who can then provide individual mixes of the overall sound tailored to the needs of each musician. The diagram on page 173 shows the layout for both front-of-house and monitor PA systems.

THE TRANSMITTER ALTERNATIVE

Over the last decade, a new solution to the problem of monitoring has evolved, through the use of radio or "wireless" transmitters on stage. Using this system, monitor outputs from the mixing desk are connected to a transmission unit that relays the sound to a wireless "invisible" earpiece worn by the musician. In this way, the performers can hear mixes tailored to their own preferences in much the same way as if they were listening to music on a personal stereo.

Transmitter systems can also be used to send the signal from an instrument on stage to an amplifier. Although it is mostly guitarists who are able to benefit from this, so too can users of remote MIDI keyboards—the kind that are worn around the neck with a strap.

The process is relatively simple: the output from the keyboard is plugged into a small transmitter that can be worn on a belt or strap. The receiver unit is then connected to the input channel on the amplifier or mixing board. Although early incarnations of this system often suffered from surrounding radio interference transmitted by taxis and the emergency

Synthesizer star Jean Michel Jarre is famed for his spectacular live performances.

services, sophisticated frequency switching has all but eliminated this problem.

BE PREPARED

Keyboard players are often the most technically oriented musicians in a band. As such, their live set-ups are generally a lot more complicated than that of other instrumentalists. This places an extra burden of responsibility on ensuring that all of the components of their keyboard rig are not only in place but working efficiently.

Here, then, is a suggested checklist that should cater for most modern keyboard players:

- Stands for multiple keyboard set-ups.
- Portable rack-mounting for sound modules and effects.
- Keyboard amplifier (if necessary).
- In-line mixer (if necessary).
- Soldering iron, solder, pliers and wire cutters.
- Spare audio and MIDI cables.
- Reel of electrical insulating tape.
- Spare batteries for foot pedals (if used).
- Indelible ink marker pens.
- Back-up disks for data held on sequencers or computers.
- Spare quarter-inch jack plugs.
- Spare XLR plugs and sockets.
- Switch-cleaning spray.

DO-IT-YOURSELF MUSIC

It may be enough for many musicians to perform live to small audiences, or make recordings for their own amusement, but others will always have greater ambitions. For these people, the urge to commit their art to perpetuity—and unleash an album of their music—is never far away. This is becoming increasingly easy as high-quality home recording equipment becomes more and more affordable, as does the small-scale bulk manufacture of the most popular recording media.

DO IT YOURSELF

The greatest advantage of pressing up your own music is that you get to present yourself to the outside world in EXACTLY the way you want. There is no manager to make decisions on your behalf, and no music executive subtly trying to steer you in certain commercial directions. You don't have to compromise at all. The downside, of course, is that you have to pay for that privilege. And then you have to try to sell the results yourself.

Before you jump in at the deep end, over the next few pages you'll find a few considerations that might make the process a little less painful. But think carefully about what you're doing—if you're not prepared for some hard labor you can easily find yourself with a garage full of your albums that nobody wants.

WHICH FORMAT?

Your first decision is to choose your format. This may well be a forgone conclusion, depending on the nature of your music. There are five principal formats for pre-recorded music. They are compact disc (CD), vinyl, audio cassette, minidisk and MP3. CD is by some distance the most common format used commercially.

In spite of their unnecessarily high costs in music stores, CDs are the most cost-effective format to produce in small quantities. Also, they are popular with music stores because they don't take up too much space. Their size and weight also makes them cheap to send through the post—a consideration if you are planning to send out hundreds of promotional copies.

Home-recordable CD (CD-R) has become commonplace in recent years. Therefore, if you have suitable hardware for your computer it is possible to bulk-record large numbers of blank CD-Rs. This has two advantages: blank CD-Rs are cheaper than high-quality cassette tapes, and they don't need to be recorded in "real-time." This means that if you have a CD-recorder with an "eight-times record" capability,

you should be able to record a full-length CD in something like ten minutes. CD-Rs are fine for promotional use or selling via mail order, but it's fair to say that the bigger music shops and distributors are unlikely to be interested.

If the music you want to release is in the club/dance vein, then you'll also need to consider the traditional vinyl option, since the "12-inch single" still remains the most popular format among dance music producers and club DJs. Vinyl has also enjoyed a resurgence in other specialized independent markets, such as punk and garage pop, but it has to be said that mainstream music buyers are nowadays highly reluctant to buy records.

MAKING A COMPACT DISC

Producing a CD is a relatively straightforward process. Your original stereo recording is DIGITALLY REMASTERED enabling the various codes to be added that the CD player needs to "read" the data. These codes—known as PQs—include the track numbers, index points, start times, and durations. From this new version, a GLASS MASTER is produced. This is the template from which all your CDs will emanate.

It's possible to produce a CD from any format, including cassette, reel-to-reel magnetic tape and minidisk. However, the most commonly used professional format is DAT (digital audio tape).

THE MASTERING PROCESS

The digital remastering takes place in special studio, usually referred to as a MASTERING ROOM. You should not ignore the possibilities offered at this stage in the process, and, if you get the opportunity, attend the remastering.

Hearing your music played in such surroundings will provide you with perhaps your first clear picture of how your music will sound on other systems. At this stage, you also have the option of making final audio alterations to your mixed tape. This can mean: adding compression to "tighten"

CHOOSING A MANUFACTURER

Whichever format you go with, the manufacturing process is broken down into a number of separate stages, all of which are performed by an entirely different set of people. If time is a major consideration for you—and for most semi-professional musicians, it's a major factor—it can be a good idea to find a broker.

Such companies act as a go-between among the different parties and they invariably look after every stage of the production. In fact, the ability to strike bulk deals with their sub-contractors often means that brokers can offer you a better deal than if you managed each stage yourself. Furthermore, they simplify the process, taking responsibility for any problems that might occur during the different stages of manufacture.

When you deal with a broker, you simply hand over a master tape of your release—which usually takes the form of a DAT tape—and your artwork; with any luck, a few weeks later you should receive the finished product.

Before you proceed, make sure that you understand if there are hidden costs for any of your requirements.

It's not too much fun driving 50 miles to collect a couple of thousand CDs from a pressing plant simply because you hadn't realized that the price you agreed excluded the cost of delivery.

It's worth putting a bit of thought into the way you present your artwork to the broker (or printer, if you go it alone). There are two basic possibilities. One is to provide "camera-ready" artwork that is then photographed and "scanned" for printing; the other is to use computer graphics software that is used to generate the film from which the printing plates can be made. This latter option can save considerable sums of money.

Manufacturing brokers often advertise in the back pages of music and technology magazines, or can be found in music industry directories.

It's always sensible to get quotes from different suppliers. You'll be surprised at the variance in price you might find over a pressing as small as 500 copies. As always, it's best to get recommendations from other satisfied customers.

---

up the sound; taking advantage of the professional-quality equalization facilities that the mastering board can offer; altering EQ between tracks; matching relative volumes between tracks; and tidying up ("chasing") fade-outs. Any of these features will help make your final product sound more polished and professional. The mastering engineer can also act as a useful second set of ears, recommending possible courses of action. Don't expect miracles, though—if the original material is poor, it won't be magically transformed.

CD PACKAGING

If you manufacture a CD you have a number of options in the way it is presented to the outside world. More often than not, the plastic "jewel" case is the most commonly used form of packaging. And because they are so widely used, they are the cheapest to produce. The sleeve design usually doubles as the front page of a small booklet that slots into the front of the case. This means that you can include up to 24 pages of information with your CD.

The simplest type of packaging features a basic cardboard "record-style" sleeve. However, these are unpopular as they are too thin to show information on a spine. An increasingly popular compromise is the "Digipack," which features a cardboard flap that when opened reveals the disc inside.

VINYL ISSUES

The mastering stage of producing a record is similar to that used in CD production, and offers the same kind of scope for alteration. In a vinyl CUTTING ROOM, the original recording is played back through a mixing console linked to a lathe mechanism. This cuts a groove into a blank lacquer disc.

PLATING

After the lacquer has been cut it is sent off for plating. This is a process whereby the lacquer is coated with a thin layer of silver and then electroplated in a solution of nickel. When the nickel plating is stripped away it holds a negative impression of the original lacquer. This is used to make the stamper, which holds a negative impression of the original lacquer which is then used to PRESS the vinyl.

PRESSING

During the pressing process, molten vinyl and heat-resistant paper labels are compressed hydraulically between the two stampers (there is one for each side of the record) to create the finished record.

Once set, the records are then "bagged up" in paper inner sleeves and are inserted into cardboard outer sleeves.

DISTRIBUTION

Once you've taken the plunge and bulk-manufactured your music, you have to face the difficult task of "shifting your product." Although you may be able to sell some copies at gigs, or directly to local stores, the only way you can really cover large territories is by using a DISTRIBUTOR. These companies simply act as a middle-man who steps in between you and the music store. In short, they buy from you and sell your products on to shops at a higher price.

Distributors have the benefit of market knowledge and connections, with links to a whole array of music stores and distributors in other countries. Your distributor will be responsible for letting these outlets know that your recording exists, and offering it to them. If successful, they do the selling, posting and packaging.

Most independent distribution works on what is called a "sale-or-return" basis. The harsh reality of this system is that if after a period of time your music remain unsold, they are returned to you. But with so much independent music now available, there's no guarantee that a distributor will want to handle your music. For this reason, it can be a good idea to try to find a distributor before doing your pressing.

Distributors very often specialize in particular types of music, so it's always a good idea to find out who distributes the artists or groups whose music most closely resembles yours.

The past decade has also seen a major growth in the development of small mail-order outlets. These operations are usually fan-based and geared towards certain types of music and artist. If you can get onto their lists, this can help to build up a following: people who buy via mail order are often the most fanatical, and likely to remain loyal to your cause.

PROMOTION

The most difficult aspect for D-I-Y musicians is letting the world know of their existence. This means some form of promotion. Clearly this is important: why else would the major record companies devote MILLIONS of dollars to marketing a new album by a major artist if it weren't? Although there are few corners that you can cut in doing the job properly, there are a few common sense steps you can take.

Be prepared to give copies of your music to ANYONE who might be useful. When you've put up the money yourself, it can sometimes be tough to give away "freebies," but this is a basic necessity. Think in terms of writing off up to 20 per cent of your pressing for promotion.

Put together a press pack. This should at the very least include the music and a basic press release. Photographs and other promotional aids can be effective, but are not worth doing unless they're done professionally. Also, try to back up new releases with as many live performances as possible.

Build up a list of music journalists and radio DJs who might be interested in your work. Keep them informed of your activities. remember, anything that helps to imbed your name in the music industry's collective brain. And always follow up your mail-outs. Many music journalists and DJs get hundreds of new releases sent to them every week, and even if they like your music they're probably not going to make the effort to let you know their feelings. If you don't hear anything, don't be afraid to hassle them for a response.

COPYRIGHT ISSUES

Whilst there is not too much the law can do to protect a musician from making a poor business decision, there are formal ways in which an artist's intellectual property—the music—can be protected. This process is known as copyright, and it can work in a number of different ways. When an artist writes a piece of music he or she is also entitled to both mechanical and performance copyright protection.

Mechanical copyright refers to an original song being used on a commercial release. Each time an album is "pressed," the songwriter (and, if relevant, the publisher) is eligible for a small percentage of the retail price. Payments are made based on returns completed at the pressing plant.

Legally, a musician wishing to cover someone else's song on a recording needs to file a request for a mechanical license from the publisher of the song.

The other kind of copyrighting covers the public performance of a song. Any piece of music that is played on the radio, television, or in the cinema is entitled to a performance payment. For some popular composers, this can bring in millions of pounds each year. Performance royalties are based on returns completed by the TV or radio stations.

Payments are made to composers and publishers by ASCAP and BMI in the United States, the PRS in the UK, and GEMA in Germany and Central Europe.

USING THE INTERNET

Within the course of less than a decade, the Internet has gone from being an obscure buzzword overused by computer nerds, to radically altering the way we communicate with one another. The fact that you rarely encounter a television or billboard advertisement that doesn't end with a "www" web address is evidence that the Internet is now very much a part of the mainstream.

THE MP3 REVOLUTION

The influence of the Internet has made itself felt in many different ways to the music world, initially in the way information was disseminated, and latterly in the way music has been sold.

The great buzzword of recent times has been MP3. This is a file format that allows music to be downloaded from websites and played back using specially made MP3 hardware or software. The key has been in the compression of data. A song held in traditional file formats such as ".WAV" or ".AIFF" could be downloaded from the Internet, but could take up to an hour to complete; most computer users armed with a standard 56K modem connection can download an MP3 file in a tenth of that time. As "broadband" Internet connections gradually become the norm over the next five years, there is a very real potential for being able to download an album in MP3 format in a matter of minutes.

The downside of MP3 is that whilst the sound quality is superior to previous attempts to use the Internet in this way, the levels of compression used mean that whilst MP3 provides "near-CD quality," most decent hi-fi systems would be able to distinguish the MP3 sound from a genuine CD.

Nevertheless, in some form or other, this concept clearly charts out the way that "e-commerce" is going to take the music industry in the future. And it's an idea that scares the major record labels, who sense a loss of control over their markets. In theory, this is all good news for the forward-thinking independent musician who doesn't have to battle to get his or her product in the music stores, when it can be made available from "cyberspace."

Of course, one clear advantage of only taking the MP3 route is that you don't have to pay out any manufacturing costs. Your only overhead is in acquiring software to convert your audio master into MP3 format (you can find a variety of downloadable freeware or shareware that performs this function) and uploading the files to an Internet site. However, since MP3 is still in its early days, by ignoring the usual methods of presenting pre-recorded music, you will be severely limiting your audience.

COMMUNICATING WITH YOUR AUDIENCE

But one of the great things about the Internet is the way that you can find a new global audience. No matter how strange and obscure your music might be, you can be guaranteed that somebody somewhere will be interested in it, and "understand" what you're getting at. So even if you don't want to bother with MP3 just yet, if you're serious about reaching an audience, getting your own web page set up is a must. This will allow anyone in the world with access to the Internet to follow your activities.

Setting up a home page on the World Wide Web can be as simple or as complex a business as you want to make it. HTML, the computer language at the heart of all web pages, is very easy to learn. But you don't even need to bother with that if you don't want to, since the two most popular web browsers—Internet Explorer and Netscape Navigator—also include features that allow you to create and upload pages at the click of a button.

At its simplest, your website should be an engaging information sheet. Remember, your activities are there for the whole world to see. It's always a good idea to register your site with the most important search engines, such as Lycos and Altavista. Also look out for "index" sites—"web signposts" that deal with your kind of music.

One of the most satisfying elements of using the Internet is that you get to communicate directly with your audience. At best, you can sell your music directly to the customer, cutting out the shops and distributors. Some cult artists, whose music sales would rarely reach the mainstream, have used this system successfully. When you build up a substantial mailing list it's easy to keep your audience informed of new developments, recordings, or live performances.

Even if you don't bother with the MP3 format, you can still include snatches of your music for downloading. There are two distinct approaches to this. The first is to simply include files that can be downloaded and then played; the second is to use an audio streaming system like RealAudio that enables a suitably equipped computer to play the music while the song downloads.

GLOSSARY

ACCENT

A dynamic playing effect that places an emphasis on specific notes of chords within a sequence, making them louder or creating rhythmic effects.

ACCIACCATURA

An ornamental effect sometimes referred to as a "crushed note." The acciaccatura "prefixes" a regular note, but is shown in small type to indicate that its duration is not included in the value of the bar. In practice, it represents a very fast move between the two notes so that the acciaccatura is barely perceptible. It should be played on the beat of the principal note.

ACCIDENTAL

Symbols used in written music to raise or lower the pitch of a note by one or two half steps. A sharp (♯) raises the pitch by a half step; a double sharp (𝄪) raises the pitch by two half steps; a flat (♭) lowers the pitch by a half step; and double flat (♭♭) lowers the pitch by two half steps. The effect of sharps and flats can be "switched off" with the use of a symbol known as a natural (♮).

ACOUSTIC(S)

A non-electric instrument; the science of the behaviour of sound—crucial to a musician's aural perception.

ADAGIO

Performance mark literally meaning "at ease," a slow tempo that is faster than *andante* but slower than *largo*. Its diminutive form is *adagietto*, which is slightly faster than *adagio*.

AIR

A tune— vocal or instrumental.

ALLEGRO

Played at a fast tempo, literally meaning "quickly." Its diminutive form is *allegretto*, which is quite fast, but not as fast as *allegro*.

AMPLIFIER

Unit designed to convert electronic impulses so they can be heard through a loudspeaker. Some form of amplifier is necessary for the signal from any electronic keyboard to be audible.

APPOGGIATURA

A grace note or "leaning" note, distinct from the accacciatura, receiving half the value of the principal note. It can also be used to indicate pitch bends on stringed instruments.

ARPEGGIO

The notes of a chord played in quick succession rather than simultaneously. Commonly notated using a wavy line. Also known as a "broken chord."

ARTICULATION

The attack with which single notes or chords are played and the length of time over which they are allowed to decay. Articulation symbols written on the staff can include the slur, which marks out phrases, and staccato, which shortens the length of a note.

AUGMENTED

Interval created by raising a perfect or major interval by a half step.

BACKBEAT

Term used in modern music to describe the rhythmic effect of a heavy snare drum beat on the second and fourth beats of a bar.

BAR

Sometimes referred to as a "measure," a unit of musical time in which the notes contained within total a fixed combined value defined by the time signature. Bars are separated by bar lines.

BEAT

A metrical pulse grouped together to form recurring patterns or rhythms.

BIND

See tie.

BOOGIE-WOOGIE

Style of jazz piano playing that emerged in the 1920s featuring a repeated "walking" bass motif.

BRACE

Symbol used to join together staves that are to be played simultaneously. Piano music usually shows a treble staff and a bass staff played by the right and left hands respectively.

CADENCE

A musical phrase that creates the sense of rest or resolution at its end.

CHORD

The sound of three or more notes of different pitch played simultaneously. A chord made up from three notes only is called a triad.

CHORUS

Electronic effect that combines delay with modulation to simulate the sound of two different instruments playing simultaneously.

CHROMATIC

A scale that includes all twelve pitches from tonic to octave with each degree separated by a half step.

CIRCLE OF FIFTHS

Closed circle of all twelve pitches arranged at intervals of a perfect 5th. First devised by Johann David Heinechen in the 18th century.

CLAVICHORD

Gentle, but highly expressive keyboard instrument that dates back beyond the 15th century.

CLEF

Symbol placed at the beginning of a staff or bar line that determines the pitches of the notes and lines on the staff that follow. Three types are commonly used: the G or treble clef; the F or bass clef; and the C clef. The C clef as shown is termed the alto clef and when centred on the fourth line it becomes the tenor clef.

CODA

The concluding passage of a piece of music.

COMMON CHORD

A major triad.

COMMON TIME

Alternative name for a piece of music written with a time signature of four-four. Can be shown by the symbol "C" instead of the traditional two numbers.

COMPOUND INTERVAL

An interval— a half-step gap between two notes—of greater than an octave.

CONCERT PITCH

The set of reference tones to which all non-transposing instruments must be tuned. A common scientific definition is that the note "A" below "middle C" is measured as having a frequency of 440 cycles/second.

COUNTERMELODY

A subordinate melody that accompanies a main melody.

COUNTERPOINT

Two or more lines of melody played at the same time.

CRESCENDO

A performance mark that indicates a gradual increase in loudness. The opposite of *diminuendo* or *decrescendo*.

CRISTOFORI, BARTOLOMEO

Harpsichord maker, generally credited with having invented the piano.

CROTCHET

A note worth one beat within a bar of four-four time.

DA CAPO

Literally meaning "from the head," *da capo* is an instruction that the performer must return to the beginning of the piece. The term is usually abbreviated as *D.C.*.

DAL SEGNO

Literally meaning "from the sign," an instruction that the performer must repeat a sequence from a point marked by the sign "𝄋." Abbreviated as *D.S.*.

DAT

Digital Audio Tape; universal stereo mastering recording format.

DEMISEMIQUAVER

A note worth an eighth of a beat within a four-four bar.

DIATONIC

The seven-note major and minor scale system.

DIMINISHED

An interval created by lowering a perfect or minor interval by a half step; also a term applied both to a minor chord with a lowered 5th note and a chord that comprises minor 3rd intervals.

DIMINUENDO

A performance mark that indicates a gradual decrease in volume. The opposite of *crescendo*. Sometimes also referred to as *decrescendo*.

DISCORD

The description given to note intervals that are deemed to be dissonant in character. Specifically this refers to the intervals between the root note (1st) and the second and seventh notes respectively.

DOMINANT

The fifth degree of a major or minor scale. The triad built on this degree is the dominant triad; the seventh built on this degree is the dominant seventh.

DOTTED NOTES

A dot positioned after any type of note that increases its value by half. A second dot can be added to increase the value by a quarter; a third dot added increases the value by an eighth.

DOTTED RESTS

A dot positioned after a rest to increase its value by half. Most commonly found in compound time.

DOUBLE BAR

Two vertical lines drawn through the staff to indicate the end of a piece of music or a movement.

DRUM MACHINE

Programmable unit that allows the user to create electronic rhythms without the need for a drummer. This function is more often carried out by a hardware or software sequencer "triggering" digital samples of drum sounds.

DYNAMIC MARKS

Terms, symbols and abbreviations used in written music to indicate different levels of volume or a transition from one level to another.

ELECTRIC PIANO

Electronic simulations of a traditional acoustic piano. The original models, built in the 1960s, used a regular piano action to strike magnetic metal "reeds" or tone bars causing them to vibrate. Modern electric pianos use digital samples—recordings of "real" pianos.

ENHARMONIC

A set of different names that may be applied to the same pitches. For example, the notes C♯ and D♭ are deemed to be enharmonic equivalents, even though they share the same pitch

ENVELOPE

Controls featured on any synthesizer governing the attack, decay, sustain and release of a note when played. Sometimes referred to as "ADSR."

EQUALIZATION (EQ)

Tone control filters. In a recording studio or electronic keyboard equalization is a more sophisticated form of the "bass" and "treble" controls found on a domestic hi-fi.

EXPRESSION MARKS

Words or symbols written on a score to guide the player on matters other than pitch or rhythm—dynamics, articulation and tempo, for example.

FORTE/FORTISSIMO/FORTISSISSIMO

A set of instructions for the performer to play louder, of which *forte* is the quietest and *fortississimo* the loudest. The terms are abbreviated using a stylized script as *f*, *ff* and *fff* respectively.

FORTE-PIANO

An instruction to play loud then soft. Shown in a stylized script as *fp*.

GATHERING NOTE

The note given by an organist to provide a choir with a reference tone for the singing of hymns.

GLISSANDO

A continuous sliding movement between two different pitches. On a piano keyboard the effect can be produced by running the nails of a finger along the black or white notes, creating a very fast scale of discreetly pitched notes.

GRACE NOTE

See Appoggiatura.

GRAND PIANO

The largest of the piano family, with a range of over seven octaves.

HALF STEP

US term for a semitone interval.

HAMMOND ORGAN

Pioneering electronic organ that creates sound using a system of rotating electronic "tone wheels."

HARMONIUM

Reed organ in which sound is generated by foot-pedal-operated bellows.

HARMONY

The effect of a set of notes played simultaneously, and the way in which these intervals and chords sound in relation to each other.

HARPSICHORD

Precursor of the piano; keyboard instrument in which a mechanism plucks rather than hammers the strings.

HEMIDEMISEMIQUAVER

A European term for a sixty-fourth note within a bar of four-four time—a note worth a sixteenth of a beat.

INTERVAL

The relationship between two different pitches numbered in terms of the degrees of the diatonic scale system.

INTONATION

The degree to which tuning and pitching is accurate among the musicians in an ensemble.

INVERSION

The order of notes in a chord from the lowest pitch. If the root is the lowest note, the chord is said to be in the root position. If the third note is the lowest, the chord is a first inversion; if the fifth note is the lowest, it is a second inversion; if a seventh note has the lowest pitch, the chord is called a third inversion.

KEY

The reference pitch for a diatonic scale.

KEY SIGNATURE

An arrangement of sharps and flats on the staff that defines the key.

LARGO

Slow or stately.

LEADING NOTE

The seventh degree of the diatonic major scale.

LEDGER LINE

A short line that allows notes to be transcribed outside of the range of the five-line staff.

LEGATO

An instruction to play a sequence of notes as smoothly as possible with no separation between successive notes. Often indicated within the boundaries of a slur but also sometimes abbreviated as *Leg*.

LENTO

Instruction to play extremely slowly.

MEASURE

Alternative name for a bar.

MELLOTRON

Electronic keyboard from the 1960s that used loops of magnetic tape to recreate the sound of acoustic instruments. In principle, the precursor of the sampler.

MELODY

A pattern of single notes that forms a coherent musical sequence. Often simply described as a tune.

METER

Alternative term for tempo.

METRONOME

Mechanical device used to denote the tempo of a piece of music in beats per minute. Often known as "Maelzel's Metronome" after the man who patented the idea.

M.M. ♩ **= 120**

MICROPHONE

Unit that can convert sound into electrical impulses for the purposes of recording and amplification.

MIDDLE C

The center note on a piano keyboard that is also an important reference tone for other orchestral instruments. It is notated on a ledger line below a staff anchored by a treble clef.

MIDI

Musical Instrument Digital Interface; a universal "systems protocol" that allows suitably equipped electrical devices, such as keyboards, sequencers, computers, drum machines and samplers to communicate with one another.

MODE

A series of fixed scales that were predominant during the Middle Ages. The modern-day diatonic system of major and minor scales evolved from their existence. The seven modes that can be built from the major scale are Ionian (I), Dorian (II), Phrygian (III), Lydian (IV), Mixolydian (V), Aeolian (VI) and Locrian (VII).

MODULATION

Movement from one key to another within a section or piece of music. Often wrongly confused with transposition, in which a complete piece of music is moved to an alternative key.

MOOG, DR ROBERT

Inventor of the first analog synthesizer. His first production-line models were built in 1964. Like his keyboards, Moog's name is often mispronounced—it rhymes with "vogue."

MORDENT

An ornamental instruction to play a single note as a "trill" with an adjacent note. An upper mordent alternates with the note a semitone higher; the lower mordent is played with the note one semitone lower.

NATURAL

See Accidentals.

NOISE GATE

Electronic effect that cuts out an incoming audio signal until it reaches a set level.

NOTES

Symbols used in written music to indicate the pitch and duration of a sound. The principal note names are whole note, half note, quarter note, eighth note, sixteenth note, thirty-second note, and sixty-fourth note. In Europe, an alternative system is used, based around centuries-old terminology: semibreve, minim, crotchet, quaver, semiquaver, demisemiquaver, and hemidemisemiquaver.

OCTAVE

An interval the pitches of which have the same note name but the frequency of the lower note is half that of the upper note. Abbreviated as *Ott., 8va or 8ve*. When these marks are written above a staff, the notes should be played an octave higher in pitch; when written below the staff they should be played an octave lower.

ORNAMENTATION

The alteration of a piece of music to make it sound more effective or beautiful, usually through the addition of notes or dynamic changes.

PCI SLOT

Peripheral Component Interconnect. Connection found on most computers; used in music production as a means of connecting sound cards to a computer.

PEDALS

Foot controls on a piano. The "loud" pedal releases the dampers inside the piano, increasing the volume; the "soft" pedal pushes a piece of cotton between the hammer and strings, damping the sound. The "sustain" pedal which "undamps" the keys being played can also be found on the grand piano.

PEDAL TONE

A bass note that sustains beneath any shifting harmonic structure, such as the bass "drone" produced by bagpipes.

PENTATONIC

A set of scales based around five notes. Among the oldest of scalar systems, pentatonic scales can be heard in musical cultures all over the world. The minor pentatonic "blues scale" is commonly used in Jazz, R&B and rock music.

PERFORMANCE MARKS

Words or symbols written on a score to indicate aspects of performance not covered purely by pitches on the staff.

PHASING

Electronic simulation of the "sweeping" effect of two out-of-phase sounds being played simultaneously.

PHRASE

A self-contained musical sentence that can be viewed as a coherent and identifiable "whole" within the context of composition. Usually no more than a few bars in length, phrases are identified in written music within a slur.

PIANO/PIANISSIMO/PIANISSISSIMO

Instructions for the performer to play more softly, of which *pianississimo* is the quietest. Shown in a stylized script as *p*, *pp* and *ppp* respectively.

PIANOFORTE

The technically correct name of the piano; also a performance instruction to play loud and then soft immediately afterwards. Usually shown on the score in a stylized script as *pf*.

PITCH

The frequency of a note in terms of the number of times it vibrates each second.

PLUG-INS

Small computer programs that can add functionality to other software. For example, add-on sound effects that work with computer audio recording systems.

POLYPHONY

Any type of music that combines two or more different lines.

PRESTO

An instruction to play very fast—faster than *allegro*.

PRIMARY TRIADS

Term describing the three triads built from the tonic, subdominant and dominant degrees of a diatonic scale.

QUAVER

An eighth note.

QUINTUPLET

A group of five notes played in the time of four.

REFRAIN

A segment from within a piece of music that is repeated at various times throughout. The chorus from within a pop song is a typical example.

REGISTER

The range of pitches playable by a voice or instrument.

RELATIVE MAJOR/RELATIVE MINOR

The relationship between major and natural minor scales: the pitch of the notes and chords built on any major scale are the same as those on a natural minor scale built from the sixth degree of the major scale.

REPEAT/REITERATE

An instruction to reiterate a piece of music within the bars specified by repeat symbols.

REST

A symbol placed on the staff to indicate a period in which no notes are played. Each of the different note types has its own equivalent rest.

REVERBERATION

The natural effect of sound bouncing off surrounding surfaces, such as walls, floors and ceilings; generally simulated digitally in recording studios.

RHYTHM

A pattern or movement in time of notes and accents.

SAMPLER

Electronic keyboard or studio device capable of replaying digital recordings. Most commonly used to create authentic reproductions of acoustic instruments.

SCALE

A collection of notes laid out in a predefined sequence from the lowest pitch to the highest pitch.

SCALE DEGREES

The position of each note within a scale. Can be shown numerically using Arabic or Roman numerals. Each degree can also be named: tonic (I); supertonic (II); mediant (III); subdominant (IV); dominant (V); submediant (VI); and leading note (VII).

SCORE

The notation of an entire piece of music for an ensemble written out so that the simultaneous parts are aligned in a vertical manner.

SEGNO

Literally meaning "sign." The symbol ("𝄋") is used to mark the beginning or end of a repeated section. The sign must be paired with either a *dal segno* instruction, "from the sign," or an *al segno* instruction, meaning "to the sign."

SEGUE

A term indicating that the next piece of music follows immediately with no interruption.

SEMIQUAVER

A sixteenth note—a note worth a quarter of a beat.

SEMITONE

European terminology for a half step. The interval between two adjacent pitches on a keyboard, representing one twelfth of an octave. The smallest interval used in the vast majority of music in the western world.

SEQUENCE

The repetition of a musical phrase at gradually increasing or decreasing intervals.

SEQUENCER

MIDI computer software or dedicated hardware unit that allows a MIDI keyboard performance to be captured, edited and replayed.

SILBERMANN, GOTTFRIED

The first notable pianomaker, who introduced the instrument to Germany where it flourished.

SOFT SYNTHS

Fully functional synthesizers that use computer software to create sound.

SOUNDCARD

Printed circuit board that plugs into the back of a computer allowing sound to be recorded and played back. A basic necessity for any computer hard disk recording system.

SOUND MODULE

Synthesizer or sampler that takes the form of a box or rack-mounted unit, but has no keyboard of its own. Requires external MIDI keyboard or input from a MIDI sequencer to create sound.

SPACE

The gap between the lines of a staff.

STACCATO

Literally meaning "detached," staccato notes or chords are dramatically reduced in length creating a "stabbing" effect. Usually shown in notation by a dot or an arrow head above or below the note.

STAFF

A group of horizontal parallel lines and spaces on which notes are placed to define their pitch. Sometimes also called a "stave" in the singular, but always "staves" in the plural.

STEM

The vertical line attached to the head of the note. The value of the note can be progressively halved by adding a tail (or flag) to the tip of the stem.

SYNCOPATION

A rhythm that runs against the prevailing meter or pulse, emphasizing the off-beats.

SYNTHESIZER

Electronic keyboard designed to produce synthetic sounds. There are two basic forms of synthesis: traditional analog models built from the mid-1960s use "subtractive synthesis" filters to create sound; digital synths uses "additive" systems in which sounds are built from the bottom up.

TEMPO

The speed at which the music is performed, usually measured in beats per second for a specific note type; see also Metronome.

TIE

A curved line joining two notes of the same pitch that indicates the value of the second note must be added to the value of the first, and that the second note itself is NOT played. Mostly used to sustain notes across bar lines. Also known as "binds."

TIME SIGNATURE

The numerical symbols positioned at the beginning of a staff to indicate its meter. The upper number indicates the number of beats in the bar; the lower number shows the type of note that make up those beats.

TONE

An interval of a major 2nd (two semitones), known in the US as a "step"; a description of the colour or quality of a sound. Also known as a whole tone.

TRANSPOSITION

A piece of music rewritten at a different pitch to the original. Usually defined in terms of the difference in interval between the two.

TRIAD

A chord made up of three notes separated by intervals of a third. There are four fundamentally different forms: major triad; minor triad; diminished triad and augmented triad.

TRILL

A rapid alteration of two notes over a distance of a step or half step.

TRIPLET

A group of three notes played in the time of two.

TUNE

A melody; adjusting an instrument to concert pitch.

VOLTAGE CONTROLLED FILTER

Function of analog synthesis in which tonal aspects of a sound are "filtered" out by sophisticated tone controls—also known as "subtractive synthesis."

VOLTAGE CONTROLLED OSCILLATOR

Part of a traditional analog synthesizer that generates soundwaves.

INDEX

BIBLIOGRAPHY

Derek Bailey—Improvisation
(Moorland, 1980)

David Bowman and Paul Terry—
Aural Matters (Schott, 1993)

Terry Burrows—Total Guitar Tutor
(Carlton, 1998)

Robert Dearling—The Ultimate
Encyclopedia of Musical Instruments
(Carlton, 1996)

Don Randall—The New Harvard
Dictionary Of Music
(Harvard University Press, 1986)

Darryl Runswick—Rock, Jazz and
Pop Arranging (Faber and Faber,
1992)

Erik Satie—A Mammal's Notebook:
Collected Writings… (Atlas, 1996)

Nicolas Slonimsky—Thesaurus of Scales
and Melodic Patterns (Scrivener's,
1947)

Eric Taylor—The AB Guide to Music
Theory (Associated Board, 1989)

ACKNOWLEDGMENTS

The author would like to thank the following people for their help with this project: Jenny Olivier, Penny Simpson and Trevor Newman at Carlton Books; Lucian Randall; Nick Kaçal for helpful hints and answering the usual dumb questions; Jim Barber; Chrys&themums; Richard Chapman; Ralph Denyer; Joachim at JAR Music; Stewart at Flamingo in New Mexico; R. Stevie Moore, king of home-brewed pop; sticksmeister supreme Andy Ward; Vladimir of the Mumz; Atomdog; Dave Gregory (late of XTC); SJ and JSJ; Los Bros Dillingham; and, above all, Junoir.

This book is dedicated to Peggy Burrows.

PICTURE CREDITS